HANDBOOK
FOR
CARE
ASSISTANTS

G000320478

HANDBOOK
FOR
CARE
ASSISTANTS
Edited by Sue Benson

a practical guide
to caring for
elderly people

A Care Concern Publication

First published in 1989 by
Hawker Publications Ltd
13 Park House
140 Battersea Park Road
London SW11 4NB

Reprinted 1990 (twice), 1991
2nd Edition 1992

© Hawker Publications 1992

British Library Cataloguing in Publication Data

A catalogue record for this book is available
from the British Library

ISBN 0-9514649-7-3

Designed by
Richard Souper
Phototypeset by
Just Words Ltd, Brighton
Printed and bound in Great Britain by
Biddles Ltd, Guildford

*Illustrations in chapters 9 and 17 are redrawn
from Keeping the Elderly Moving in Old People's Homes by
Helen Ransome, published by the Centre for Policy on
Ageing, and How to Save a Life by Alan Maryon Davis
and Jenny Rogers, published by BBC Books.*

Contents

Contributors

Rosemary Ashbee is manager of the Royal National Institute for the Blind's Westcliff House, Westgate on sea, Kent. She began her career as a care assistant with RNIB 12 years ago, and has trained in social work and communication with the deaf-blind.

Richard Banks BEd (Education and Applied Social Studies) is Programme Head for Social Care at the Central Council for Education and Training in Social Work.

Elaine Barratt BA SRN MSc is a research nurse with special interest in pressure sore prevention and treatment. She wrote this chapter while senior nurse (research) in the Dept. of Public Health, Parkside Health Authority, London.

Sue Benson BA RGN has been involved with *Care Concern* magazine for eight years as editor and features editor, and is editor of Care Concern Books. She also works on the nurses' bank at Atkinson Morley's Hospital, Wimbledon.

Karen Bryan PhD BSc (Hons) MCSLT is a lecturer in acquired communication disorders at the National Hospitals College of Speech Sciences. She previously worked as a speech therapist with elderly people.

Margaret Cheetham is Inspector of Homes with Scarborough Social Services, Yorkshire. For eleven years until 1988 she was officer in charge of a voluntary home for 79 residents in Scarborough.

Paul Julian Fletcher BSc MA CQSW is Head of Direct Services for the Northern Division of Buckinghamshire County Council Social Services Department. Before this he has worked in service planning, been a team manager, managed a group of homes for elderly people and been an officer in charge.

Claire Hale BA PhD RGN RNT is a research associate at the Centre for Health Services Research at the University of Newcastle upon Tyne. She was previously a nurse tutor at the Lakeland College of Nursing, Cumbria.

Una Holden Cosgrove is a clinical psychologist specialising in work with elderly people. She has written several books on the practical management of confusion and difficult behaviour.

Brenda Hooper MA is manager of Libury Hall, a residential care home in Hertfordshire. She was previously a training adviser at the Centre for Policy on Ageing, and is author of *Home Ground*, a handbook on staff training.

Judith Kemp MSc SRCh wrote this chapter while a chiropodist with City and Hackney Health Authority and research officer with the Age Concern Institute of Gerontology, King's College, London.

Alastair Kent MA MPhil DipCG wrote this chapter while director of residential, education and employment services for the Royal National Institute for the Deaf. He is now director of Action for Blind People.

Sheila Mackie Bailey BA SRN RCNT DipNEd RNT is a freelance lecturer consultant and author. Her special interests include elderly people, nursing ethics and nursing research.

Ruth Manley MBE RGN RCNT RNT worked for many years in the NHS and later with the Royal College of Nursing. She currently acts as an independent nurse adviser on health care projects for older people.

Jane Maxim PhD MA DipCST MCSLT is a senior lecturer at the National Hospitals College of Speech Sciences. She is a speech therapist whose research area is language change in dementia, and she runs a group for elderly stroke patients.

Teresa Mearing-Smith BSc MB BCh DCH MRCGP is clinical assistant in geriatric medicine and dermatology at St Peter's Hospital, Chertsey.

Eric Midwinter wrote this chapter while director of the Centre for Policy on Ageing. Now "retired" he works as consultant to projects in a wide variety of fields, including older age and education.

Sue Millward SRN is senior clinical nurse for the National Society for Epilepsy at Chalfont St Peter, Buckinghamshire, where she is in charge of the Nursing Unit and teaches on the in-service training course for care staff.

Joan Mitchell BSc BA MB BCh studied medicine at Newnham College, Cambridge and The London Hospital, Whitechapel. For the last 26 years of her career she was a general practitioner in Crayford, Kent, and is now retired.

Helen Ransome (Dip. Physio. Victoria, Australia) wrote this chapter while district physiotherapist for Lewisham and North Southwark Health Authority.

Gwyn Roberts DMS is general manager for Tadworth Grove nursing and residential home, part of the Court Cavendish group.

Sue Thomas SRD is a dietitian with special interest in the nutrition of older people. She has worked in the geriatric unit at St George's Hospital, London, and the Gerontology Nutrition Unit of the Royal Free Hospital, London.

Helen White RGN RHV is continence adviser at the Dene Centre, Newcastle-upon-Tyne Council for the Disabled.

Deirdre Wynne-Harley, lately deputy director of the Centre for Policy on Ageing, is now an independent consultant/adviser. In 1982-84 she co-ordinated the DHSS sponsored working party which produced *Home life: a code of practice for residential care*.

Foreword

By Peter Millard, Eleanor Peel Professor of Geriatric Medicine,
St George's Hospital Medical School, London.

Ageing is universal. Nothing escapes. Animals, motor cars, buildings, bridges and elastic bands age. Why ageing occurs is beyond the scope of this book, but the fact that all of us have aged, are ageing and will (if we do not die first) become old is inescapable.

To live to be old one must not die young. The number of old people in our country is increasing because at the turn of the century children stopped dying in the first year of life. Yet the number being born did not decrease until the 1930s. As well as an increase in absolute numbers, the proportion is increasing because for the last twenty years fewer children have been born. Thus we have more old people with a decreasing labour force.

Most do not need care. Reflect that much of the voluntary work being done in the homes, churches, clubs and societies of our country depends upon the enthusiastic contribution of those who are chronologically old. Their bodies show age but it is not the years they have lived but the sickness they have had which hampers them.

The ill-informed say if only we were like the East we would have no need for care homes. Yet those who say that, betray their ignorance of life in both countries. People in Western society are in care mainly because they have no families. You cannot slaughter a million men in the First World War and expect all the eighty and ninety year old women to be married and have families. Nor do all married couples have children.

I used to think that others should change their attitudes. Later as my knowledge increased I realised that people's attitudes reflect their knowledge. Unless they are sick in mind, people do not willingly harm others. Therefore if people in care in rest homes, nursing homes, and hospital wards are being badly treated it is not because the people employed to look after them don't care, it is because they don't know *how* to care. Ignorance is nothing to be ashamed of.

At one time I knew nothing about geriatric medicine. At school the subject was not mentioned. Indeed even at my Medical School, which in the 1960s was the only London Teaching Hospital with geriatric medical wards and a consultant, I still did not know, for I was not taught. I was taught anatomy, physiology, biochemistry, obstetrics, medicine, surgery, paediatrics, and psychiatry, but no one mentioned old age.

By the age of twenty four I had gained sufficient knowledge to be given sole charge of a 100-bedded African Hospital. There I made many mistakes but I knew what had to be done. However, two years later as a junior doctor in a geriatric ward in this country, standing with four others around a cot-sided bed, I did not know what to do.

Twenty five years later as a Professor of Geriatric Medicine I now know something, but not everything, about the care of the aged. I research and study because I want to do the job better.

Age changes are universal, intrinsic, progressive and deleterious. Yet the rate of deterioration is influenced by genetic, nutritional, environmental, social and psychological factors. Elderly people when they are admitted to hospital usually have something wrong in at least seven systems of the body. Therefore to practise my subject one must know a little about ageing in all systems: skin, eyes, ears, teeth, feet, hearts, lungs, bowels, kidney, bladder, or brain. However, in addition to these organ changes that are relatively easy to understand, one has to deal with a person who has lived their life. During those years they will have learnt to cope with life's hardships. They have adjusted to success or even failure at school, at work, in marriage, and in their home life. Each one is different. Each a unique person with their life. To cope with them requires skill, tact, patience, and understanding.

In homes, in residential homes, in nursing homes and in hospital wards staff have been developing better ways of caring. Because a better way is possible we can see the poverty of management in other places. To improve standards nationally we must teach others.

Over the next decade there is no doubt that a universal training system will be established for those who tend the aged. Throughout the country there is a hunger for that knowledge. Gradually courses in gerontology and in geriatric medicine are being established, and as we teach we learn. This book represents a beginning, and I feel privileged to be asked to write its foreword. Yet in reading the chapters, each contributed by a different author, I recognise the depth of my own ignorance, the debt I owe to others and the gulf of knowledge that still exists.

I wish the book well. It represents the effort of many people who have tried in their professional lives to benefit the elderly. Within its pages you will find the perceived wisdom of many people. In reading their thoughts you will gain an understanding of the problems and how to cope with them. Each writer comes from a different professional discipline. You the reader, will have to use the knowledge they give to build on the understanding you have already gained.

That you have read this far in the foreword shows that you have a quest for knowledge. I hope that through the pages of this book you gain further insight and understanding of your work, and that through ventures such as this the home, residential home, nursing home, or ward in which you work moves towards the better world that you know awaits it.

Peter H. Millard

Introduction

E ducation is about enabling people to think for themselves. Training is imparting the particular skills a job requires. We hope this book will help provide both education and training for everyone who cares for older people. Its focus is on the care home setting, but it applies equally to a long-stay hospital ward.

No book can replace practical instruction and work experience; rather it adds an extra dimension of knowledge, and the resources to question and challenge some of the assumptions and attitudes you are all bound to meet.

I was once told by the Matron of a luxury nursing home, "They're just 80-year-old babies really". Think about it. The people in your care are not babies: they are individuals who have lived long, varied, stressful, boring, rewarding, frustrating, joyful, tragic, selfish, valuable, utterly different real lives. In other words, each one needs and deserves to be treated with respect and attention to their individual needs and preferences. Even - no, especially - those least able to make their wants known. This is the message which we hope sounds loud and clear through the pages of this book. We make no apologies for its reiteration by author after author, because it is the most important point by far.

The idea of a training handbook for care assistants grew out of my experience and that of my publisher Dr Richard Hawkins, in producing the care home magazine Care Concern over several years. Our readers have made clear the lack of and need for training schemes for care assistants, and we hope this book will be a valuable step in the direction of better training. We have planned the chapters to cover those topics which we know cause most concern to care assistants and their managers, and we have selected authors who, in our experience, are best able to answer their needs.

I would like to thank Paulette Prendergast and Veronica Carey for their secretarial help; my father Bill Thompson for teaching me to spell and acting as an extra unpaid proof-reader; and all the authors for their hard work and friendly enthusiasm for this project.

Sue Benson, London 1989

Introduction to the Second Edition

T he continuing popularity of this handbook has prompted us to produce this second edition, completely revised and including a new chapter explaining how care assistants can benefit from the developing system of National Vocational Qualifications. Changes in legislation, in particular the Food Safety Act 1990, have been taken into account; and an updated, expanded resource list includes several more useful organisations.

I hope this book will continue to meet the needs of both care assistants and those responsible for their training, as a practical teaching resource.

Sue Benson, 1992

CHAPTER 1

A healthy old age

by Eric Midwinter

Taking a broad view • active older people in the community • statistics • old does not mean ill • encouraging independence, but allowing eccentricity

B eing old is normal. What is, if any-thing, abnormal is being old in a residential care setting.

Nearly 12 million people in the United Kingdom are over 60 years of age; almost a fifth of the population. Contrary to popular belief and despite the recent boom in private residential care, the number living in care is very small. About 330,000 older people (less than three per cent of those over 60) do not live in their own ordinary accommodation, but in residential homes, nursing homes, sheltered housing and so on.

So, first of all, you are dealing with a very small minority, whether privileged or unfortunate is a matter of circumstance and opinion. But they are not, basically, different from the norm.

It is true that they tend to be older and more dependent than the wider cohort of older people, and this you would expect, for of course many residents of homes are there because of difficulties in managing alone. Nonetheless, being very old as opposed to old is not so exceptional. Nearly four million are over 75, and there are 180,000 people over the age of 90.

For every thousand people aged 65 to 74, just over six will be in residential care: for every thousand 75 and over, the figure is nearer 49. In effect, you are likely to find up to four-fifths of residents will be 75 and over.

How dependent?

It is often said that dependency levels are declining sadly, but some of the research does not actually support that view. In the residential care setting you are likely to find that out of every hundred residents, 17 would be severely dependent, 42 moderately dependent, and 41 reasonably independent. That is based on scales and tests concerning being able to look after oneself, continence, being able to mix sensibly with others, and being mentally alert.

In some people's minds this creates a dilemma, for residential care homes appear to have two distinct functions: caring for those unable to look after themselves, and providing a rational habitat for those able to look after themselves.

There is no simple answer to this. It has to be accepted that this is a fact of residential care life. What should be recognised is that the two camps – dependent and independent – are not, in practice, quite so definite in composition. In some respects, the "severely dependent" resident might

Avoid generalisations: older people are all individuals.

be fiercely independent, and rightly so, insisting on this or that personal need. A "reasonably independent" resident, on the other hand might be temporarily incapacitated or be absolutely dependent in one aspect of life-style. In the end, the blurring is such that it is much safer to take each resident on his or her own terms as an individual.

A word of warning: for all sorts of reasons, such as the number of places locally available in the public sector or the demand made evident locally in the private sector, these figures of age and dependency vary crazily from area to area. There is no prototype – the "average" home probably doesn't exist.

You will find that women outnumber men in residential care, in the ratio of at least three to one. This reflects what happens in society at large where women gradually grow in numbers compared to men.

Think of each age range as represented by a hundred people. Then the breakdown, male and female would look like this:

aged 55/64	65/74	75/84	85+
48 men	44 men	35 men	23 men
52 women	56 women	65 women	77 women

There you can easily see how, steadily, women outnumber men more and more with age.

So, again, it is quite normal to find many more women than men as residents. It follows that many women are single, widowed or divorced – nearly half of those between 65 and 69 and over two-thirds of those over 70. Half the women over 60 either have no children or, in the case of a small but crucial number, have outlived their children.

Talk of families looking after older relations is, therefore, misleading, added to which even those with near relatives may be living many miles apart. Do not be too surprised if there are few visitors for some residents: do not assume they have been ignored or deserted by their family. They may not enjoy the luxury of having one. It is worth remembering that 90 per cent of pensioners live alone or with one other, usually another pensioner. That form of social isolation is not at all unusual.

Old does not mean ill

Although many people are in residential care for reasons of ill health, it is worth recalling that "old" does not mean "ill". By the very token of increased survival into older age, it follows that a decline in health should not automatically be associated with an increase in years.

Consider the following statements, based on an over-75 yardstick, because, as we have already noted, most residents will be of that range. These are, of course, national figures, for all over-75s. Let us assume a sample group of 100 people over 75 years of age.

This 100 were asked had they suffered any "restricted activity" during the previous fortnight, any time they had been inhibited from getting about in the ordinary way. Seventy-five of them had *not* been so restricted.

Asked if they were housebound or bedfast, 90 of them said they weren't.

Asked if they were able to climb the stairs without assistance, 86 said they could manage that in reasonable comfort.

You see, if you put the figures the other way round, they do look a little sunnier and more optimistic. Of course, it is bad enough that 25 out of every 100 people over 75 have been limited in activity during the last two weeks. But it's not a complete tale of woe.

It is just too risky to assume that everyone over 75 is automatically declining in health and capability at some alarming rate.

Take dementia. The popular view is that people crumble mentally with age, and that the older you are, the dottier. But 78 per cent even of over-80s do *not* suffer from any form of dementia.

Let us not be mistaken about this. The fact that 22 per cent *do* suffer from dementia amounts to a million tragic victims, just as 13 per cent of over-65s being unable to move outdoors readily is a grave social issue. This is not whitewashing, but it is a matter of perspective.

Of course, in the residential care home, there will be some accumulation of those with needs of a mental and physical, as well as a social, kind. The lesson of perspective is that you should begin with the stance they they are alright, that they are, so to speak, normal – and then adapt according to degrees, if any, of ill health and impairment, some of which, needless to say, may or should be temporary. In short, treat them as residents, not as patients.

Remember, then, at all times that we are living in an "old" society. The chief reason why the *proportion* of older people has risen dramatically, is because the proportion of younger people has dropped melodramatically. A hundred years ago near enough to two-fifths of the population was under 14; that has halved to a fifth. It is unlikely to change with any degree of significance.

No wonder the Victorians started the Boys Brigade, football and compulsory schooling! The average age of Victorian society was as little as 25. Now it is moving toward 35 and above. There are about as many people over sixty as there are under the school leaving age of sixteen.

A long retirement

Many more people survive beyond 60 to enjoy another swathe of, hopefully, pleasant years. It is interesting to note that getting to 60 is the key. If you had arrived at 60 years of age in 1901, you could, on average, have expected another 13 or 14 years were left to you. If you reach 60 now, your anticipation might be of 15 or 16 years. Those are the male figures: females did and do somewhat better: but the point is the same. There's not that much difference. It's about survival. It is a fact that, in the nineteenth century, our grandfathers or great grandfathers scarcely bothered, even if they were able, to make plans for old age: it was, so to say, such a minority sport that one presumed it wouldn't happen.

Now, with earlier retirement – for instance, less than two-thirds of men between 60 and 65, (the official state retiring age) are still working – many, many people have a relatively long post-work span of life. Some people are retired for as long as they have worked.

This means, in turn, that residents crossing the threshold into residential care homes, increasingly, spent a long time "at leisure". They are not coming to you direct from work, as would have sometimes happened in the past, nor, equally, from completion of the happy chores of parenthood. Their children, did they exist, will be grown-up and away, and their jobs, did they have one, long ago over.

This raises an important issue. You should understand that, over the past years, the involvement of retired people in what might be called "constructive" activities (sports and pastimes, educational and recreational concerns) has been remarkably low. People take retirement all too seriously. They retire. They withdraw. They do very little.

For instance, only two out of a hundred of those of pensionable age use parks and allied amenities with any regularity; only one in a hundred, despite matinée concessions, as opposed to 11 out of a hundred of

the population, go to the cinema regularly. They do watch, on average 26-28 hours television a week, and two-thirds of older people claim this as their chief leisure pursuit.

There are all sorts of reasons for this: lack of money, fear of going out, impaired health, poor transport, and so on. The cultural factor – just, simply, retiring – must be also taken seriously into account. Without the structure of work or of family life, many older people allow the organisation of their lives to become passive and flabby.

Add to this that, among over-65s:

a tenth visit neither friends nor relatives
just under a third receive no visit from friends
a fifth are visited by relatives less than once a month
a twentieth never receive visits from relatives
a quarter receive no visits from doctor, home help or other officers.

You can see that it may not be easy for them to adapt to the public business of living cheek by jowl with ten, twenty or forty others, with staff hopeful that they will "join in" and be one of the large family. Many have been, in a word "counter-institutionalised": they have been ingrained into a lonely and negative lifestyle. Don't be surprised if they are not eager for bonhomie.

Playing out roles

Some experts speak of a "fitness gap", a widening gulf, as people grow older, between what they can do and what they do do. There are two or three explanations for this, and one of them is cultural. People do play out the role they have been cast in: old people do not run after buses; therefore, old people stop running after buses; therefore old people lose the capacity to run after buses.

Other people play their role, offering the helping hand that seems chivalrous and appropriate. One moves to help the old lady peeling carrots because she has lost some power in her fingers and hands: next time she wants to peel carrots, a little more power may have been lost. "Here, let me do that for you" can be a blood-curdling saying.

This applies, of course, to mental affairs as well as physical matters, but it also applies, apropos institutional life, to what might be termed social fitness. The habits of involvement and of activity are as easily lost as the habits of exercising arms and legs, and maintaining some mental agility.

In the residential care setting, it is as important to recall that older people may have jettisoned some of the habits of physical, intellectual and social activity, as it is to note that opportunities should be provided for them to become involved again.

Choice and opportunity

Opportunities is the operative word. If one is a believer in giving maximum dignity and independence to older people in residential care, then the critical thing is choice. Old people must choose to do this or that. If, acting with all the sensitivity to their previous perhaps negative background and offering the most tastily tempting of chances, the resident still hands you the frozen mitt of refusal, that is her or his right.

If they do not want to do keep fit (to improve and maintain their physical suppleness), if they do not want to join in the quiz about World War II (designed to keep them mentally alert), if they do not want to create an Easter bonnet and process in an Easter parade (in the interests of social

cohesiveness) so be it. They have made an informed choice, offered proper opportunities, and that is their civic right.

Some residential homes, rebounding from the autocratic model of yesteryear, have gone to another extreme, practically forcing residents to do things, either by ruling, like the washing up, or by social pressure, like joining in collective activities. That is wrong. You cannot twist people's arms into dignity. You cannot frogmarch people into independence. You can request, persuade, even plead, but self-determination involves the resident's right to say "no" and lead a life as eccentric as is compatible with the safety and comfort of others.

That also entails the need for as much consultation as possible with residents. They are citizens, not clients. As far as possible, they should make the decisions, either the individual ones, like when to take a bath, or the collective ones, like what should be the character of the Christmas party. Chapters that follow go into practical detail on this subject.

They are not children

There is a tendency to see normal ageing as a decline rather than a continuation. But frailty and weakness are not vices. Unconsciously, sometimes consciously, some treat very old people as children, as being in their "second childhood". This too has its attractions, but unluckily it is misleading. In any event, people do not always treat children as if they were "normal" and human: they do patronise them and assume responsibility for their rights; at worst, they humiliate them.

When this is applied to equally normal older people, the insult is compounded, for here are experienced veterans of life, who have grappled doughtily with all kinds of social problems, and who have perhaps remained resilient in the face of hammerblows – losing spouse, home, income; suffering pain, hurt and indignity – each of which would floor many "ordinary" individuals.

One observes the trait in the forced ebullience with which residents are sometimes approached: in the use of forenames and endearments in a discourteously familiar way; in the presumption of decisions; in entering rooms without knocking; and in a score of tiny ways. By all means develop a close and warm, if not sentimental (they are not "family") relationship, but do not assume it before it occurs, anymore than you would in the work place with a forty-year-old or in the local tennis club with a thirty-year-old.

It is not a geriatric Maplins you should aim at, with shrieks of "Hi-de-hi", and a dreary attempt at synthetic jollity in the Hawaian ballroom. Old people are normal. They are saints and sinners; more usually, mixtures of both. Some are cantankerous and quarrelsome and bloody nuisances, not because they are old, but because they probably always were. Old age does not confer a second childhood, and it does not convert to a benign mellowness. There will be rows. There will be good times, and bad.

No generalisations

In a single word, there will be life. So, presume nothing. Have no preconceived ideas and make no generalisations. Let me give just three illustrations of what this means.

First, a popular view of older age is that it involves loss of memory. When a twenty year old forgets something, it is a "lapse" of memory, but when a seventy year old forgets something, it is a "loss". As an automatic and exclusive assumption, this could be misleading.

Memory proceeds by way of screening, often dependent on value and interest. The fifth birthday is remembered because there was a lovely party and fifty-fifth forgotten because, sadly and frankly, nothing happened. An old person who forgets the name of the Prime Minister may recall the date of her grandson's birthday. It is, then, a complicated business, and it is best probably just not to entertain a presumption about it.

Secondly, it is popularly thought that older people grumble a lot and tend to whinge. If anything, the research suggests that older people are the world's worst consumers: they don't complain enough, tending rather to be deferential. That is mentioned as a salutary warning: on balance, again, it is preferable to avoid those staff common room exchanges which begin "Old people are all . . ."

Thirdly, one occasionally hears of residential care staff being thrown by signs of romantic emotion and involvement among older residents. Older sexuality, in our culture, is often perceived as either offensive or comic. Yet again, the moral is that some older people may be romantically inclined, and others not. Make no prediction. This example is especially interesting, because it reverts back to the "second childhood" syndrome: I have, in the residential care setting, heard of sexuality berated as one would scold the young for what the "normal" adult sees as premature enlightenment about the birds and bees.

Dozens of other instances could be listed, but the conclusion remains the same. You are dealing with individuals, and they should be approached as individually as possible. It is important to have some grasp of the general national background of older age, and to use that for reference and judgement. Beyond that, the individual is and should be sacred.

Age does not necessarily bring a decline in health and fitness.

The acid test

The pundits say to architects now that the acid test is: would you live or work in the building you designed? The rule of thumb for staff in residential care is sometimes said to be: do you look after the residents as you would look after your own mother? That's fine, but, first, another question must be put: have you, as a person, the self critical faculty which enables you to assess how well or badly you did or do look after your own mother? For a kick-off, did or do you *like* your own mother?

This is important. Please be honest. Care is about the whole person, not just about washing that bit or bandaging this bit. It is about enabling the full person to be as autonomous and, yes, as happy as possible.

We should emphasise the old saying that every age has its compensations. This is very true. It should be the aim of the care assistant to help guarantee that each resident's compensations are entirely realised.

Resources
Centre for Policy on Ageing, 25-31 Ironmonger Row, London EC1V 3QP. Tel: 071 253 1787. Publications and information on old age, policy and service provision, including practical handbooks on aspects of residential care.

CHAPTER 2

Coming into care

by Gwyn Roberts

*Imagine how it feels • welcoming a new resident • preserving
self-respect • relatives • personal belongings and pets*

Have you ever tried to imagine what it is like to go into residential care for the first time? From being surrounded by your own belongings, living life according to your own rules, you are suddenly catapulted into a new environment where everything and everyone about you is strange and different.

This is not easy for anyone, regardless of age. We all tend to be suspicious of strange places and people. It is not surprising then that many elderly people initially find the transition from their own home (where they may have lived for many years) to a residential home quite a difficult one to make.

It is undoubtedly one of the major decisions people make in life – and almost certainly the last major decision.

Going into care is surrounded by all the sorts of fears and doubts that everyone – young or old – feels when they are faced with a momentous change in their way of life.

All elderly people are not the same, any more than all young people are all the same. They have different hopes and aspirations, uncertainties, capabilities, levels of intelligence, background and indeed everything else that distinguishes one human being from another. It is crucial that we do not lump our residents together as being simply "old".

Gains . . .

Of course, "going into care" is not all bad. For many it represents relief from worry about cooking, housework, dealing with finances and loneliness. From time to time, most of us feel pressured by modern life and the thought of being cared for by other people is idyllic. Imagine never having to worry about putting aside money to pay bills or going shopping when it is bitterly cold outside. These can be positive benefits of going into residential care, especially for those elderly people who are physically quite frail.

. . . and losses

On the other side of the coin are the losses people endure when they make the decision to leave their own homes for good. They will never have quite the same freedom of choice or action again; they may miss their gardens or their pets, or having meals whenever they feel like them.

Those of us who work in care homes should be constantly aware of these feelings of loss and try to strive to minimise them as much as possible. Perhaps it is possible for the resident to help in the garden; maybe there is a pet belonging to the home that could be "adopted" by the resident – keeping one's mind and imagination open can provide all sorts of possibilities for reducing a person's feeling of loss.

Staff should be aware of the circumstances leading up to the admission into care. Why was it felt necessary for this person to leave his or her own home? What were the problems? How was he or she failing to cope? Who was involved in the decision? Answers to these questions give valuable clues to the future happiness of the resident.

For example, they may be feeling inadequate because they have been told they are unable to look after themselves. It is quite a shock to people who have spent a lifetime looking after their families to be told they can no longer even look after themselves. As carers, we have a responsibility to try and reverse this feeling of inadequacy. We should try to support and encourage the things that they can do for themselves, rather than emphasising their frailties.

It is important for all people to feel needed and loved, to have a place in the world that is recognised as their own. Therefore, all carers must be aware all the time of the *individual* needs of the people for whom they care.

As an exercise, try and make a list of the "losses" and "gains" you personally would feel about going to live in a large house with a number of other people who are strangers to you. It can be very enlightening!

Receiving a new resident

The first few days in the home are very important in setting the scene for the future; *and* in making the resident feel comfortable and at home. Even more important in some ways, though, are the first few hours.

Try to think how you would feel leaving your own home and moving to a totally strange environment where people seem preoccupied with their own activities and hardly notice your presence. It does not take much imagination to realise how sad and vulnerable you would feel.

When someone comes into care there are always various administrative tasks that have to be carried out and it is easy for staff to become absorbed in these and seem to forget the new resident. It helps a lot if one member of staff can be designated to sit with the resident for a while; to help unpack clothes and belongings; to make a cup of tea or even to introduce other residents if this is appropriate. How you behave on the first day can make all the difference to the long-term wellbeing of the person coming into care.

Do not try to give new residents all the information about the home that they are eventually going to need. All that matters in the first instance is vital and immediate information like where the toilet is, and what time and where the next meal is being served. Everyone going into strange surroundings need to cling onto familiar things and helping to unpack or even just sitting in the room while the new resident unpacks gives the opportunity to talk about items being brought out of the suitcase. Of course, some people may actually prefer to be alone when they are unpacking. Give the new resident the opportunity of being alone if that is what he or she wants, but be on hand in case there are any queries or problems.

It is important also not to assume that new residents are unable to help themselves. People come into care for all sorts of reasons; many are able to undertake daily tasks of living quite independently and this ought to be encouraged. So, again, on the crucial first day, try to establish by observation how much new residents can do for themselves and let them do those things. If it takes a little longer, so what?

A calm, relaxed atmosphere will help in settling in, rather than one of bustling efficiency. It is likely that in our own homes many of us are not very efficient in carrying out household tasks, yet we manage to muddle through in the end. Remember that a care home should be a substitute for the person's own home and should provide the same sort of relaxed and homely environment with opportunities for independence and choice.

Of course, some residents will need more help than others; this is dependent on their level of physical or mental disability. Good observation and listening skills at the start should make it reasonably clear how much help is going to be needed. Having said that, however, do not forget that people change when they become more comfortable and used to an environment and it may be that they are capable of doing much more after a few days than you had first thought. The trick is to review constantly and update your impressions about the residents. Nothing is cast in concrete!

Independence

It is tempting to try to do everything for people in care, especially if they are very slow or very forgetful. But if we do not think carefully about how much we are doing, it is possible to make people entirely dependent upon us for every aspect of life. Naturally, there is a fine line to draw between leaving people to their own devices completely and doing everything for them ourselves, and only by careful assessment of their capabilities can we draw this line with any accuracy.

For example, give them the chance to wash themselves, to choose which clothes to wear and to make their own hot drinks. Obviously, in many homes this is self-evident – many residents are quite capable of undertaking all self-care tasks without supervision and for these it is easier to organise a programme of care that suits both carer and cared for.

However, it is not always so clear cut. Where people are physically frail, staff are inclined to offer a great deal of help, perhaps without thinking how much those people may be able to do for themselves. This is not cruel or hard-hearted: it is a common-sense approach to helping people keep their independence as long as possible.

Even with mentally frail residents, we may underestimate their ability to do simple tasks. Of course, the end result may not be as good as we would like, but at least they will have put some effort into their own care. For example, people with dementia often develop poor eating skills; their table manners deteriorate and they may forget how to use a knife and fork properly. It is often easier and quicker to place people like this on the "feeders" list, and once this is done it is unlikely that they will ever return to feeding themselves.

Instead, have heated plates, give them spoons and leave them to get on with it. Does this sound hard? It isn't really – it is giving those people the opportunity to do something independently.

Dignity

Perhaps the most important aspect of all of residential work is the preservation of dignity – or self-respect – for the residents.

Of course, many elderly people going into care are in need of help and supervision, particularly if they are suffering from mental confusion. Victims of Alzheimer's Disease or senile dementia may be incontinent or prone to behaving in a sexually uninhibited way, and it is difficult to help them maintain dignity in these situations. However, the fact that it is difficult is no excuse for not trying *at all times*.

Indeed, if the carers regard the need to preserve dignity as a constant challenge rather than as a problem, the whole thing takes on a different perspective. Remember that the confused resident could be your grandmother, your mother or even you, one day, and act appropriately. Ensure that residents are always appropriately and cleanly dressed (even if that means their being changed several times a day); that they are led gently and quietly away to privacy if there are signs of sexual disinhibition and that incontinence is dealt with quickly and patiently when it occurs.

Another all-pervasive human need is that of privacy. Living in close proximity to a lot of people can be stressful and most of us (particularly those with unimpaired mental faculties) will need time to "do our own thing". Do not push people into joining in – perhaps they have never been the type to join clubs and mix socially with others. Everyone deserves to make their own choices about their daily lives – even if for the confused residents it is necessary to impose some routine to help them with reality orientation and mental stimulation.

It is worth thinking about how you will address a new resident. Never assume that using their first name is acceptable. Many of the people now coming into care are from a generation that used formal names even with long-standing acquaintances. They may be used to being called "Mr" or "Mrs" and may resent the use of their first name by a total stranger.

Certainly everyone should be asked what form of address they would prefer. Calling people 'darling' or 'love' should be avoided at all times unless they themselves use such expressions and are comfortable with them.

It is particularly important with confused people not to speak to them as children. Although their actions may be child-like sometimes, this should never be an excuse for communicating as one would with a naughty child. Remember that these people are all adults; that many of them have been highly intelligent people and that all have led lives as full and useful as anyone else.

While it is commendable (even necessary) to feel compassion for the elderly confused, over-affection is out of place. We cannot know how much demented people are aware of and they all deserve the courtesy of dignified speech. Of course it is necessary to speak simply and slowly, but this can be achieved without resorting to childish words and phrases.

Relatives

It is important to remember that relatives must always be treated with respect and friendliness.

The decision to place someone in care is often one that is taken by the whole family and usually after much soul-searching. There are unfortunately occasions when the elderly person may be the only one who has *not* been involved in the decision-making process and may thus feel shunned or neglected by the family.

Even if they have been involved and have accepted the need for residential care, there may still be feelings of being unloved and unwanted. Imagine if it were you. Even if you knew that you were physically very difficult to care for and understood how much it was taking out of your family, you would still dislike the idea of their suggesting you should go to a residential home to live with strangers.

As carers, we must understand that there are two sides to every story, and that to remain impartial is crucial. It is wrong to make judgements on family situations about which we have little background knowledge. It is more important to try and promote a feeling of being wanted and needed in the home than to suggest any criticism of the family.

Remember that for many people the decision to place a member of their family into a Home is a very traumatic one – loaded with guilt and negative emotions. If the elderly person has become confused the move can be even more difficult because he or she probably has little insight into the problems that the family are coping with and any attempt to explain and involve the person fully in the decision is met with a total lack of understanding.

Occasionally, the guilt feelings that relatives have are transferred to the carers, and it can happen that whilst 99 per cent of residents' relatives are totally happy with the care we are giving, there are one or two people who seem to have lists of complaints every time they visit.

Obviously, every complaint must be taken seriously and investigated, but if you and the other staff are quite satisfied that they are not justified, try to look behind the actual words and discover if there is a deeper problem. Talk to relatives about how they feel; ask them if they are happy with the care and be sympathetic to complaints. Never argue! Remember that whether in the public sector or the private, our residents and their relatives are our customers and have every right to a say in the service that is being provided.

Activities

What should we as carers be offering our residents? Warmth, comfort, nutritious food – yes, but there is more to it than that. People need to be thought of as individuals with different interests and personalities. The subject of providing and encouraging residents' interests and activities is dealt with fully in Chapter 5, but I would like to add some points from my own experience with elderly confused people.

A short attention span, difficulties in communication and failing memory all make it much more of a challenge to organise a meaningful programme of activities for this group, but it can be done with a little thought and imagination. Treat everyone as an individual with his or her own specific limitations, and it is possible to think of things to do.

Many elderly confused people are physically fit, and escorting them on walks or trips to the local shops can be very stimulating for them. Simple games like dominoes or draughts can be organised and collage-making is usually quite within the scope of many sufferers of senile dementia.

Sing-songs and music and movement are popular, and it is surprising how people with little memory for today's events will be able to remember the words to old songs and dance steps they may have learned fifty years before.

The secret of providing activities for confused residents is not to expect too much of them or of yourself. Even ten minutes spent doing something – no matter how basic – is better than nothing and perseverance can often lead to quite surprising results.

Take time to find out about the social history of residents. This will often provide a lot of information to use during conversation. Never give up entirely because every bit of effort you put into providing entertainment is helping that person achieve something that makes them still human.

Belongings

The fact that a new resident is moving into strange surroundings has been mentioned several times already, and it is important to remember just what this means. A lot of elderly people have lived in the same house for many years (the generation that is now coming into care tended not to move around quite as much as we do nowadays)

The old person's love for their pet should never be underestimated.

and leaving treasured possessions behind can be very upsetting.

Fortunately, most homes allow people to bring in some items of furniture and this should be encouraged. Even just a favourite chair and a small coffee table may help transform the room (no matter how nice the room) into that individual's "space". If furniture cannot be accommodated, at least pictures, photographs and ornaments may give a feeling of homeliness.

People's belongings are important to them; they are all that is left of a lifetime and must therefore be respected. Remember that losing one's home is a form of mourning: a time to reflect on things past and, perhaps, to feel anxious and fearful of the future.

If the resident is confused, it is just as important to have familiar things around. For example, it is very useful if the family can provide a photograph album of holiday snapshots; all clearly labelled so that they can be used by staff in talking to the resident.

Confused people should also be afforded the dignity of wearing their own clothes. This can be very difficult sometimes when they have no recollection of which items belong to them, but having all clothing name-tagged is a small price to pay for helping them to look good. Appearance is important and every personal item that surrounds them – whether furniture or clothing – helps to add meaning to a life.

Pets

When people live alone they often have pets to help combat loneliness and perhaps to give them a feeling of being needed. The love that is felt for the animal should not be underestimated and any decision about going into care will obviously have to take account of the future of something that has become a very important part of that person's life.

It would be easy to say that all residential homes should be prepared to take pets – perhaps in an ideal world they would – but the fact is that there are practical issues that must be considered. Firstly, cats and dogs have to be cared for. Who will walk the dog if its owner is not able to? How will the cat get out and if it cannot, who is going to clean the litter tray? How can we ensure that the animals cannot stray to the food preparation areas where high standards of cleanliness are required by law.

Of course, there are pets that are somewhat easier to accommodate – such as budgerigars or goldfish – and it is possible that staff at a home are willing to accept at least a supervisory role in the up-keep of these animals.

But it is clear that in most instances, the beloved animal cannot accompany its owner into care. It is important for staff to realise that there will be a period of mourning just as acute as mourning for a person who has died. Sympathy, patience and understanding will go a long way to easing the grief, and you should provide opportunities to talk about the lost animal.

Photographs are useful, but by the time the person comes into care, it may be too late to organise these. The family may, of course, be able to provide snapshots, and it is a good idea to use these as conversation pieces to try and reinforce the new resident's feeling of belonging to someone or something.

Points to remember

The prospect of entering a care home means different things to different people. It can range from relief from everyday domestic worries to total supervision in every sphere of living. There are no hard and fast rules – only guidelines.

Every resident:

Is an individual with different needs;

Has led a life that is at least as full and interesting as our own;

Is right to feel strange when first coming into care;

Needs **privacy** and the **right to choose**;

Is a **customer** and should expect **good service.**

CHAPTER 3

Life in a home: balancing rights and risk

by Brenda Hooper

Choosing our way of life • residents should still have choice • privacy and dignity • active independence • the dilemmas in residential care

Every individual has his or her own lifestyle. What does this mean?

It simply means that I choose to live my life in a particular way and this is almost certainly very different in many respects from the way in which you choose to live your life.

You like dancing; I like reading. I am a "hoarder" and can't bear to throw anything away; you hate having things around that you are not actually using at the time. You like to sleep late in the morning (if you get the chance!); I wake early and like to get on with things. You drink tea; I drink coffee. You are happiest when you are with a crowd of friends; I prefer being with just one or two people.

Of course none of us is entirely free to live our life exactly as we choose. Most of us have to earn a living and this takes up quite a large part of our time (though what we do for a job is itself part of our lifestyle, and doing a job which involves shift work for example, affects our way of life considerably). How much money we have can re-strict the interests and hobbies we pursue.

We are all of us subject to the laws of the country, and if we choose to do something that is illegal, we may soon find that we are not as free as we imagined we were! Again, as a member of a group of friends, you may have experienced the pressure that can be exerted on you if you want to do something which is regarded as rather odd by that particular circle – and so you don't feel free to act as you really want to.

Physical illness or handicap, too, can restrict one's chosen way of life.

Precious choice

Despite these constraints, though, the opportunities that each of us has to lead our life in the way we choose, and just to "be ourselves", are very precious to most of us.

What then, of the elderly person who comes to live in an old people's home? Is this freedom a thing of the past for her? You might think so, to hear what some well meaning people say.

Becoming a resident in an old people's home is usually one of the most significant milestones in that person's life. It marks a huge decision: to give up her own home – perhaps the house in which she has lived for sixty years or more – and to begin living in a house which is home for possibly also twenty or thirty other elderly people.

All sorts of people have probably been involved in helping her to come to that decision. Perhaps her sons and daughters have been worried about her for a long time; if she was living alone, they may have been anxious in case she had a fall during the night. Perhaps she has gradually become less able than she was, to go out to collect her pension and to do her shopping, and the family live too far away to help her regularly. Or maybe she was coping quite well until a bout of flu took her into hospital and somehow she was never able to regain her old independence.

Assuming she has some relatives we can be certain there were endless family discussions about what should be done for the best before a decision was taken to make application for a place in a home.

The resulting wait, first for someone to come and see her at home, then for a place to become available, will have been a very difficult time for the old lady. One day she will feel that she can't wait to move; the next day, she will decide it is all a terrible mistake.

For some, of course, it will have been an emergency admission, with all the trauma involved in that. Perhaps she wasn't able even to go back and see her old home and to sort out for herself which of her possessions she wanted to bring with her.

Naturally we do not want to imply that no resident makes a calm and firm decision for herself that the choice to move into a residential home is the right one for her. It is, though, important for us to understand that such a decision is rarely as simple and straightforward as it might appear and that even where the decision seems clearcut and purposeful, there is nearly always a feeling that "this is second best". Almost everyone feels their own home is the ideal place in which to end their days. Entry into a residential home signifies the recognition that this ideal will not be attained.

No more cares?

How is life in a residential home likely to have been described to the potential resident? Almost certainly in terms of "being looked after", of being "cared for", of having all her responsibilities taken over, of never being alone – or lonely – again. Small wonder, then, if she feels as if everything that made up her old life has now finished, and everything about her new life will be decided for her.

Questions asked by new residents or their relatives about life in the home, are very frequently phrased in terms of "Will I be able to . . ." or "Will she be allowed to . . ." or even "What is the rule about . . .".

It is vitally important, therefore, that as soon as a resident comes in, and even before, everyone concerned tries to reinforce the idea that as far as possible, the aim will be to enable her to continue to live her life in the way she chooses, but with the positive addition of the particular forms of help that she as an individual needs, whether this be help with washing and dressing, assistance with mobility or with maintaining continence, or with preparation of her main meals.

Any group of residents in a home will vary considerably in terms of which activities of daily living and personal care they have difficulty with. The temptation to treat them all as equally handicapped must be resisted at all costs.

Balancing risks

A member of staff in a home where it was part of the normal pattern of life for residents to help with the washing up became anxious because a number of breakages of crockery were occurring. Her reaction was to suggest that all residents should be banned from the kitchen. Two issues are involved here. If elderly people with failing eyesight and shaky hands are handling dishes some breakages are inevitable. The importance to the person, however, of feeling wanted and useful, may far outweigh the disadvantage of the cost of replacement dishes!

There may, of course be a genuine fear of danger to the elderly person or to someone else. Proper precautions need to be taken, for example by removing obvious sources of danger, by having equipment at the right height, by installing non-slip surfaces etc. But to prevent a whole group of residents from helping in the kitchen may be quite unnecessary when all that is needed is to provide gentle dissuasion and alternative activities for the one or two residents who are getting beyond being able to cope in the kitchen.

Independence

Again staff may be heard to say that a particular resident has become more frail, and now needs "total" care. What does this mean? Someone who is completely paralysed and in a coma may need total care. But the most frail elderly person will be able to do some things for herself, whether it be, for example, choosing which dress she wants to put on, turning over the pages of a book of pictures, straightening the cover on her bed after it has been made for her, taking a cake from an offered plate of cakes.

The approach needs to be to look for the things that a person can do, and to build any necessary help around her capabilities rather than concentrating exclusively on her disabilities. Assessment needs always to be on an individual basis, and it is unhelpful to fit residents into broad categories of "independent" or "needing full care".

If a resident is unable to wash herself all over but can manage to wash her hands and face if the soap and flannel are handed to her, to encourage her to do this is an important contribution to her dignity and self worth. The fact that it would be quicker for the care assistant do do the task for her is quite beside the point.

If someone is too shaky to pour a cup of tea out for herself, but is able to put the sugar in the cup and stir the tea (even if some goes in the saucer!) then it is important that she is encouraged (not just allowed) to do so. In other words, it is as important not to do for someone what they are able to do for themselves, as it is to help someone with a task that is clearly beyond them.

Don't patronise

Everyone has a right to be treated with dignity as an independent adult. Just because someone needs help with certain tasks of daily living this is not a reason for presuming to treat them like a child. "That's a good girl" is an insulting way to speak to an elderly person, even if her memory is bad and she is more than a little confused from time to time. To have a friendly approach and manner is of course a very good thing, but the care assistant should beware of letting this degenerate into a patronising over-familiarity.

In most homes the use of first names among both staff and residents will be common, but some elderly people will not have been used to being addressed by their first names by younger people, and the care assistant should therefore wait for an invitation to abandon using "Mr" or "Mrs".

The aim must be to establish in the home relationships of mutual respect. (A good Head of Home will be as concerned to deal with incidents of residents treating members of staff rudely or inappropriately as she will be to ensure that staff always speak and act towards residents in a proper manner).

The right to privacy

As we have seen, the transition from living on one's own or with just one or two other people to living in a building where there are maybe twenty, thirty or forty other people can be very traumatic. It can mean having to carry out many of the activities of daily living in the presence of other residents and staff.

For a very "private" sort of person, the thought of eating her meals regularly in a large dining room, and of having to share a table with strangers, can be quite terrifying. Knowing that everyone in a large lounge is watching and listening when one's visitors arrive or when the doctor calls may be another source of embarrassment for some people. And of course, for many elderly people, the most feared aspect of residential care may be the prospect of someone seeing them undressed while helping them to have a bath.

While, as we shall see, the communal aspects of a residential home may be very stimulating to some people and the fact that there is always someone around to talk to may be a source of great thankfulness to them, it is evident that the right to privacy must be preserved at all costs. Some ways of achieving this will be considered below.

Encouraging a person to remain as self-sufficient as possible, even if only in very small ways, can be a means of helping them

to come to terms with the humiliation and embarrassment they may feel about being dependent on others for help with what we all regard as very personal bodily functions.

Of course, residents in a home will, like any cross section of people, include those who will decide not to exert themselves at all when "the staff are paid to do it for me" as well as those who will struggle indefinitely before asking for help. But getting to know the residents as individuals and adjusting one's intervention accordingly, is part of what the professional task of working in a residential home is all about.

Everyone is individual

Fundamental to this is understanding something about the resident's background and emotional needs which are a part and parcel of her behaviour and attitudes towards staff. For every resident is an individual, and has a right to be treated as such. Indeed one of the satisfactions of working in a residential home can lie in establishing real relationships with a number of elderly people who are all different and who have a wealth of experience of life by which the staff and fellow residents can be enriched.

The danger is to try and make everyone fit into the same "mould", and so lose out on the potential of the variety among the residents. Encouraging residents to talk about some of their past life experiences (using reminiscence material like Help the Aged's Recall slide-tape sequences can be stimulating) may help them establish themselves as individuals in the group, as well as being very illuminating for the staff whose own experiences may be so different.

To maintain individuality in the group it is essential that residents have real opportunities to continue to make their own choices about the way they want to spend their time and otherwise live their lives. Ways in which they may be helped to do so, will be considered later.

A full life

Residential homes should not be places where people are waiting to die! They should be places where people are enabled to live their lives to the full despite the limitations which frailty or weakness may place upon them. And this is the rewarding role that staff can play – to encourage and make possible a positive approach to life.

Staff can sometimes get so anxious about caring for the residents and protecting them from potentially risky activities that they are in danger of making it almost impossible for the elderly people to keep hold of the very things that for them make life worth living.

A "home", then can never be exactly the same as the residents' own previous home. But it can become, for an individual, "my home". An old lady, who had been most reluctant to enter the Home in which she had been a resident for several months, had to be admitted to hospital after a heart attack.

After her return to the home, she recounted that while she was recovering in hospital, she found herself "longing to go home", and added that before she became a resident, she would never have imagined that she would "ever say that about this sort of place". It was clearly not just a natural reaction to being in hospital. She genuinely felt that this was her home.

Home sweet home?

What is it that will make "A Home" into "my home" for an individual elderly person? Much will depend on the extent to which

the principles which we have already touched upon are put into practice. It is likely to be achieved if the staff ensure that the resident's needs for assistance are met, but also that she is encouraged and supported in continuing to do for herself everything that she is able to do; if each resident is accorded dignity as an independent adult person, and if the relationships staff have with her are characterised by friendly respect and equality; if her right to privacy as and when she chooses, is ungrudgingly preserved; if she is treated always as an autonomous individual, with the right to choose for herself how to live her life, subject only to the inevitable constraints of living within a community; if she is given every opportunity to lead as fulfilling a life as possible, and encouraged to be outward rather than inward looking.

In the remainder of this chapter we shall look at some aspects of life for residents in a home, and see further how these principles of independence, dignity, privacy, individuality, and fulfilment, may be put into practice.

Private space

The majority of residents will have their own rooms. For someone living in a community, this, their only "private" space becomes all important. Even a small room, or even a part of a shared room can be personalised by pictures, photographs, ornaments.

If there is not room for a lot of furniture, one favourite armchair, and a shabby but well-loved cushion, can make the room feel immediately more like home. Having a second comfortable chair can encourage the resident to think of her room as a place where she can entertain a friend – whether someone from inside the home or from outside.

To rearrange furniture so that the room

can truly be used as a bedsitting room, ie somewhere to live as well as just somewhere to sleep may also make a lot of difference.

Above all, the resident must be able to feel that it is her room and that her privacy in it will at all times be respected. A very timid resident suffered agonies during her first few days in a home, since she had not realised that she could slip the catch on the inside of her door to ensure that no one would walk in unexpectedly, while she was undressing.

Every resident should have the confidence of knowing that she can secure the door from inside (a master key will always be available in a case of emergency), and that in any case, no one will enter her room without knocking – and waiting for an invitation to come in!

Of course some residents are deaf, and will want to give permission to known people to come straight in. But to deny all residents privacy in their rooms because some are deaf is unacceptable. Each resident should be provided with a key for her room and not made to feel a nuisance if she decides to use it – or if she sometimes loses it!

Staff who clean residents' rooms have a particular part to play in ensuring that rooms are regarded as private, by respecting residents' patterns of life when choosing times of day for cleaning. Staff have their own work to get through, but to make a mutual agreement with a resident as to a convenient time for the room to be cleaned is to treat that resident with equality and as an individual.

Again, the interest in and respect for the resident's possessions, shown by the person doing her cleaning or washing can do much to affirm the resident's worth as an individual.

In one home, several different colours were available in the bedlinen used. A particular resident had a great dislike of the colour yellow. She never failed to express her appreciation of the fact that a new member of staff had discovered this and subsequently ensured that when she was on duty the lady's bed was never made up with yellow sheets. A very small thing, but a recognition to that lady that she mattered as an individual, and that she was not just "one of the residents".

Bedtime habits

Getting up and going to bed can be crucial times in the life of a home. People tend to have very individual and sometimes very firmly set habits here. Fortunately, these different preferences can be more easily accommodated than some other aspects of daily life in the home. A flexible breakfast time together with the opportunity and encouragement to get one's own breakfast for all those able to do so, ought to be possible to achieve in most homes.

Few elderly people want more than a simple breakfast, which makes it quite possible to cater, for example, for the one man in a particular home who likes his bacon and eggs every morning. It seems hard to ask someone who has had a cooked breakfast for the last eighty-odd years to change his habits at the age of ninety-one because he has come to live in an old people's home.

Certainly there ought to be no restrictions at all about times of rising or of going to bed. The fact that there are staff on duty 24 hours a day ought to make this not a problem, but it will only happen if routines of staff work are considered to be secondary to residents' chosen ways of organising their lives, and not vice versa.

In the bath

The significance of this is seen in the way staff give help to residents with bathing – a task with which most residents will need

Sitting down Keep Fit is a popular group activity.

some assistance. Privacy and dignity can be maintained by keeping doors shut, by the same care assistant being involved regularly whenever possible, by staff not talking to one another over the resident's head if more than one are present.

Giving only what assistance is actually needed – and for some this will just be seeing them safely in and out of the bath – and encouraging them to do the rest for themselves in privacy will be a valuable contribution to maintaining their independence.

Respecting personal preferences as to how often to have a bath and whether to take it in the morning or just before going to bed demonstrates a recognition of that person as a unique individual. Of course, demands upon staff time may determine how far resident choice can be completely catered for, in relation to those who need help with bathing as well as with getting up or going to bed, but a "negotiation" between resident and staff on the arrangements implies a healthy mutual respect.

It is good, too, to see bath time not just as a chore, but as an opportunity for getting to know one another which often comes more easily in the intimate setting of the bathroom, and which again reas-

sures the resident that she matters as a person.

Focus on food

Food can loom large in any residential home, and is often a focus for complaints! Sometimes, it would appear, because residents have too little otherwise to occupy their thoughts; sometimes because complaining about food may be "acceptable", whereas complaining about the "real" cause of discontent, (perhaps a feeling that residents' views are not being sufficiently considered in decisions about the running of the home), is thought to be too threatening.

Thus, as with a small child and its mother, complaining about food can be a weapon used by residents against staff who can take it as a personal insult to have their best efforts constantly criticised! Sometimes, therefore, criticisms need to be taken lightheartedly, or attention given to other apparently unrelated aspects of life in the home.

However, food is important to most people, and it can be one of the more difficult areas in which to avoid an institutional approach far removed from someone's own home. The aim should be to arrange for each resident to be able to choose, as far as is possible within the constraints of communal living, when they eat, what they eat, where they eat, and with whom they eat!

You may immediately say, that this is impossible. Perhaps the most helpful way to approach the subject is to think about your own experience in your own home. In any family, certain patterns will have become established about times of meals, type of food served, and when people eat together or separately. These patterns will almost certainly have been set, however, as a result of the personal preferences and commitments of different members of the family, with compromises where the choices of some members conflict with one another. Special dietary needs will, it is hoped be certainly catered for, but over and above this, as much choice as possible should be built in to meal arrangements.

Getting to know likes and dislikes and what for an individual resident makes a "special" meal, is another way of treating someone as an individual. Birthdays are obvious times to mark with chosen meals. It is good, too, if the special days which are celebrated in families, are marked in some way. One home had a very successful Pancake party on Shrove Tuesday, complete with a game of tossing the pancake!

Staying active

The whole area of activities for residents can become a very vexed one, with staff complaining that residents don't want to do anything, and residents refusing offered outings, while spending much time asleep apparently out of boredom. The issues are complex, but some guidelines could be considered.

Every resident has a right to choose whether to participate or not in any particular activity. However there will undoubtedly be some who, because of failing eyesight or arthritis, for example, are no longer able to pursue hobbies they previously enjoyed. Some of these may positively welcome the opportunity to take part in activities which are only possible because they are part of a group. Sitting down Keep Fit classes are one example. Chapter 5 gives detailed ideas for encouraging activities and outings.

Normal life

As much "normality" as possible should be the aim. If an outing to the theatre is being arranged, don't assume that of course it will be the matinée. It will probably be much more of an excitement to go to the evening performance and arrive home late and in the dark!. It is too easy for staff to assume that they know what is good for residents instead of really asking them what they would like.

Perhaps the crucial question to ask is always "Whose home is it?". Most residents will have previously been used to running their own homes and there are many ways in which they can be involved in making decisions about the way in which the home in which they are now living is organised.

Each home will need to discover for itself the best way of finding out residents' opinions on relevant issues. Residents' meetings will be successful in some cases; in others a more individual approach will be needed.

What is important is that staff do not act as if they have the right to decide on matters which affect all residents, and as if any consultation is a privilege. If each resident is truly treated with dignity and respect as an independent, adult individual, there is a very good chance that she will soon come to feel that the "Home" is her home.

CHAPTER 4

Life in a home: as clients and carers see it

by Paul Julian Fletcher

How your behaviour is seen • how your attitudes show • rules ruled out • what to do about bad practice • a framework for care • the keyworker role

Let us begin with an example: the old lady who comes to a home for a two-week stay while her family, with whom she lives, go away for a holiday.

The family bring her with a packed case at 11.00am and it's a busy morning as mornings usually are. It takes a few rings of the bell before someone can get down to answer it. She is welcomed with a smile by a care assistant who shows her and the family into the hallway, and then shoots off to fetch the officer in charge who is busy elsewhere. She looks around warily while the family try to reassure her.

The officer in charge arrives and welcomes her, again with a big warm smile, but quickly gets into conversation with the son and daughter-in-law, reassuring them that she'll be alright, asking about her clothes, her tablets, her money and when they will be collecting her again.

Our lady gets distracted by the care assistants and other residents that pass and as someone else is helped by in a wheelchair. The officer in charge asks her if she would like to see her room, adding that it's on the first floor but she's sure to be able to

manage the lift. It's a slow walk with her walker to the bedroom and it seems a long way down great corridors and around many corners to get there.

Forty people live here, the officer in charge mentions, and she also talks about the mealtimes, the buzzer system and the laundry arrangements as they walk along. She talks in a nice friendly way and introduces her to other care assistants and residents as they make their way. She catches glimpses into sitting rooms, other people's bedrooms and a bathroom with a hoist as they go.

They arrive at her room which is OK though not like a bedroom in an ordinary house. The officer in charge leaves them for a moment while her son and daughter-in-law unpack and talk to her about the room. She mentions that she will never remember how they got to the room!

Everyday event

For most of us this is a familiar picture. I am sure we have all showed someone new to their room at some time. It's not an example of how not to do it either. It's just a familiar event in our work, though we know it's special for this lady and for her family. But let's go through that again and think what some of those events might have meant to the new lady: what could she be thinking while we would be talking and showing them around?

	What she might have thought
The packed case	they are going without me: I must be a nuisance.
Few rings of the bell	they are not ready for me – we're too early.
The hallway	it's so strange . . .
Officer in charge talking to son	I'm as much use as that suitcase . . .
Care assistants/other residents	so many faces, and none familiar. Do they think I'm like that?
The lift	does she think I can't press a lift button?
The long corridors	it's no use; this will never work.
Other rooms and bedrooms	it is strange . . . it's frightening.
The hoist	I'm frightened.
Unpacking	they will be leaving soon . . .

What has happened is that this lady, like all of us would do, is making sense as best she can of what she sees around her. She makes sense of it by relating it to what she had known in the past, from ideas that she has, and to how she feels at that time. She is interpreting what she sees and hears, making her own sense of it, as we do all the time.

Picking up clues

In just the same way we all interpret the attitudes of other people towards us – what we think they think about us. We interpret attitudes from what someone says, how they say it, from their "body language" (with a smile or an outstretched hand, or looking away with their back turned) and from what they actually do.

So we pick up someone's attitude towards us in many different ways from the clues we are given. The attitude can sometimes be quite clear, or it can be open to misunderstanding. Either way it can be very powerful, and quite change the meaning of something that is said.

For example, if someone says to us "Nice to see you again" it can be enthusiastic and sincere, or it can be said routinely and without much feeling, or it can be muttered while they roll their eyes up to heaven. The words are the same, but those are three quite different attitudes towards us, at that moment.

Some attitudes demonstrate positive feelings and make the day nicer for anyone, like:

interest; affection; respect; patience; kindliness; generosity; energy; enthusiasm; helpfulness.

There are lots more. They make people feel comfortable about being with that person and in that situation.

Other attitudes will be understood to show less kind feelings. From these we will believe that that other person:

is not interested in us
does not like us
thinks we are worth nothing
has no time for us
is unkind

is mean

can't be believed

is bored

does not want to help

is condescending and thinks they are better than we are.

In our work our attitude towards clients is crucial – either what we mean, or what our clients think we mean. People we help may be frail, vulnerable and dependent. They may need our help and may need it every day that we are there. If a request is met by a negative attitude, how can they ask for help again? How must that feel? On the other hand what pleasure the positive attitudes can give: to feel worth something, that people do care, and that they really will help.

Actions speak louder

What we say and how we say it is important if we are helping someone, but the many small actions imply an attitude too. For instance

• do we knock on doors?

• do we close doors? That means respect and privacy, especially in bedrooms and bathrooms.

• do we make time for people? showing that they are worth our time?

• are we polite and respectful – even when we are rushing to do something else?

• do we look happy to be doing something, even when it is not our favourite task?

• do we sit with people, or stand and "talk down" to them? Do we talk to other staff given the chance, over our clients' heads?

• do we always treat old people as adults? Nothing else is good enough even if they do need our help.

The "positive" attitudes are positive and the "negative" are negative whoever the client may be. The most able, alert, inde-pendent and jolly person to be helped deserves no different an attitude from someone who may be disabled, confused, demanding or "unresponsive". All are adults and deserve our respect whatever the assistance they need.

Elderly people who are confused deserve special mention. Too easily attitudes can creep in which suggest that it somehow "matters a bit less" how they are helped or treated. It sounds shocking but it's true. For example, the bedroom or sitting room that is bare and unattractive; less careful attention to clothes or hair or personal possessions; undignified toileting routines; less patience; less attempt at conversation or finding out their pleasures; fewer outings; less knocking on the door before entering . . .

For the most confused clients there is sometimes the terrible tendency to "babify" which is no way to treat an adult even when well intended. Baby talk, baby bibs and baby nappies are strictly for babies – not for handicapped adults. There are decent adult solutions to adult disabilities.

Consider the messages that treating someone like a baby contains: you are not an adult anymore: you no longer have the rights or the respect that an adult can expect, to be helpful I expect you to be-have like a "good baby". The devastation of Alzheimer's Disease does not need to be compounded by loss of dignity, respect and civilised behaviour by those around you.

The rot spreads

It is also worth considering two other points: what are the effects of attitudes also (i) on other people being helped and (ii) on us, the helpers.

For other clients, it is degrading and frightening to witness a fellow client being treated as they would not want to be treated

The best homes stress the rights, individuality, independence, choice, strengths, privacy and dignity of every single person.

themselves. The phrase "I hope I never get like that" also means "I hope I never get treated like that".

It also encourages fellow clients to adopt negative attitudes about a confused member: "Poor thing, she's no idea what she is doing".

This also serves to justify poor staff behaviour, like asking in a loud voice in a room full of other people, "Have you been to toilet this morning? Have you wet yourself again? Come on, you'd better come with me". We can all think of more discreet, adult and respectful ways of asking, or places to ask this, once we accept that it does matter how we do it.

For us as staff or helpers there is also the danger that treating one person inappropriately can spread so that all clients being helped get similarly treated; everyone gets cared for as if they were incapable of thinking for themselves or doing anything properly. Just think how many negative attitudes this demonstrates and what its effect on people must be, even when it is well-intentioned "caring".

This is far removed from the attitudes expressed in the practice of many enlightened homes that stress the rights; individuality; independence; choices (however big or small); preferences; abilities and strengths; privacy; dignity; of every single person, regardless of their specific disabilities. After all, our role as helpers is only to assist residents with the things that they cannot do for themselves. We are not in the business of somehow changing people into what we think they ought to be, or doing what we think they should do. Our role is about helping to fill in the gaps in what our clients or their families or friends can manage, it is not about taking over and running other people's lives regardless.

That is why I have never had any time for the rules and regulations that some homes have dreamt up, that say what you can/can't, or must/mustn't do, or where you can or can't be at any time. These are repressive, institutionalising and unnecessary. A set of rules can be a set of negative attitudes too!

A special difficulty that we as helpers face is that so many things that are crucial to our clients do become routine to us. It is just normal to us to do things in the way we usually do – without checking first that that is what we ought to be doing.

We cannot assume that a client wants us to do what we think they want us to do, or what we would routinely expect to do for them. If we do, our attitudes are showing. We are giving them a message about what we think of them – or what we think they are capable of – and these are likely to be negative attitudes. Perhaps this is the difference between "doing to" and "doing for" the client.

If something is wrong

The attitudes of our colleagues are something that will affect us as well. We too can be pleased, upset, amused, saddened, infuriated . . . by the attitudes of our colleagues. In an ideal team all the members would be sharing broadly similar positive attitudes to the work and clients, but it does happen that one member of the team may be expressing attitudes, and demonstrating them in their work, that you feel are clearly going against the interests of clients. It could be about their behaviour to a particular client or to a particular task for example.

What can you do about it? Firstly, if you are sure you are right and you really care for the people you help, you know you cannot just forget it or pretend it didn't happen. You cannot keep it to yourself and stay worried or unhappy about it: that solves nothing. You have to do something about it; you must confront bad practice even in the face of "group pressure" from colleagues. But how?

The only answer is by talking to someone who can do something about it, although it may not be easy. Can you talk to the person who did whatever it was? If not you must talk to your supervisor or officer in charge. Do this as quickly as possible: it can be very difficult to do anything positive about something that happened weeks ago.

If you feel bad about doing this you must remind yourself of why you came into this work, of what you believe in and why. We all have a duty to safeguard the rights of clients and to maintain the professional standards of our work. If your boss will not listen to you, you must go to your boss's boss, and so on. You may feel you need

support in this, and may find it helpful to enlist the help of another colleague, a friend, another "professional" you may know (nurse, GP, vicar), or a representative of a professional organisation (SCA, BASW) or a Trades Union.

Large organisations usually have a complaints procedure you can use, and all private or voluntary homes for the elderly with four or more residents are visited by a Registration Officer of the Local Authority Social Services Department who can be consulted. If you are an outsider of the organisation go straight to the officer in charge or the director of that organisation. You may not be able to change the world, but you must satisfy yourself that what you have to say has been fairly heard by a person who is in a position to do something about it. Try and deal in facts as far as possible, not in personalities or "rumours", and find someone you can talk to for your support.

A framework for care

In this chapter we have looked at a number of pitfalls. I hope that nevertheless my own attitude to residential work is clear. As someone who has worked as a care assistant, assistant officer in charge, deputy officer in charge, officer in charge and as a manager of a group of local authority homes for the elderly, I can say that I have a great love for this work, respect and admiration for the many people I know who are engaged in it at every level, and a true belief in the positive opportunities it provides for the clients who choose to join a comfortable, stable and unrestricted community where they can find the services and companionship they seek without being diminished as individuals.

Attitudes and feelings however do not exist in a vacuum, and for the best service to our clients they need to be harnessed together in a "framework of practice" where every helper is clear about their role and the overall aims of the establishment. If we are trying to establish a professional framework here are thirteen key features of it that I would list first. None is imaginary; each is well developed in one of the homes I know well, and all are in everyday practice in a few excellent establishments.

1. A clear **delegation of duties amongst senior staff** – real responsibilities allowing for real satisfaction and opportunities for creative working.

2. **The key worker role** to offer more individual support to each client, but balancing these individual staff responsibilities with the wider **residential worker role** (the shared team responsibilities).

3. Regular, well established, personal **supervision** for each member of staff.

4. Properly planned **induction programmes** and probationary interviews for each member of staff, introducing them to their individual and team responsibilities. Ongoing staff development courses continue this process.

5. Planned **admission procedures** for each new resident (including relief care and day care clients) involving social worker, senior staff, key worker, the resident and their family.

6. **Care plans** for each resident. A statement of how we can offer as normal, adult and enjoyable a lifestyle to that resident, with attention to the details that are important to him or her.

7. **Home as "home".** This is about power. It is a rejection of all the old ideas about "rules" and do's and don'ts, and is seen in returning decision-making to the resident. This is observable in the ways residents use their rooms, what they bring with them, flexibility in meal times/bed times/bath times, how residents and their families come and go about their own lives and establish their own unique lifestyles within the home with our help. Residents' meet-ings are also a part of this.

8. **Programmes of social events**: although some clients will choose to avoid these, as they are free to do, for others they provide stimulation, entertainment and fun. They can also foster a feeling of belonging, a sense of community and something to look forward to. The contribution of voluntary organisations or individual volunteers can be invaluable in this. Without these diversions life in a home can be boring and empty. Summer holidays are also increasingly popular.

9. **Communicating and recording**: how best to use staff meetings, co-ordinating work "as a team", the value of written records, and making the best use of them. Regular senior staff meetings are essential too.

10. In an attempt to bring all these together in the form of a policy for the establishment, homes are increasingly writing **Operational Policies** to define clearly just what it is they are aiming to achieve, and how they intend to set about it.

11. **Annual residents reviews** – with the resident and family/friends: a friendly but "formal" annual meeting with staff of the home to discuss just how far the services provided meet the desires and needs of the client.

12. **Annual staff appraisals**. A discussion sheet prepared by the care assistant and their supervisor provides the basis for this annual review of their work by the officer in charge; a chance to thank and congratulate staff on all their good work and to help work on any areas of weakness. Similar systems are used for senior staff.

13. **Annual Establishment Reviews**. A cycle of meetings brings together discussions with clients, families and friends, fellow "professionals" (doctors, nurses, occupational therapists, physiotherapists, social workers etc), volunteers and staff, about what the home is trying to achieve and how, and welcoming their views.

CHAPTER 5

Life in a home: interests and activities

by Margaret Cheetham

Apathy – "the enemy within" • encouraging residents' interests • communications • the right to opt out • group activities and outings • fund-raising and social events in the home • everyday activities • education and discussions • a sense of purpose

This chapter is based on my ten years experience as officer in charge of a voluntary home for seventy-nine elderly people. It is a large purpose-built home in extensive grounds, but it has no special facilities for activities other than six useful sized lounges. Nor does it have staff who are particularly trained to be activity leaders, although the care assistants' training course which all the care assistants have attended does emphasise the importance of helping residents to remain mentally active and physically fit.

The home is therefore typical of many throughout the country. Its residents come from a variety of backgrounds with differing interests and abilities.

Although she may have lived alone for a number of years prior to admission to the home, loneliness for a new resident can be heightened by being in a crowd of unfamiliar people in strange surroundings. It is by meeting other residents, not only at meal times but also at groups and social gatherings in the home that the barriers are gradually brought down.

The enemy within

If a home does not deliberately set out to provide opportunities – social, cultural, educational, group or individual, both inside and outside the home, the residents will quickly deteriorate mentally, and therefore physically, to a state of apathy. They may well become inward looking and find ailments, real or imaginary, to occupy their time. Their state of health takes on an unnatural significance in their lives.

How frequently are residents of homes for the elderly viewed (and this is the image commonly seen on television programmes) sitting in rows against the walls of large sitting rooms; the chairs arranged like this for the benefit of the staff for ease of movement with wheelchairs, medicine trolleys and so on? Although the residents' chairs may not be actually labelled with their names, they may just as well be since chairs are allocated and no one is given the option of sitting in a different chair.

There is usually little conversation to be heard. Sitting alongside someone rather than opposite tends to discourage conversation since there is not so much eye contact and therefore less need to make conversation.

Their days are spent largely unoccupied, the long hours interrupted only by meals and visits to the toilet. To give the impression to visitors, perhaps even to themselves, that something is going on, staff may have a television or a radio on to which no one is paying any attention, and some residents undoubtedly would prefer not to have it on.

There is, in this rather dismal scene, a feeling of apathy that is almost tangible, and the residents may be described as being socially dead. Apathy is the "enemy within" homes for the elderly, and we who work in these homes must continually fight against it.

Caring skills

Until recently, even among geriatricians, there were low expectations about the quality of life in old age, but it is now more widely accepted that with help old people in residential homes can progress, can even be rehabilitated into the community. It is now recognised that care assistants require special skills and training in order to effectively carry out not just the essential physical care tasks such as bathing, feeding, and attending to residents' personal needs, but also the social care aspects of their work. This is equally important and should be seen to be so.

All residents, whatever their state of health, need to fill their days usefully and purposefully. Some may require little or no assistance from care assistants in order to do this but many will need encouragement and even physical help in order to carry out particular activities. Care assistants therefore need to have a good working knowledge of the residents in their care, including knowledge of their physical and mental problems.

It is very helpful also if, on admission, a resident is asked for details of her life and what hobbies and interests she has had. (I refer to the residents as "she" only because female residents are in the majority in most homes.) The information can be attached to her file and it may be possible then or at a later stage to introduce her to another resident with the same interest, to form the basis of a new friendship. One of the main objects of organising activities is to bring people together and ease their loneliness.

Communicate

Especially in a large home, such as the one I work in, communications are vital to the smooth running of the establishment. In the context of organising activities good communications are also essential, so that everyone knows what is going on and where. We have a large notice board on which notices of external events as well as those within the home are pinned.

Local theatre productions, fund-raising events in the area, holiday post cards from staff and residents – all these are alongside a weekly diary of events and activities in the home. The residents have become accustomed over the years to studying the notice board each day for any additions or alterations. It is helpful to residents with poor sight if the notices are written in black marker pen on white paper for clarity.

Another interesting and useful way we have of keeping everyone informed of future and recent past events is by the monthly production of a newsletter. This is compiled, edited, and produced by the residents and circulated to all the residents and staff free of charge. Additional copies can be purchased to send to friends and relations. The newsletter contains detailed accounts from individual residents of all happenings and developments inside the home, as well as reports on outings in the minibus, visits to the theatre, and family affairs. In most editions there is a crossword for which a prize is awarded for the first correct entry.

A third way by which residents may communicate with administration, staff, and other residents, is by holding regular residents' meetings. As well as the criticisms and compliments which are handed out by the residents at these meetings, ideas are put forward for new activities and arrangements are made for parties, fund-raising events, and so on.

Opting out, or in . . .

It is important to point out that in every group of residents there will be a few non-participants. It is every resident's right to opt out, if she so wishes, of any organised activity without being made to feel an outcast of the community. As staff we have a duty to provide opportunities for enjoyment and creativity, and encourage residents who show any interest, however small, but certainly not put pressure on them in any way.

We have to accept, reluctantly perhaps, that there are those who wish to keep out of social activities and have no intention of doing anything whatsoever. There are others, however, who whilst saying they are loners because they do not wish to commit themselves, or through lack of confidence, can with help be drawn into a group and encouraged to join in. For example, by suggesting that they just watch an activity such as Keep Fit or singing, or make up the numbers at a card game to assist the others,

they may find themselves irresistibly drawn into the group. By such devious means reticent residents may find enjoyment in pastimes that normally they would not have attempted.

Activities may be categorised in different ways – individual or group, indoor and outdoor, social and educational, physical and mental. Many activities fall into more than one of these categories. I would also suggest another way of classifying activities – into those which are organised by the staff for the residents, and those which the residents organise for themselves or which when carried out in some way improve the quality of their own lives and the lives of their fellow residents.

The following activities are all organised in the home, some weekly, some at less frequent intervals, but regularly:

Keep Fit

As well as being a popular group activity this also is beneficial to health. Residents who suffer from conditions such as arthritis, and come to Keep Fit, tend to complain less than those who do not take any kind of regular exercise. They maintain that the exercises help to reduce joint stiffness, keep them mobile, improve circulation, and give them a feeling of well-being. These sessions are combined with techniques in relaxation which aids reduction of tension and stress.

Occasionally other physical activities are incorporated into the more formal Keep Fit. There can be a great deal of movement involved in the throwing and catching of a large ball or bean bag, or kicking a football around in a group. Keep Fit is very enjoyable, especially when the exercises are performed in time to music with a group leader who has the necessary enthusiasm and personality to encourage those taking part.

There are other pastimes which are

physically beneficial to residents as well as giving pleasure and companionship. Snooker, darts, indoor and outdoor bowls, putting and croquet, are all games which improve fitness whilst socialising. Our garden is very large and residents who lack confidence to go further afield enjoy walking in the grounds with staff on fine days.

Handicrafts

Weekly handicraft sessions are run by an outside volunteer and are very popular. Residents bring their own knitting, sewing, or whatever they are working on, or if there is a fund-raising event coming up they work together as a team to make items to sell on their stall. These afternoons are as popular for the social opportunity they provide as they are useful. A tea trolley is provided midway through the afternoon from which the residents serve each other.

Fund-raising

Each year there are at least three fund-raising events for the residents' Amenities Fund which provides the "extras" for the residents – large print books for the library, garden furniture, Christmas decorations etc. The residents help a great deal before and during these Coffee Mornings or Christmas Fairs or Garden Parties. They donate items for the stalls, design publicity posters, man the stalls, sell raffle tickets and encourage many of their friends and relations to attend. Normally a large number of people from the area attend, and again these events are very much a social occasion with the home as part of the wider community.

We should never forget that the home is part of the community and ought to make efforts to be involved in outside affairs, by fund-raising for example. In recent years this home has been involved in raising

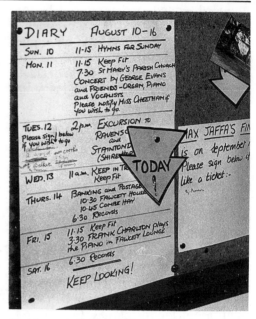

Residents study this noticeboard every day.

funds for two local churches, the hospice, and equipment for the hospital, as well as supporting efforts by individuals such as helping to fund participation by a young woman in Operation Raleigh.

Social Events

Purely social events – parties – play an important part of the life of any home. They are another link with the outside world and give residents the opportunity they would otherwise miss of dressing in their best clothes and acting as hosts and hostesses to their guests. Parties are occasions when staff, residents, and outside people can socialise together and get to know each other better.

Playreading

This may appeal to some residents who can read and hear well. They can have a great deal of fun choosing and rehearsing plays. We find that the most popular plays are comedies and these are eventually performed for the rest of the residents.

Outings

There is another way of keeping in touch with the outside world. After a winter of intensive fund-raising the home was able to buy its own minibus which had been adapted for use by disabled residents by the addition of a folding step at the side and a ramp for wheelchairs at the back. Having the bus has added another dimension to the lives of the residents who now enjoy regular outings such as twice weekly shopping trips to town and on fine days trips to the countryside. These runs out of town usually include a stop at a cafe or perhaps for a picnic in the summer.

Twice a year the bus is used for taking residents away on country or seaside holidays. Outings provide residents with something new to talk about as well as a complete change of scene. Some have not been able to go out at all prior to coming to the home and are a little afraid of venturing into the outside world again, so frequent short trips may be necessary to restore their confidence. As well as catering for all tastes, outings should include visits to new developments and buildings in the area to help to keep residents abreast with what is going on in their town.

Shopping

Even though the regular visits to town mean that a number of residents can choose what they want to buy, some housebound residents would have to depend on the choice of others for their shopping if it were not for the fact that local shops are willing to visit the home. Exercising choice, and making a decision about what to buy is something the majority of us take for granted and so it is important that the element of choice should be maintained in the lives of all residents.

Particularly around Christmas time we have found several shops prepared to come on the same afternoon with a range of their goods to put on display, to form a mini-market in one of the larger lounges. Cosmetics and toiletries, jewellery, leather goods and stationery are placed on tables all round the room to give residents plenty of choice when buying gifts for loved ones, or simply treating themselves to something.

Several firms of clothiers, some who specialise in clothing for the elderly and/or disabled, visit during the year with the changing seasons and show appropriate clothes for the coming season.

Education

Continuing education for residents may mean they widen their knowledge by attending activities outside the home, and they should be encouraged to keep up with their attendance of any societies or courses that they were involved with prior to coming to the home. For many though this will not be possible, so the provision of informal educational and cultural opportunities within the home helps to keep up existing interests and possibly develop new ones.

We offered the local University of the Third Age (U3A) branch facilities at the home for meetings some years ago, and it has been mutually beneficial to residents and members of the outside community alike. Courses held at the home enable both sides to exchange ideas and points of view, and have included music appreciation, painting, dressmaking, local history.

The U3A is run by and for retired people, with tutors taken from among the membership. Any person who has a particular skill or is knowledgeable about a subject and is willing to pass on this knowledge to a small group is a "tutor". So it is that one of our residents who has always been a skilled soft toy maker is now a tutor and holds her small class in the home each week. The emphasis here as with other activities is the social side. Each afternoon session provides a good reason for coming together with people of similar interests.

Religion

Religion can play an increasingly important part in the lives of older people and each person's spiritual requirements should be accommodated as far as possible. Those who are able and who like to attend church are taken by car or minibus each Sunday.

For the housebound Holy Communion is brought once a month and one of the lounges temporarily is converted to a chapel for the occasion. In addition once a month a service is taken by a local minister, and the Gideons also hold a monthly meeting in the home.

Reminiscence

Many old people have no difficulty at all in remembering the distant past, but find remembering what they did yesterday very difficult indeed. Apart from being very frustrating this can be demoralising and add to a feeling of worthlessness. Holding a small group where they are encouraged to remember the past can help them, they can contribute something worthwhile again, and others can learn from them.

In order to get a discussion started there are aids in the form of slides or photographs of days gone by, or old fashioned household objects. Care assistants, especially the younger ones, find that they can learn a lot from these mentally frail residents about their youth and the times they lived in.

Discussions

Initiating and sustaining a discussion is one of the hardest exercises to undertake, but if it can be done successfully it is very rewarding. Apart from reminiscence discussions we have found it difficult, partly because residents are unwilling or unable to advance beyond their own set ideas. We have had some limited success using television programmes as a basis for discussion. Programmes which are designed especially to interest elderly people are recorded and later watched by a group of residents, who enjoy discussing what they have seen together.

Passive entertainment

Watching television occupies much of residents' time; it may be classed as passive entertainment. Passive entertainments are those in which the residents do not take an active part but nevertheless provide them with a new experience to think and talk about.

In this category of organised activity in the home, there are weekly slide shows or talks by invited speakers on different parts of the world or local familiar places. At the end of these sessions residents may take a more active part by asking questions if they wish to.

As an alternative to slide shows or talks about travel, we have invited guests who have interesting collections or who are willing to come and talk about their hobbies, for example collecting Eskimo carvings, glass ornaments, or stamps. We also invite people who have a special art or craft which they are willing to demonstrate, such as portrait painting or flower arranging.

Concerts regularly occupy an afternoon or an evening. Soloists, music ensembles, or choirs give great pleasure, and those who come to entertain in this way come

Encourage residents in the activities that interest them.

from local schools, churches, and surrounding villages. We are also very fortunate in having a resident organist and a resident pianist – both of whom live close to the home and give regular concerts to our residents.

Self-starters

All the activities mentioned so far have been arranged by the home for the residents, but there are many other activities which residents have initiated or have been encouraged by staff to take up, and have then developed themselves.

Experience shows that the happiest and most fulfilled residents are those who are actively involved in the daily life of the home which includes helping others. We all need to feel that we are of value and worth to the community and should accept responsibility for what goes on in that community. As staff we should actively encourage independence and allow some risks to be taken towards that end.

We should also promote self-help amongst the residents and there should be an atmosphere in the home that welcomes initiatives and offers of practical help from residents. The activities which follow are those which are carried out by residents in the home, and they all in some way contribute towards improving the quality of life for all residents.

Daily life

We are fortunate in having a large well-stocked library containing many large print books. (We have noticed that even residents with good sight prefer to read these.) The library is completely run by two residents who check the incoming and outgoing books, and periodically present an order for new books to replace those which they have discarded. Other residents select books and take them for residents who are unable to leave their rooms.

It is residents who tend the plants which adorn every window sill and table top in the home, and also see to it that there are fresh cut flowers placed in the entrance halls and lounges.

Other residents, on receiving the next day's menu from the cook, make up the menu board for the next day and display it in the entrance hall.

In the evening the local newspaper is read to residents who are not able to see the small print, or who simply enjoy being read to. This is done each evening by two or three residents in turn. This practice incidentally can give rise to lively comment, discussion, or reminiscence.

The home has a pond with goldfish, two budgerigars, and a golden retriever bitch. These are cared for by several residents, and as is well documented pets have a therapeutic value all of their own.

The large garden needs a great deal of attention to be kept tidy. The heavy work of grass cutting, edging, and digging, is carried out by a firm of gardeners, but there is still much to be done in growing seeds in the greenhouse, planting seedlings out, and weeding, and it is the residents who undertake this kind of work. With the recent addition of raised flower beds in part of the gardens this activity has now been opened up to more residents who may be interested.

Of the more active residents there are several who help the staff in different ways by assisting frailer residents. They may accompany residents on outings or appointments, help with wheeling chairs or just walking alongside someone to give confidence, or even assist a resident to be dressed if through arthritis or as a result of a stroke this is a problem.

Some residents organise their own small parties in one of the lounges, with no staff help. They invite friends from inside and outside the home and these events give great pleasure to residents who prefer smaller numbers of people to the larger social gatherings.

We have amongst our residents three pianists who give impromptu recitals to entertain residents. Another two alternate to provide evenings of playing records each week.

One gentleman is on hand to help any resident with an electrical or any other kind of appliance which needs repairing.

One lady makes sloe gin, and although unable to go out herself, she has regular supplies of the necessary ingredients brought to her. She enjoys providing the sloe gin as presents or for fund-raising events.

All used envelopes are kept and people from outside the home bring in theirs too. The residents cut the stamps off and these are sent to local charities.

Jigsaws are a pleasant way of occupying spare time. The residents have a large collection and leave one out in a lounge for all to complete; they then replace it with another.

Residents organise for themselves and for others afternoons of games such as Bingo or Trivial Pursuit or Bridge – games which aid memory or concentration.

Sense of purpose

All activities, whether provided by the staff of a home or by the residents themselves, are there to help residents to remain motivated and interested in life.

With better provision in the community fewer older people in the future may be compelled to leave their homes, and the option of residential care may be a matter of positive choice in many instances. Those people, or their relatives, will look only at homes that look beyond catering for the obvious physical comforts and give to their residents the opportunity to reach their maximum potential.

Resources
Activities for the Frail Aged, Patricia M. Cornish. Winslow Press, Telford Road, Bicester, Oxon OX6 0TS.
Older Learners, edited by Susanna Johnston and Chris Philipson, published for Help the Aged Education Dept. by Bedford Square Press, 26 Bedford Square, London WC1 3HU.
Encouraging Residents' Activities (Booklet No. 4 Home Work), Judith Hodgkinson, and Staying Active, June Armstrong, both from the Centre for Policy on Ageing, 25-31 Ironmonger Row, London EC1V 3QP.

CHAPTER 6

Talking and listening

by Jane Maxim and Karen Bryan

Good listening • speech and understanding • conversation and relationships • confusion and dementia • language and speech difficulties

What is communication? What can make communication difficult for an elderly person? What can be done to make *communication* easier?

These questions all use the term communication. It is often said that someone is a good communicator when they can talk well and interest their listeners. But there are two sides to good communication: being able to make the meaning clear, and being able to listen and understand what is being said.

In working with elderly people it is often listening which is by far the most important part of good communication. Listening can be done well or badly: think of how annoying it can be when someone does not appear to be listening to what is being said. To be a good listener it is important that your conversational partner can see that you are attending.

For most people, good communication is a very important part of their lives. For many elderly people it is particularly important because they have limited mobility and are restricted in their activities. For

example, the frail elderly person, the person with arthritis, the person who has difficulty walking after a stroke – talking and listening are vital ingredients in their everyday lives.

How can people be good communicators and good listeners?

Of course good communication does not mean just speaking clearly. It means using an appropriate tone of voice, making eye contact with the listener, perhaps using gesture to emphasise a particular point, perhaps altering body position to show someone that you are talking to them rather than someone else. In other words most people, including elderly people, listen with their eyes as well as their ears.

Some elderly people have hearing difficulties or cannot see well. Communicating with them requires the same set of good communication skills but with a different emphasis.

An elderly person with hearing difficulties will be much more reliant on their eyes when listening. They will only know when someone is speaking to them because that person is facing them. They may be able to lip read and so need to be able to see the person's face well, in good light.

They need to see normal speech to be able to lip read. This comment may seem strange but when someone is shouting they distort their normal speech. Not only is lip reading then more difficult but, if the person listening can hear something, it is much more difficult to understand and it can even be painful to the ears.

In much the same way the elderly person who has poor sight needs alerting to the fact that someone is talking to them, rather than anyone else. It often helps to call their name or to touch their arm so that they are alerted and ready to listen. But even someone who cannot see is helped by the same good communication skills. Tone of voice becomes very important but, because they are relying on their ears, it is also important to face them so that your speech can be heard clearly.

Do elderly people speak and understand in a different way from younger people?

The answer to this question is, probably not. Some research has been carried out which shows that elderly people hesitate and pause more when they speak. Elderly people themselves say that they sometimes find it difficult to remember a particular word, often a name. But everyone has this same difficulty from time to time.

Sometimes elderly people do not understand what is being said to them, but they usually have no difficulty when something is repeated. Part of this difficulty may be hearing loss, but part of it is due to *psychomotor slowing*. Psychomotor slowing is the slowing down of thought and the following action. Elderly people may be somewhat slower at understanding what is said to them than younger people.

One of the few changes which definitely does occur with age is a change in voice quality. Given a choice between an elderly and younger person speaking, it is usually easy to tell who is older. In elderly men the voice often becomes higher and in elderly women it sometimes becomes lower.

Of course elderly people do have difficulty communicating at times. Illness, fatigue and anxiety all make talking and understanding more difficult for an elderly person. An elderly person with bronchitis, for example, or in pain with arthritis may find communicating more difficult temporarily.

Do people speak differently to an elderly person?

Yes, they can do. Most people adopt different tones of voice depending on who they are talking to. People may sound very different when they are speaking on the telephone.

People often speak very differently to small babies and dogs. They make their voice higher, they speak more slowly and their voice often has a different rhythm. Researchers call this "motherese" because mothers of small children use it a great deal. Some research has shown that people use the same sort of voice when talking to elderly people.

This is not a good idea. It may be very irritating to some elderly people. To make sure that you are not using motherese, make a tape recording of yourself and your colleagues when you are talking to elderly people, and then listen.

What helps good communication in a residential home?

It is very easy for communication to go wrong between the carer and resident in a home, but it is also quite easy to put it right. One of the delicate balances in looking after someone is the relationship between the resident's needs and the carer's time and interest. Good communication needs some time and a genuine interest between the people who are having the conversation.

It is quite easy to have low expectations about how elderly people communicate. It is also quite easy to forget that they may have a great deal to contribute to a conversation. As well as asking the elderly person how they are, encourage them to ask how you are. Ask for their opinions about the weather, politics, sport, the newspaper or television and give them yours.

This is real communication and it is quite unlike the passive communication which sometimes can happen. Real communication includes the kind of teasing and telling jokes which is natural between friends.

Most human beings like change. Change stimulates conversation. Going for a walk, meeting a new person or old friend or changing activities can all start a conversation.

What about television? Television can be an excellent activity but it needs to be watched actively. It is much better to turn on the television for a particular programme and then turn it off at the end. Television requires concentration and, if it is left on all day, it becomes just another noise. It is easier to listen to music, but make sure it is appropriate for that age group.

Language

Before considering specific problems that the elderly may have in communicating, a brief description of the constituents of language may be useful.

Communication is made up of many parts. Before communication there needs to be a thought or idea. That thought or idea then needs words which are arranged into an appropriate order for what is to be said. Then the arranged words are spoken. The muscles of the face, tongue and larynx move in a co-ordinated manner to pro-

duce speech. The larynx produces the sound while the tongue and facial muscles shape it into speech. Communication can go wrong at any of these points.

What specific problems can affect communication?

• Confusion

• Dementia

• Language problems

• Speech production problems

Confusion

Confusion arises due to alteration in a person's mental state. This alteration is often variable; the person may be disorientated in time and place (perhaps insisting that he is in another place) and may fail to recognise familiar faces or surroundings.

He or she may say a mixture of quite sensible and very odd things or take offence through failing to understand what has been said. Confusion is commonly associated with illness such as urinary tract infection, changes in medication and life events such as entering a residential home.

When communicating with a confused person, it is helpful to provide information about the here and now, to assist in orientating the person to the present. It is advisable to confine speech to the essentials that need to be understood. Understanding will be helped by clear informative speech produced in short sentences, allowing time between sentences for understanding the meaning.

Repetition may be needed to clarify the meaning. Normal voice and expression should be used and it is helpful to face the listener since understanding is aided by the additional information gained from the speaker's facial expression and gestures.

Particular effort to help re-orientation

is needed when confusion recedes. The person will need to be reassured about where he is and what is happening to him. Discussion of this and daily activities and pastimes will be beneficial.

Dementia

Unfortunately, for some elderly people, confusion represents an early sign of an underlying dementia – a general intellectual impairment (see Chapter 15). Brain mechanisms for speech are eventually disrupted by the loss of brain cells. As well as confusion, early signs of dementia are short term and recent memory loss and a general slowing up, with difficulty in carrying out activities of daily living as the disease progresses.

There are a number of specific changes in speech and language abilities which occur in most people with dementia. In the early stage speech is fluent, words are spoken normally, comprehension remains intact. However, difficulty in thinking of words can occur. This is often seen as a "tip of the tongue" state when someone can't think of the right word although they know it. Even at an early stage communication is affected by short term memory loss, which means that the person may well not remember what they have just done.

As the disease progresses, naming becomes more impaired. The fluency of speech increases so that speech becomes rambling and fragmented. Here is an example from an eighty-two year old lady with a two-year history of dementia, describing a picture of a busy high street. She has been widowed for twenty years:

"Two ladies, baker, somebody leading a little baby. I had a little baby. I don't see much of my husband now. She turned around and looked at me. Supermarket".

Understanding becomes moderately impaired and problems with reading and writing occur.

In the later stages of dementia the person becomes non-fluent, speaking only occasional words. Sometimes a word may be repeated many times. Some people also produce echo-speech, repeating what has been said to them. By this stage the person has severe problems with understanding and is probably only able to understand a few conversational points. Reading and writing become impossible for them.

It is obviously difficult to communicate with a person suffering from advanced dementia. However, the early and middle stages can last for many years, and during this time effective communication can be achieved. There are five basic points to consider in order to assist communication with someone who is suffering from dementia:

1. Do not assume that any aspects of meaning which are not specified will be understood. For example, you may talk about the next meal and be very well aware that this must be breakfast because it is 7am and the elderly person is just getting up. But you must make this clear, perhaps by using the word "breakfast".
2. Be very direct – cut out unnecessary details.
3. Keep the content direct. For example, the remark "I imagine its like flying" would be very difficult for a dementia sufferer to understand.
4. Do not assume that the person remembers – he or she is likely not to, even though what you refer to may be a daily event.
5. Try to give additional facial and gestural clues.

Although communication with a person suffering from dementia may be difficult it is important that these people are encouraged to talk, discuss and remember. With a little extra effort on the part of the listener it is usually possible to understand what the person is saying, to extend their topics of conversation and to communicate effectively. This helps the confused person to stay in contact with daily activities and surroundings. It also makes caring for the person far more rewarding, as a relationship between staff and elderly residents is primarily maintained through their communication.

Language problems

Damage to certain areas of the brain can cause an adult to have an acquired language disorder, called dysphasia: the ability to understand and express meaning through words is disrupted. This may affect speech, reading and writing. The most common cause of this would be a stroke affecting the left side of the brain.

The exact effect of such an injury on speech and language ability will vary from one individual to another depending upon their injury, their previous education, work and experiences, their personality and their present communication needs relating to their environment.

Recovery can occur after such an injury although previous levels of language ability are not always achieved. Many of the residents entering elderly persons homes may have had their dysphasia for many years so that further recovery cannot be expected. But where someone becomes dysphasic in the residential home some degree of recovery would be expected.

Dysphasic adults may have non-fluent speech: they have difficulty producing sentences, or even words in severe cases.

For example, they might say "walk", where "I went for a walk" would be expected, or "ki" to mean cat.

Sometimes errors are made. These may involve changing sounds – "tat" for "bat" – or use of an incorrect word – "dog" for "cat", "sugar" for "salt".

Other dysphasics may have fluent speech but difficulty in finding the right words. For example, "Thats a, oh yes, it's a, you know, cut, cut with it, fork no knife".

In other cases, although speech is fluent, it is not correctly structured so that little meaning is expressed.

A person's understanding of language can also be disrupted by dysphasia but not necessarily in the same way as their expressive speech. Thus a person who is only able to utter the occasional word may have very good understanding, while someone with fluent speech may have great difficulty in comprehending other people's speech. Reading and writing are usually affected in the same way as speech, but occasionally someone is able to write down what they can't say. On the other hand in some cases, reading and writing can be much more severely affected than expressive speech.

Where possible a speech therapist can be asked to give details of a dysphasic person's speech and language abilities, and to give advice on the most effective ways of achieving communication. Staff can also observe a dysphasic patient and note the difficulties that they have in communicating and what helps them to achieve this. In addition the following general guidelines are helpful to remember when speaking to a dysphasic person.

1. Slow down
2. Remove distractions, eg TV.
3. Break any speech into stages. For example:

    – "It's getting cold, isn't it?" –

    – "Are you cold?" –

    – "Do you want a jumper?" –

4. Try and understand the person. Asking questions which only need a yes/no answer may help to give you clues. For example "Is it red?"
5. Maintain contact with the person while they struggle to speak: look towards them, look interested and wait patiently.
6. Give the person time.
7. Commiserate with the person if he gets upset or frustrated.
8. The person is not stupid – speaking loudly and very slowly does not help. Use

normal voice and expression.

9. Ask the person's opinion.

10. Use gesture – "Would you like a cup of tea?" – point to the tea pot while speaking.

11. Remember that speech is a great effort so try to break up interviews etc. Do not expect a dysphasic person to talk for too long and watch for signs of fatigue.

Speech production problems

Another form of acquired speech problem is called dysarthria. This is a disorder of speech production with no disruption in comprehension or reading and writing skills (unless other physical problems such as poor eyesight cause these). In dysarthria the nerve supply to the muscles is disrupted so that speech production is difficult. There are a number of forms of dysarthria, the main ones being:

1. Flaccid dysarthria – where the muscles are weak and floppy. The person may have a very quiet voice making them difficult to hear, and their speech may sound slurred.

2. Spastic dysarthria – where the muscles are very stiff making movement difficult. Speech is therefore very jerky with sudden changes in loudness.

3. Parkinsonian dysarthria – here the muscles are stiff and uncoordinated due to Parkinson's disease. This can cause the person's speech to speed up, and the speech is often difficult to hear at the end of a sentence.

Dysarthria can be caused by a number of diseases which affect the brain or central nervous system including strokes, Parkinson's disease, motor neurone disease, multiple sclerosis and several infections or viral diseases.

However, the most common cause of a motor speech problem is ill-fitting dentures or no dentures at all. This makes speech production difficult and results in speech that can be difficult for the listener to understand.

A person with dysarthria can understand language fully and has no problem in thinking what to say or in formulating a sentence in his head but has a physical difficulty in speaking the words because the speech muscles are not working normally. In some cases very little speech can be achieved, or the speech is unintelligible. It is often the case that people in everyday contact with a dysarthric speaker can "tune in" to their speech and understand them very well. Some dysarthrics are able to use writing or a communication aid such as a pointing chart or an electronic device to augment or be a substitute for speech.

Feeding difficulties

Many dysarthric people and some dysphasics have difficulty with feeding. Many of the muscles used for speaking are also used for eating. Problems can occur with getting food into the mouth, holding it in the mouth, chewing, moving food to the back of the mouth, swallowing and control of saliva. Expert advice from a doctor or speech therapist should be gained if the resident appears to choke on food or drink or reports that food is sticking in his or her throat.

There are a number of ways in which eating and drinking can be assisted:

1. Ensure that dentures are worn and are correctly fitted.

2. Posture – ensure that the resident is sitting up and that the head is slightly flexed forward. Food or drink should never be "poured down the throat" while the head is back. This is likely to cause choking.

3. Give food in small amounts using a normal fork if possible. Give food in single textures per mouthful, ie give meat, or potato, or vegetable. Mixed textures are more likely to cause choking.

4. Encourage chewing and allow enough

Communicating with a person suffering from dementia may be difficult, but it is important to encourage them to talk, discuss and remember.

time for this.

5. Ensure that the patient has swallowed the food before giving another mouthful.

6. Mixed texture goods, such as soup with pieces of food in it, and dry crumbling foods such as peanuts, crisps, dry biscuits etc, should be avoided where a person has difficulty swallowing.

7. Try to make mealtimes calm and re-laxed, and food interesting and tasty, to increase motivation where feeding is slow or difficult. Keeping food hot will also help where feeding is very slow.

Drinking thin liquids such as water and tea is often more of a problem than taking solids. Again posture, taking small amounts and giving enough time to achieve a swal-low are important.

CHAPTER 7

Personal hygiene

by Sue Millward

*A trusting relationship • bathing, showering and the strip
wash • shaving • giving a bed bath • hair washing • mouth
care and dentures*

To help elderly people in residential care maintain good personal hygiene requires a great deal of tact and skill on the part of the carer, but it can be extremely rewarding.

Accepting the need for help can be difficult for anyone, even for a short time. In a residential situation, where the invasion of privacy will seem likely to go on, the need to establish a relationship of trust between client and carer is absolutely vital.

Elderly people can develop quite negative feelings about themselves when they have to rely on other people. This may lead to their "giving-up" and becoming even more dependent. So it is important that clients are given as much choice as possible in all matters of personal care. Deciding whether to bath or shower and at what time of day, choosing favourite toiletries and which clothes to wear, will all help to minimise these feelings.

If the client retains a degree of independence and the carer experiences job satisfaction, any "generation gap" between them will not matter. In fact, it may have advantages for them both. A trusting relationship with good communication can be the foundation of happy and dignified residential care.

The bath

No topic, except perhaps the day's menu, is guaranteed to arouse such strong feelings among people in residential care as the timing and frequency of their baths. But it is unlikely that everyone, given the choice would want to have a bath at the same time of day, and a little negotiation will usually maintain harmony.

Having a bath should be a pleasant experience in a relaxed atmosphere. It provides a good opportunity for a chat and time for reminiscing.

Get organised: Everything needed should be assembled at the outset. No one wants to wait unclad while the talcum powder is retrieved from the other end of the building. All toiletries, flannels, towels and clean clothes should be taken to the bathroom with the client and the door closed to maintain privacy. The bath should be run to the preferred temperature and depth. This is largely a matter of common sense and individual choice but it should be deep enough to cover the legs when sitting down. It is vital to check that the water is not scalding hot, and a non-slip mat placed at the bottom of the bath is a sensible safety precaution.

Help as required: Most people appreciate having their back washed, but can manage everything else themselves. If this is not possible for any reason then help should be given to make sure the client is thoroughly washed all over. The use of bath foam, liquid soap or a soap substitute is a matter of individual choice and staff should be guided by the client's wishes. Extra attention may be needed to the ears, navel and areas between the toes.

Be observant: This is a good time for the carer to look out for any skin conditions, swellings, lumps or sore areas, which should be noted and reported to the person in charge. Any necessary treatment can then be given promptly. Not only physical ailments but emotional problems will often be revealed under the relaxing conditions in a bathroom.

Once out of the bath, quick thorough drying of the skin with a warm towel will be appreciated. Extra care should be given to areas where skin surfaces touch, such as under the arms and between thighs. A light dusting of talcum powder is soothing but it should be used in addition to efficient drying, not as a substitute.

Allow enough time: Help with dressing should only be offered where necessary. The carer must avoid trying to speed up the process by doing too much. It is better to clean the bath and tidy the bathroom while the client dresses at her own pace.

Be familiar with guidelines: Whether or not a client should be left unattended during bath time will depend on the policy of the home. All care staff should be familiar with their own relevant guidelines.

If someone is taken ill in the bath, pull out the plug, support the head above the water level, then call for assistance and keep the client warm.

Care of nails: General care of nails is easier after a bath as they are softened by soaking in warm water. Finger nails can be trimmed if necessary, and a little hand cream applied to counteract dry skin. Toe nails should be kept short, cut straight across at the top. However, if the nails are really tough, the services of a chiropodist may be essential, as there is risk of injury to a toe from inexperienced hands.

Vigilant attention to feet is an essential element in the care of the elderly. Many problems of mobility can be eased by competent treatment of corns and bunions.

Extra care must be taken if a client has diabetes. The circulation of the blood is usually less efficient: any cuts or wounds will take longer to heal and be more liable to infection.

Use of bath hoist: If a client is unable to step in and out of the bath for any reason and a mechanical hoist is provided, it should always be used. Instruction and advice will be given by a senior member of staff. It is foolhardy to lift anyone alone as the risk of injuring your back is very high.

Tidy up afterwards: This is a vital part of any procedure, and leaving the bathroom clean and tidy is important for many reasons. Elderly people can be absent minded and items like watches can easily be left behind on a bathroom shelf. Everything must be taken back to the client's living area and put away. Any dirty washing should be dealt with in accordance with the policy of the home.

The bath must be cleaned with a suitable cleansing cream and rinsed well. The floor should be mopped and allowed to dry. This will reduce the possibility of infection being spread from one person to another and is part of maintaining a general high standard of care.

Points to remember:

• Get everything ready before you start – save your legs.

• Encourage clients to do as much as possible for themselves.

• Pay attention to details – nails, ears, navel and between toes.

The shower

A shower can be a considerably safer prospect than having a bath for any elderly person who is rather frail. It also requires less physical effort.

If a strong comfortable shower seat is provided and the water temperature properly controlled, preferably with a thermostat, then most people will enjoy a shower and find it invigorating. It is important to make sure the shower room is warm enough to avoid the client feeling chilled either before or after the procedure.

A shower may however be more difficult for people who are not able to wash themselves, and it is difficult for staff to help someone else to shower without getting very wet themselves! Some homes provide wellingtons for them to wear, and it has been known for carers to don swimsuits.

Some elderly people are very resistant to the idea of showering. It may just be that they did not have one at home and have never used one before. Others just prefer the soothing effect of a bath. The final choice must be made by the client. But as long as there is sufficient time and the individual does as much as possible for herself, a shower can prove a very satisfactory alternative.

Care of the skin: Once again, it is a good time for the carer to be observant. Remember to be gentle when drying elderly people; the skin becomes less elastic with age. Apply talcum powder sparingly as it can make the skin even drier.

Clearing up afterwards is most important. The shower should be cleaned after use and the floor mopped to avoid the risk of anyone slipping over. Accidents can happen so easily to staff or clients that this cannot be stressed too highly.

Points to remember:

• The client should be happy about having a shower.

• Check water temperature.

• Dry skin gently but thoroughly and be sparing with talcum powder.

• Clear up carefully; alert others if floor is wet.

The strip wash

Most residential homes now provide facilities in each room for clients to wash themselves. If this is not the case, a screen should be placed around the sink so that privacy is maintained.

Some elderly people may have difficulty turning taps on and off. Providing special taps with large handles can mean the difference between managing themselves and relying on others – a great advantage at modest cost.

A strip wash can be done sitting down on a seat or wheelchair beside a sink or with a wash bowl on a convenient table. Help should be given where required.

Care of flannels: It is a good idea to remind people occasionally that face flannels need regular laundering. There is nothing worse then finding a soapy, soggy mess at the bottom of a toilet bag when helping someone freshen-up.

The bidet: This can be a very useful item for making a wash of the genital area much quicker and more thorough. It is not easy to wash this area while standing up, if the client is unsteady and needs support.

The bidet could be more widely used in residential homes particularly for the frequent washing sometimes needed when there are incontinence problems.

Shaving: There should always be a mirror

available for men to shave in a good light. The routine of shaving does not get easier with age. Sometimes folds of skin under the chin are impossible to flatten out with one hand and a little tactful assistance may be welcomed. it must be a firm rule that razors are never shared. Each client must have his own shaving equipment, and never lend it or borrow from anyone else.

Facial hair: The Volunteer Beauty Care Service of the Red Cross is skilled in providing help to remove unwanted facial hair. This caring service operates throughout the British Isles. The teams are controlled by each county branch headquarters and will help elderly people who are not able to care for themselves. They will also give a relaxing massage of the face and neck, hand care and cosmetic camouflage. Provided volunteers are available, the service is free.

Points to remember:

• Maintain privacy.

• Clients can wash sitting down if it is easier.

• Mention to senior staff if more toiletries are required.

• Help with details – make-up for ladies, after-shave for men – can boost morale.

A bed bath

From time to time it may happen that a client is confined to bed although not be ill enough to need admission to hospital or a nursing home. Extra care will then be required, of the kind of caring that a relative would give at home.

A bed bath is simply a way of bathing someone in bed. It is not an awesome task, and if two people can work together it should only take about 20 minutes.

Begin by placing everything that is needed at the bedside: bowl of water; soap,

two flannels and towels; brush and comb; toiletries; toothbrush and paste with beaker and small bowl; nail scissors; barrier cream; clean night-wear and bed linen.

Principles:
1. It is a good idea to ask the client if she would like to use the toilet first. A commode at the bedside is probably easiest for someone feeling unwell.
2. Ensure privacy. Screen the bed if necessary.
3. Remove top bed clothes carefully, leave client covered by a cotton blanket, and take off night dress or pyjamas.
4. Wash and dry face, then neck and ears followed by arms.
5. Expose only the part being washed. Pay special care to under arms and apply deodorant if used. The area beneath the breasts in a woman may need a light dusting of talcum powder.
6. Use a separate flannel for the genital area. The client may be able to do this herself if the blanket is held up. Again a light dusting of talcum powder can aid comfort.
7. Change the water and with the first flannel, wash legs and feet. If possible, rinse feet in the bowl. Cut toe nails straight across if necessary.
8. Roll client over gently, wash and dry the back, massage a little cream to base of spine, heels, elbows and hips. This may be a convenient time to insert a clean sheet.
9. Help the client to put on clean night-wear, then re-make the bed.
10. Trim finger nails and tidy hair.
11. Clean teeth and give a mouth wash.
12. Leave client warm and comfortable. Clear away and tidy up. Make sure bed-table and locker are within reach.

Points to remember:

• The temperature of the water should be as hot as is comfortable for the carers' hands.

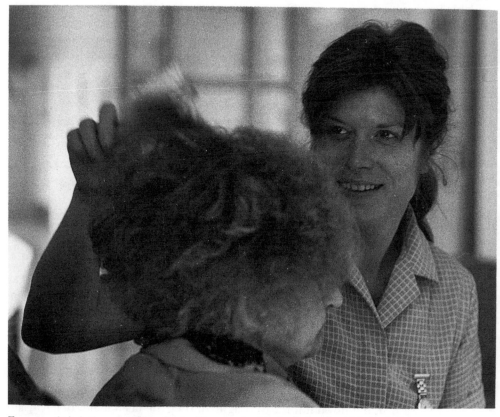

Everyone feels better when they are looking good with the hairstyle of their choice.

• A separate flannel is always used for the groin.

• The client is exposed as little as possible at all times.

Care of the hair

Hairdressing is a skilled occupation. Cutting and setting hair with all the extra treatments available today, is best done by a professional. Many salons have special reduced prices for senior citizens on certain days. Most ladies will enjoy a regular outing for a "hair-do". Alternatively, a hairdresser can be found who is happy to visit a residential home for regular sessions. Men can equally enjoy a trip to the barbers. Everyone feels better when they are looking good with the hairstyle of their choice.

Hair may need washing in between visits to the hairdresser but it can quickly become dry and brittle if shampooed too often. It is *not* necessary to wash hair at every bathtime. If a client has paid for a shampoo and set, she will not be pleased to have it washed out a day or two later by an over-enthusiastic member of staff!

Older people often say their heads are more tender than they used to be, so massage shampoo into the scalp very gently. (If someone with a tender scalp also complains of a headache, inform the staff member in charge, as it could be a sign of a serious illness.) Rinse thoroughly and pat dry with a towel. Set the hair in the preferred style and dry with a hair dryer if available.

Points to remember:

• Hair care is best dealt with by professionals.

• Be gentle, older heads are often tender.

• Observe the condition of the scalp.

Washing the hair in bed: If a client is confined to bed for a short time, the use of a dry shampoo may be sufficient to leave the hair clean and manageable. However, after a longer period it may be necessary to wash the hair while the client is in bed.

The most comfortable position depends on the condition of the client. It may be sitting up leaning forward over a bed-table or lying flat with the mattress pulled down. The bed should be protected with a plastic sheet.

A plastic cape and towel should be placed around the client's shoulders, and eyes protected with a flannel.

Hair is washed, rinsed and finally gathered up into a towel.

Use a hair dryer if available.

Brush and comb hair so that it looks attractive.

Remake the bed, use plastic pillow case if hair is still damp.

The client must be left comfortable.

Points to remember:

• The head must be adequately supported throughout.

• Report any dryness or flaking of the skin to the person in charge.

Head lice may occur in any community. They can be a source of embarrassment, which is really unjustified. Lice seem to like clean, healthy hair and pass easily from one person to another when heads touch. Treatment, with special shampoo, is simple and effective.

Inspecting the head for lice or nits requires patience and great care. If care staff are asked to assist with such an inspection, which is done with a special comb, the following points should be remembered:

• Maintain strict privacy for the resident.

• Be as kind and tactful as possible.

• Staff are as likely to be the source of infestation as clients.

Care of the mouth

Mouth care tends to be rather low on the list of priorities involved in giving personal care. By the time a client has bathed, put on clean clothes, had a shave or applied some make-up, it is all too easy to forget about the mouth and teeth.

But taking care of teeth and gums is important all through life. It should be part of the routine involved in getting up in the morning and preparing to go to bed at night.

The sort of advice given to children at school applies equally to elderly people:

1. Regular visits to the dentist to check for tooth decay and gum disease should continue.

2. A healthy diet should be encouraged with no sticky, sugary snacks between meals.

3. Thorough brushing of the teeth at least twice daily will remove particles of food which can decompose and cause infection.

4. Change toothbrushes as soon as they begin to wear and ensure that clients are able to obtain supplies of toothpaste or powder.

Complications of neglected teeth include:

• Tooth decay.

• Unpleasant taste leading to refusal of food.

• Spread of infection to other parts of the body.

Denture cleaning: Most clients will have

their own established routine for dentures. However, if help is needed, the best method is to place them in a container, rinse under cold water, then brush with special denture cream or powder.

To remove stains the dentures should be soaked or scrubbed in a proprietary solution. Bleach should never be used on dentures as it can damage their surface.

Avoiding misplaced dentures: Great care must always be taken to keep dentures in a container at the client's bedside when they are not being worn. Never leave them in a bathroom or beside a wash-basin which may be used by others. Considerable confusion can be caused as one set of dentures looks very like another. The story of the new student nurse who collected all the dentures she could find on the ward, cleaned them all thoroughly in a bowl and was then unable to match them up again with their owners, is a salutary reminder to us all!

Caring for an ill person's mouth: During illness the mouth can become very dry. If the tongue gets furred and the breath offensive, they will feel even worse.

It is important that the sick person has enough to drink. Sharp-flavoured drinks such as lime juice can be refreshing and leave a pleasant taste.

Extra mouthwashes, in addition to the usual care, can be helpful.

A little vaseline or lip-salve can be applied to the lips to counteract any dryness.

Points to remember:

• "Prevention is better than cure" when caring for the mouth.

• Regular dental checks should continue. If the client has dentures, they should be checked regularly for correct fit and any damage.

• Extra attention is necessary if a client is ill.

Problems

If a client obviously needs a bath but refuses to have one, it is better to "take time out" and avoid a head-on confrontation. Where a good relationship exists between client and carer, this type of problem is rare. With good communication and some skill at negotiation, a compromise can usually be reached. This avoids loss of dignity for anyone.

The carer who is skilful at managing those who are less than enthusiastic about personal hygiene, will always be appreciated by everyone else in the home. A sense of humour is also a great asset when coping with this type of problem.

Sometimes a written care-plan related to hygiene needs can be helpful so that progress can be assessed and recorded. Advice can always be sought from a more senior member of staff.

It is important to keep a sense of proportion. Many older people will recount how they were brought up to have one bath each week. For them it may have been a major operation involving a lot of hard work. Although modern appliances make the procedure a lot easier, this memory remains. The most protracted negotiations may not produce any desire to change the routine of a life-time. A thorough daily wash may have to be accepted as a reasonable alternative.

To conclude, maintaining good personal hygiene contributes to a healthy life. Clients have the right to expect proper care and attention, to help them achieve the proverbial "health and happiness" so often expressed as good wishes on special occasions.

Resources
British Red Cross Society, 9 Grosvenor Crescent, London SW1X 7EJ. Tel: 071 235 5454.

This chapter was typed for the author by a young lady with cerebral palsy using a peg held between her toes.

CHAPTER 8

Promoting continence

by Ruth Manley and Helen White

*Bladder control and incontinence • different types of incontinence and
how they are caused • continence training and management • catheter
care • faecal incontinence, causes and treatment*

Continence is the ability to control the desire to pass water (urine), or faeces (pronounced feeseez), until both time and place are convenient. Once control is successfully established, usually before school age, it becomes an automatic response and the person with a normal bladder or bowel seldom gives more than a passing thought to the act, unless something goes wrong which disrupts regularity.

A urinary infection causing pain or a burning sensation when water is passed, diarrhoea or severe constipation - all these increase individual awareness of bladder or bowel activity because they interfere with normal working or social life, and may disturb sleep.

Some people can never achieve continence because of imperfect development or birth injury; spina bifida for example affects the nerve pathways between brain and bladder, preventing voluntary control.

Bladder control

Continence of urine is a complex process controlled by the part of the brain which interprets sensations transmitted from the bladder where urine is stored, warning of the need to pass water. These messages usually give sufficient notice to enable the individual to delay emptying until it is convenient - a meal break for example - or until a suitable place is reached, such as a motorway service station. If the time is convenient and the toilet at hand the bladder can be emptied with the minimum of fuss.

An adult bladder holds 400-500mls of urine. The sensation of fullness may occur at half capacity, about 250mls, but this is very individual. If the time and place is not convenient it is possible to ignore the desire to pass urine, and it will fade from consciousness. Then it returns at intervals until the need is so urgent that emptying can no longer be delayed. Control is possible because messages between the bladder and the brain can be blocked by conscious (voluntary) control - called inhibition - preventing the bladder from contracting to squeeze out urine). Most people produce about 1,500mls of urine a day depending on how much they drink.

There are two kidneys situated in the lower part of the back on either side of the spine. They act as a filter and remove waste products from the blood. These, in the form of urine, pass down two tubes, ureters, into the bladder. The bladder is an "elastic" bag made of muscle which expands to store the urine and contracts to squeeze the urine out through a narrow tube, the urethra, which is 4cm long in women, 20cm in men. The bladder and urethra are supported in position by a band of muscles, the pelvic floor muscles.

Passing urine

When the bladder fills to about 250-350 mls, it sends messages to the nerves in the lower part of the spine. These messages travel up the spine to the brain. The brain responds by sending the appropriate message back to the bladder. If the time and place is convenient, the nerves send the messages back down the spine to the bladder muscles. The bladder muscles contract, the urethra relaxes and the urine is squeezed out.

Loss of bladder control

Continence is seen as a major milestone of normal child development. Society expects it to be maintained once it has been achieved, isolating or rejecting those who are not continent.

Urinary incontinence means the uncontrolled (involuntary) loss of urine. It is not a disease but is a symptom of an underlying problem which can happen to anyone at any time of life. It affects more women than men but it is not an inevitable consequence of old age. Indeed the majority of old people remain continent all their lives.

Incontinence at any age causes physical, emotional, social and financial hardship and severely disrupts people's lives.

The effects may be particularly harsh for older people: influencing where and with whom they live, creating dependence and loss of individuality when they cannot continue to live in their own homes. Many see incontinence in older people as a natural stage of regression to infancy and treat them accordingly, increasing

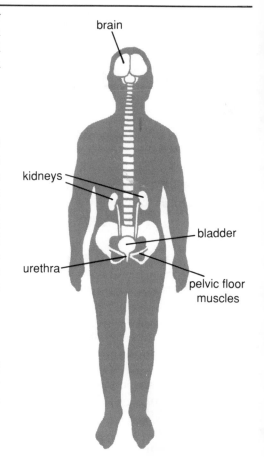

dependence and loss of adult status.

There are many causes of incontinence and an individual can suffer from several symptoms. **Treatment or management must be based on individual assessment and investigation** to discover the type of incontinence and possible causes. Basically there are three types of urinary incontinence; the names indicate the symptoms which are experienced with each type.

1. Stress incontinence is a common complaint among women of all ages who have weakened muscles of the pelvic floor. Those who have had several children are most likely to suffer from this type. Any extra effort or strain, such as lifting a heavy object, increases pressure within the abdomen, causing urine to leak from the bladder because the muscles which normally squeeze the sphincters shut at each end of the urethra have become inefficient. These women are afraid to laugh heartily, to cough or sneeze, or to enjoy dancing or active sports without fear of leaking into their clothing.

If the condition remains untreated it will tend to worsen following the menopause (change of life) when muscles lose their tone. Constipation should be avoided because a full bowel increases pressure on pelvic floor muscles during exertion, making the condition worse.

The bladder does not empty completely during the stress incontinence episode and the amount of urine lost may produce no more than a small damp patch on underclothes. Sometimes the loss is much larger and requires a pad to contain it.

2. Urge incontinence occurs when there is too little time between the first feeling of bladder sensation and the onset of urine flow. Those affected have no time to reach the toilet or to remove clothing and position themselves before they are wet. Normally the first indication of the need to visit the toilet can be controlled (the ability to hold) until a suitable time and place, but the bladder contracts before it is full, (an unstable, irritable bladder). It is associated with a number of medical conditions.

Sometimes anxiety may be an underlying factor. Accidents may have happened in the past which produce fear and tension, so that every bladder sensation is interpreted as a potential accident. The person rushes to the toilet immediately they are aware of the bladder, in an effort to prevent urine loss. The bladder seldom holds more than a few ounces of urine because it is emptied so frequently, and this quickly becomes a habit, the time between voiding intervals being reduced until the individual may be frightened to move too far from the toilet or to move about freely.

This type of incontinence is a common complication following a stroke, or affects elderly people suffering from dementia. It is associated with other illnesses such as brain or bladder tumours, or stones in the bladder. Infection or inflammation of the bladder may also cause it.

3. Overflow incontinence describes the condition in which there is a dribble or continuous leakage of urine: the bladder does not empty properly and the person is always damp or wet. It is a distressing condition, sometimes leading to sore skin and itching, or unpleasant odour. There are several possible causes which can be treated and cured or greatly improved:

If the cause is loss of the nerve supply, the bladder is unable to contract and empty completely becoming large, distended and full of stale urine which overflows causing a constant dribble. As a consequence of this condition the urine left in the bladder is likely to be infected and may be very offensive. Any outflow obstruction of the bladder (such as enlargement of the prostate gland, a condition affecting older men which prevents the flow of urine through the urethra) will cause retention of urine, leading to overflow incontinence when bladder capacity is exceeded. Diabetes and some drugs given for medical conditions affect the nerve control of the bladder, reducing the bladder's ability to contract and empty, and are potential causes of urinary incontinence.

4. Night incontinence - bedwetting - occurs most commonly in children, particularly those who sleep very heavily. The condition may continue into adult life, or occur for the first time in old age, especially when elderly people take sleeping tablets at night, which prevent them from responding to the need to get up and empty the bladder.

Factors which may lead to urinary incontinence

Frequency

Everyone passes urine at regular intervals during a 24-hour span but each individual has different drinking habits and bladder capacity. Someone with frequency may need to visit the toilet more than the average of 5-7 times a day and some take every opportunity to do so. The cause may be one of the following:

a) Drinking a higher than average amount of fluid each day
b) Taking water pills (diuretics) prescribed by the doctor which increases the amount of urine produced by the kidneys
c) An infection which irritates the bladder and increases sensitivity
d) A smaller bladder capacity than other people
e) Habit, which has trained the bladder to empty at a low volume.

Urgency

This is an intense desire to empty the bladder immediately. If the feeling cannot be suppressed, urge incontinence of either a small amount of urine or the entire bladder results. Most people with urgency make a dash for the nearest toilet and breathe a sigh of relief if they reach it in time. Many do not make it in time , however, and would be better advised to wait until the feeling fades before making their way more slowly; the dash seems to make matters worse by raising anxiety.

The most likely cause is uncontrolled contractions which happen even when the bladder is not full, producing the acute sensation of imminent emptying. This condition, sometimes called an "unstable bladder" is a major problem for older people who are unable to move as a result

of painful joints or other conditions and who risk a fall if they try to do so.

Infection

An infection may cause both frequency and urgency, as many women who have had cystitis will testify. A severe, acute bladder infection can lead to incontinence in young people and almost certainly will do so in an older person, when it often also causes confusion or disorientation and a raised temperature. Low-grade urine infection, however, is a common finding among older people as a result of incomplete bladder emptying. This does not usually cause incontinence.

Incontinence in older age

Although age is not a cause of incontinence, some changes in later life make control rather more difficult.

1. The ageing kidney is less efficient. It produces large quantities of dilute urine, so **increasing the urine volume**. In addition, some people have medical conditions which are associated with extra urine production, such as diabetes.

2. After the change of life (menopause) there is a gradual reduction in the female hormone levels which influence the delicate lining of the urethra and external female sex organs. **Soreness, redness or itching** may result and infection follow. Treatment of these conditions will often improve incontinence.

3. Obstruction may sometimes be caused by stones or a growth in the bladder, but the most common cause is **severe constipation** leading to a hard mas of faeces impacted in the rectum, with seepage of diarrhoea (liquid stool) around it. This quickly causes bladder infection in women because their short urethra enables the bowel organisms, which are harmless in their own environment, to reach the bladder where they multiply rapidly.

4. With age the bladder loses some of its elasticity and becomes more rigid, unable to stretch to accommodate the same volumes of urine as previously, and needing to be emptied more often. **Loss of elasticity** also means that the bladder does not empty so efficiently; older people often have a larger residual urine after voiding than younger people.

5. **Mobility may be reduced** with age, preventing someone reaching the toilet unaided. Unless the necessary help is readily available, incontinence will frequently result.

6. **The ability to recognise that the bladder needs emptying may be lost** because the nerve supply between the bladder and the brain is interrupted due to a stroke, multiple sclerosis or dementia.

Other factors

1.Inadequate or inappropriate toilet facilities:

a) Lack of signs to the toilet

a) Lavatory too far away

b) Lavatory seat too low/too high

c) Lack of privacy

d) Too few toilets or commodes (someone with frequency or urgency is unable to "hold" until a toilet becomes free.

2. Drugs may affect bladder control:

a) Those which cause drowsiness (sedatives - sleeping tablets)

b) Those which increase urine output (diuretics - water tablets).

3. Mental state has an important influence on continence:

a) Boredom or apathy

b) Depression

c) Loneliness or rejection may lead to loss of individual motivation and acceptance of the incontinent state.

4. Confusion and dementia are major causes of loss of control, requiring special skills in management.

Disease processes

Micturition, the act of passing urine, can be controlled by someone with normal development and intact nervous pathways between bladder, spinal cord and brain. Imperfect development or interruption of the nervous transmission to the brain by disease or injury leads to uncontrolled micturition. The site of the problem may lie in the brain itself or in the spinal cord, or between the bladder and spinal cord.

Conditions such as spina bifida are present from birth; others associated with incontinence may develop later: multiple sclerosis, Parkinson's disease, strokes, or injury to the spinal cord leading to paralysis, for example.

Among older people the most common cause is undoubtedly progressive brain failure. The severe memory loss associated with dementia makes it impossible for the individual to plan ahead and anticipate bladder emptying, for example before going to bed or on an outing. They cannot remember where the lavatory is situated, or even recognise it. Some retain bladder sensation but are unable to interpret it correctly or control spontaneous bladder contraction, leading to incontinence.

Alert staff are sometimes able to recognise cues indicating that a mentally impaired person has a full bladder, preventing accidents by taking the individual to toilet. Passing urine in inappropriate places suggests that sensation remains intact, but the ability to discriminate between the correct place and an unsuitable place is lost.

Continence training

Successful continence training has two main prerequisites:

First, staff need to receive adequate preparation to gain the appropriate level of knowledge and to become familiar with the training material. A team leader should be appointed to coordinate and support staff, and advise on the selection of the group to receive continence training.

Secondly, people should be assessed for the appropriate care programme. Continence cannot be imposed on an unwilling or uncooperative person, even if they are intellectually competent. It is therefore important that both staff and clients are convinced that success is achievable.

Continence training is based on individual programmes rather than on a general approach for a group of incontinent people. Perhaps the exception to this rule may be in the development of behavioural training for groups of mentally handicapped people, or regular toileting regimes for elderly mentally frail groups in residential settings.

Staff preparation should include a study of the environment to identify factors which may encourage incontinence. For example:

Environmental factors
a) Lavatories which are too far from sitting or bed areas, or are too few for the population being served
b) Toilets which do not admit a wheelchair or a helper
c) Toilet doors which cannot be safely secured to afford privacy
d) Inadequate support rails to enable people to be independent
e) Insufficient lighting or toilet identification

Problems of mobility or dexterity
a) Difficulty in getting out of bed or chair
b) Inability to adjust clothing
c) Total dependence upon staff support
d) Joint stiffness, especially of the hips and knees which prevents a person getting on to or off the toilet
e) Pain on movement which discourages cooperation with staff

Mental state
a) Insufficient stimulation leading to boredom

b) Depression causing loss of motivation or poor self image
c) Confusion or memory loss, and the inability to concentrate
d) Loneliness, especially following bereavement or entry into residential accommodation.

Staff attitudes and behaviour
a) Expectancy and acceptance or incontinence for disabled or elderly people
b) Routines which ignore individual client need
c) Failure to respond to requests for help
d) Over-protection which creates dependence
e) Widespread or inappropriate use of "incontinence aids".

Promotion of a continence programme is a team effort, including all grades of staff working in the home. Each team member contributes from their own particular knowledge or skill, offering support and encouragement to each other. A medical and nursing assessment must be undertaken. Community nurses assess patients in their own homes and often provide teaching or support for residential or nursing home staff in the development of "in-house" programmes. Many health districts appoint continence nurse advisers to provide a wide range or services for professionals working with incontinent people and their carers.

Care assistants make an important contribution to client assessment and continence training implementation. Careful observation combined with accurate recording and reporting are essential features of individual continence management strategy. You may be asked to note some or all of the following points during contact with a client:

1. Expressions of anxiety about loss of control and the way this affects normal activity. If the person denies the condition

or refuses to discuss it, this should be noted.

2. Comments on how the individual copes with the problem. For example, passive acceptance - "What can you expect at my age?" - or a more positive response seeking information on how other people manage. They may be able to provide a clear picture of when and how the problem arose and suggest a possible cause.

3. Staff should try to establish a relationship between the onset of incontinent episodes and a change of environment, such as a recent spell in hospital or admission to residential accommodation. The resident may be unable to move as quickly as usual because of an accidental injury, or painful condition which prevents the removal of clothing in time.

4. An alert care assistant will note whether the "wet" episodes are preceded by feelings of urgency causing a rush for the toilet, or of being unable to "hold" until help is available. Unusually frequent use of the toilet, or increasing episodes of incontinence or night disturbance, should be recorded. The introduction of a new drug, for example water pills (diuretics) may be blamed for the condition.

5. A complaint about constipation must be taken seriously as it may be a "trigger" factor in causing leakage of urine. Any changes in diet or fluid intake should be noted.

6. Sometimes clients are able to recall previous occasions when they have experienced bladder or bowel problems, for example during pregnancy or following an operation, which may have some bearing on current events.

Occasionally an older person is reported by a relative as having recently developed incontinence, but will themselves reveal a long-standing history of bladder leakage which they have hidden successfully for years. Staff need to ask if the condition is better or worse, or much the same.

8. If it is important to know how much urine is actually lost during each incontinent episode, you may be asked to collect and measure the urine passed and to record the amount accurately. As part of the procedure the urine can be observed for colour, odour, or any obvious abnormalities: for example it may be very dark as a result of not drinking enough, or smell fishy due to an infection.

When incontinence aids such as absorbent pads are used, staff need to be clear about how the amount of loss is to be estimated. For example, when using plus signs:

+= slight loss or dampness

++= moderate loss which is contained in the pad without leakage

+++= heavy loss of an amount too large for the pad to contain and leakage has occurred.

All staff must use the same method of indicating the amount.

The care assessment includes the compilation of individual voiding charts - daily records of bladder emptying. Staff note the date and time of day or night and whether the urine is passed into the toilet. If the urine is being measured a column for the amount is also needed.

Some commercial companies produce special charts as part of their service. These charts are often ticked in columns titled "dry" or "wet". Charts are usually compiled for 5-7 days, but others used in treatment may be maintained for several weeks. Interpretation of the chart forms the basis of individual care plans, but it requires a sound knowledge of bladder disorder, and experience in using the charts. Nevertheless, obvious patterns can soon be recognised by most staff after familiarisation, and they are useful indicators of client progress.

Objective : Continence

Name_____ Week beginning_____

KEY ▦_____ ☐_____

SPECIAL INSTRUCTIONS

Coloplast Ltd

	SUNDAY	MONDAY	TUESDAY	WEDNESDAY	THURSDAY	FRIDAY	SATURDAY
6am							
7am							
8am							
9am							
10am							
11am							
12am							
1pm							
2pm							
3pm							
4pm							
5pm							
6pm							
7pm							
8pm							
9pm							
10pm							
11pm							
12pm							
1am							
2am							
3am							
4am							
5am							
TOTAL							

Management

The most suitable method of training is started once the assessment has been completed, with the client's cooperation whenever possible. Sometimes all that is required is to change the environment so as to help someone with mobility problems to reach the toilet more easily, by providing a commode for example, but most clients need more help than this.

Bladder training aims to promote continence in people suffering from urge incontinence who have developed a habit of emptying the bladder at very short intervals, maybe as often as every 15-30 minutes. This method requires experienced staff support to offer reassurance to the person trying to regain control. The period between visits to the toilet is gradually extended until a more normal voiding pattern is achieved.

The client must be cooperative and motivated, and this method is not suitable for every person with urge incontinence. Charts are kept for the whole period of training and for some weeks afterwards to monitor progress. A successful outcome is to re-establish normal voiding patterns of every 3-4 hours.

Individual toileting is based on anticipatory toileting. The individual's chart is used to establish the times when incontinence is most likely to occur and how long control can be maintained between episodes. The client is taken to the toilet some 20-30 minutes before the next incontinence episode is expected. Charts are maintained during the training period to assess the effectiveness or the interventions.

Set interval toileting is used when the person is forgetful or there is no regular pattern for passing water. The person is reminded or taken to the toilet at regular intervals, between two- and four- hourly depending on circumstances.

This does not train the bladder and is not based on individual needs, but can substantially reduce the number of incontinent episodes among groups of confused elderly people, creating a pleasanter environment free from odour, and reducing laundry costs.

Controlling incontinence

It may be necessary to provide protective garments or urinary appliances for people who cannot be completely dry. The choice of product will depend on the quantity of urine loss, and the dexterity, mobility and mental ability of the individual. For men and women who have a light loss, machine washable pants with an absorbent gusset can give that extra feeling of confidence. Where the loss is more severe, there is a range of disposable or reusable liners which can be worn inside the person's own pants. Men may prefer to wear an appliance which is available on prescription. There are also highly absorbent washable bed sheets which can help to improve sleep patterns because they keep the person warm and dry. It is important to follow the manufacturer's instructions to obtain the maximum benefit. The continence adviser can advise on the selection, although this is often restricted by cost and purchasing policies by health or local authorities, and some products are expensive for regular use if they are bought independently.

Catheter care

Sometimes a hollow tube called a catheter is placed in the bladder in order to drain the urine away. A catheter may be used once and then removed, or left in position to drain continuously and changed at intervals.

The in-dwelling catheter is attached to a drainage bag to collect the urine, and it is important always to ensure that the connecting tubing is not kinked or compressed so that the urine can flow freely, and that the bag is below the level of the bladder, as urine cannot flow uphill.

Hygiene is particularly important: the area surrounding the catheter must be kept scrupulously clean. A daily bath or wash is essential to prevent bacteria entering the bladder alongside the catheter. Nursing staff are responsible for the management of catheters and drainage bags, and care assistants should seek advice from a senior member of staff if any problems arise in relation to the client with a catheter. Make sure that someone with this device drinks an adequate amount of fluid - about two litres a day - as this helps to prevent infection.

Bowel control

Faecal incontinence is fortunately less common than urinary incontinence. It is unpleasant for both the recipient and giver of care because of the problem of adequate cleansing and the accompanying odour. Although the highest incidence is usually found in severely mentally handicapped or elderly mentally infirm people, there are some medical conditions associated with faecal incontinence - such as disorders which produce diarrhoea or severe constipation resulting in overflow.

In normal bowel action, the stool should be soft, well formed and pass easily out. The formed stool is pushed into the lower part of the bowel called the rectum by contraction of the muscular walls of the bowel, triggering sensory receptors in the wall of the rectum which are felt as a desire to empty the bowel. Sphincters controlling the anus (the back passage outlet) are relaxed if the time and place is convenient, and the stool is passed, sometimes with the assistance of the muscles of the abdomen.

Loss of bowel control

With ageing the sphincter muscles may become lax and less efficient, and certain changes in the rectum make faecal incontinence more likely. A lifetime of straining to open the bowels, or persistent use of laxatives are known to contribute to loss of control. Recently new methods of surgical intervention have been developed to help some sufferers from this condition.

The most common cause is **severe constipation.** This often leads to "faecal impaction", when a hard mass of stool plugs the lower part of the bowel. Liquid stool then trickles past the mass as a continual faecal leak. It is important when caring for someone with this type of incontinence to keep the skin as clean and dry as possible, in order to prevent soreness or infection of the urine from organisms present in the stool.

Some elderly people find it hard to wipe themselves properly after having their bowels open, and staff need to give help when necessary to prevent soiling of underclothing.

Treatment

Treatment of faecal incontinence is based on identifying the possible cause. Then dietary measures are taken such as increasing high fibre foods or fluid intake. Prescribed drugs may be used to soften the stool making it easier to pass. If these measures are not effective, suppositories or enemas will be used.

Persistent diarrhoea requires medical advice on management techniques.

In conclusion

Older people, especially those living in rest or nursing homes, are at risk to bladder and bowel problems. However with an assessment of their individual needs together with appropriate care the majority can remain continent. For the minority who may have to accept a degree of incontinence, their problem can always be made more manageable.

Staff attitudes are important, in reassuring people that their problems are recognised and will receive sympathetic consideration. Advice and support in setting up a training programme can be obtained through health professionals who are members of the Association for Continence Advice (the Association will supply a local contact), through the local District Health Authority, or one of the organisations listed below.

Further reading

1. *Nursing for Continence*, Christine Norton ISBN 0 906584 15 9.

Resources

Association for Continence Advice, 380-384 Harrow Road, London W9 2HU.

Age Concern England, Astral House, 1268 London Road, London SW16 4EJ. Information and publications. Practical volunteer services through local groups.

Alzheimer's Disease Society, 158-160 Balham High Road, London SW12 9BN. Tel: 081 675 6557/8/9/0.

Incontinence Information Helpline - for people with bladder and bowel problems. Tel: 091 213 0050, weekdays 2-7pm.

Multiple Sclerosis Society of Great Britain and Northern Ireland, 25 Effie Road, Fulham, London SW6 1EE. Tel: 071 736 6269.

National Action on Incontinence, 4 St Pancras Way, London NW1 0PE. Support group for people with incontinence problems and their carers.

CHAPTER 9

Keeping older people mobile

by Helen Ransome

Be alert to signs of disease • loss of activity when in care • assessing the level of help needed • walking aids and how to use them • motivation, risk and independence • getting up after illness • getting into and out of a chair or bed, on and off the toilet • lifting techniques

Does old age cause decreasing mobility?

Many old people enjoy very active lives – physically and mentally. By doing this they prove to us that there is no direct link between old age and declining mobility. However, certain changes which occur in the body as people get older make them likely to become immobile if they do not keep moving. This should persuade us all to encourage old people to keep active because **"What you don't use, you lose".**

Why?

If active young people become noticeably less mobile it is correctly assumed that a disease process is the cause. When old people become less mobile it should also be assumed that a disease is responsible. Therefore if a resident gradually or suddenly loses his/her usual level of mobility the logical response is to refer the resident to the GP for diagnosis and treatment.

Unfortunately, like most of the rest of us, GPs sometimes find it difficult to accept that many of the immobile old people they see have become like that not because they are *old*, but because they have either spent too much time sitting about or they (or their carers) have not sought diagnosis and treatment for a disease, or both.

However, hospital doctors who specialise in the care of old people (physicians in geriatric medicine or geriatricians) believe that old age does not inherently mean disability, ill-health and less activity. On the contrary they believe that early medical treatment of the disease causing the deterioration can weaken or delay its disabling effects.

It is thus vital to refer residents whose mobility is *just beginning* to show a marked deterioration, to the GP who in turn can refer the resident to the geriatrician for early diagnosis and treatment. Early referral is essential, because if nothing is done and immobility sets in, it is usually very difficult, if not impossible, to restore mobility again.

You can help

Here is an example of how care assistants helped a resident to remain more mobile for longer by early referral.

An elderly lady had real pain, not just discomfort, in her knees for a few weeks and found it increasingly difficult to get to the dining room from her bedroom. Like most older people she had a low expectation of her health and mobility and said to the care assistants, "My knees are seizing up, don't worry dear it's all I can expect at my age – just get a wheelchair for me".

Had the care staff accepted her explanation of the problem and blamed it on age, she would soon have been permanently immobile. However they understood that there was a treatable disease causing the lady's pain and difficulty in moving and told the officer-in-charge about it. The lady was referred to the GP and then to the geriatrician, and the pain was largely relieved by appropriate medicine.

Once the pain was better, walking became easier again. The community physiotherapist also visited to show her and the care staff how to strengthen the important knee muscles and how best to manage activities of daily living, despite her knees. Having been "caught early", this lady had not lost her mobility and could therefore continue to be active at or very near her previous level.

This is one example of the vital role care assistants have in helping residents to remain mobile in residential homes.

The environment

In order to consider the particular problems which make it so difficult for elderly people to keep active in residential homes, we need to look at the environment in which the majority of our residents have spent most of their lives as elderly people –

their own homes.

A group of care assistants accurately answered the question "What keeps an elderly person who lives at home mentally and physically active?" like this:

"Getting out of bed, dressing (with as much time as they need), personal hygiene, going to the toilet, getting a cup of tea, making a bed, answering the door, reading, knitting, going to meals, preparing meals, washing clothes – even if only "smalls", dusting and housework, shopping, gardening, tending the fire, looking after pets, going to bed".

Out of this rich (but by no means exhaustive) list of activities, most are lost when an older person is admitted to most homes. Apart from reading and knitting, often only getting out of bed, dressing and personal hygiene (all usually in a hurry), going to meals, to the toilet and bed are still available to old people in residential homes.

Even residents who had very limited mobility before admission and who could only potter about at home, were having regular exercise (like getting in the milk, letting out the cat and making cups of tea) which they immediately lose on admission. The long periods between meals, instead of providing opportunities for vital, varied activity are now filled with sitting – the well-known independence robber!

In addition, opportunities for mental activity are also usually lost, such as choice, decision-making, preserving self esteem and being needed/contributing. The difficulties of coping at home are removed, but because residents do not themselves have to provide the basic necessities of life (food, clean shelter, clothes, warmth), a new problem arises on admission to residential homes: lack of activity, both mental and physical. These two types of activity are inextricably linked: if an old person is physically immobile, her mental activity level will tend to decrease; if mentally unstimulated, her level of physical activity will tend to fall off.

How can care staff in homes change this independence-robbing environment into an independence-encouraging one? A group of care assistants answered this question correctly as follows:

• Assess each resident individually on admission and regularly thereafter.

• Find ways of responding to the various identified needs of each individual resident. In the case of the need for exercise, encourage the resident to remain as active as she was when admitted.

• Involve residents in making decisions about and running the home.

• Encourage them to carry out household tasks – in their own rooms, the dining room, laundry room, kitchen etc.

• Encourage group living.

• Help them to feel valued – encourage pride and independence, not dependence.

• Discover their interests and enable them to continue with hobbies and activities they enjoy.

Assessing independence

So that we can encourage each individual resident to remain as active as she was when admitted, we must know what she is capable of. An accurate assessment of each new resident's level of performance of the various activities of daily living should be made within a few days of admission.

Information is also needed as to how these activities were previously managed at home – perhaps from relatives, friends or social worker. A home-visit to a potential resident by a member of staff of the home is very helpful in this and other respects.

Some residents perform activities of daily living like getting out of bed, getting dressed, getting in and out of chairs, going to the toilet, walking etc., easily; others find them more difficult. The assessment gives a guide to this "functional level" of the new resident and care assistants can then encourage her all through each day's activities to "keep up" to this. The different levels at which activities of daily living can be performed are:

1. Alone (with the use of an aid if needed, eg walking frame). This is independence and should be our constant aim.

2. With supervision but no physical help from a person. Unhurried supervision is important as a confidence-booster. As confidence and performance improve, the care assistant will only need to "pop" back from time to time and the resident should eventually progress to carrying out the activity alone.

3. With verbal help (ie spoken instructions/advice) – but still no physical help. Verbal help also boosts confidence, and can enable a motivated resident by careful, consistent instructions to relearn how to do an activity and thus to regain independence.

4. With physical help – verbal instruction should be first tried on several occasions before using physical help. The aim should always be to give the *least possible* help to enable the resident to carry out the activity. Once physical help is used a resident is dependent, even if only partially.

For a variety of reasons a resident's functional level may fluctuate, improve or deteriorate. In order for care staff to continue to respond to these changing levels and needs with just the right amount of independence-encouraging support, regular and frequent reassessment is essential. Where this is carried out residents have the best possible chance of retaining and even improving their level of independence.

Independence in walking

Walking is the most important activity of daily living. Only if a resident can walk alone (so long as she can get out of a chair, which she can usually learn if she is capable of walking) can she make choices and be independent.

Independent walking enables her to go *when she chooses* to the toilet, meals, the sitting room, her bedroom and elsewhere in and outside the home. This means she does not have to wait for someone to take her, and the mental and physical stimulation she gains by moving about freely helps to keep her active.

Independent residents are also good news for care assistants: less exhausting work and physical risk of back strain, and more time to respond to the needs of other more dependent residents.

Lively residents are best kept independently mobile by providing lots of varied activity in the home. Frailer residents, who may have specific physical problems (eg arthritis, stroke or Parkinson's Disease) may need walking aids to help them walk independently.

It is often very tempting to "give an arm" to a frailer resident who is able to get from room to room without help but who is slightly unsteady and appears vulnerable. When care assistants yield to this temptation they instantly deprive the resident of her independence.

This kind of "help" is given with the best of intentions – because care assistants feel sorry for the resident and worried she might fall. However, if we stop and think, we realise that there is an alternative which will enable the resident to remain independently mobile. A walking aid (walking stick in this case) should always be tried before considering using the physical help of a person.

A resident who walks alone with a walking aid can move about the home when she wishes, remains confident in her ability to move alone and will not have to sit until someone comes to help her. On the other hand, a resident who is beginning to rely on care staff will sit for longer and walk less. This causes her muscles to get weaker, her joints stiffer, her balance to deteriorate and her walking to become worse.

She also becomes frightened of walking alone, as it feels so unsafe – so she sits rather than moves and as a result she becomes more dependent in all her other activities of daily living. The vicious circle of dependence has begun.

Soon she will be in a wheelchair requiring total help from the already hard-pressed care assistants, who thought they were being caring and helpful by offering her an arm, but who were actually depriving her of her dignity and independence. This lady lost her independence because she did not continue using her mind and body to accomplish activities of daily living. Another case of "What you don't use, you lose"!

So all residents who can walk when they enter the home, must be consistently encouraged to remain **on their feet** with as little help as possible. Always try a suitable walking aid before giving physical help.

A physiotherapist is the most appropriate person to assess which walking aid a particular resident needs. However if you cannot find a physiotherapist, the following will help you to do it yourselves.

Walking aids

Walking Stick

A resident who is slightly unsteady and who seems to need the physical help of one care assistant will usually be just as safe (and also independent) if given a walking stick. Before giving a resident a walking stick, carry out the following steps:

Equipment needed: Adjustable metal walking stick, saw, new wooden walking stick.

1. **Decide on the length.** Walking sticks should be individually measured. An adjustable metal walking stick is useful for deciding on the correct length for a wooden one. Adjust the metal stick to the approximate height and ask the resident to hold it in the hand *opposite* to her "bad" leg if she has one. Otherwise she will usually use it on the side best for her. With the resident standing, adjust the length so that:

• the resident's hand on the stick handle is level with the top of the thigh

• the elbow is *slightly* bent

• the shoulders are level.

When you think the stick height is right with the resident standing, ask her to walk. See how it looks and how she feels. If either of you is unhappy, move the stick down or up a notch and try again until you find a height which basically follows the rules above but which also looks and feels 'right'.

Most people have their sticks too long. The elbow is thus very bent, which makes the stick less useful, and/or the shoulder is too high which leads to a painful shoulder. You may need to persuade residents that a shorter stick is more useful and comfortable; ask them to try it and review a few days later.

2. **Measure a wooden stick** to the same length as the metal one without its ferrule (the removable rubber end). Saw off the wooden stick to the correct length.

3. **Put a strong, wide-based, suction ferrule** on the bottom of the stick.

Make sure that all sticks have ferrules in good condition. When they are worn unevenly, have a hole or no suction ridges, replace them, as they are dangerous and can lead to falls.

4. **Teach the resident to hold the stick in the correct hand.**

5. **Teach the resident to walk correctly** with the stick as follows. There are two ways of walking with a stick:

(a) When more support is needed – eg stroke, arthritis
– put stick forward slightly to the side
– take a normal-sized step with the opposite foot *to the level of the stick*
– take a normal-sized step with the other foot past the walking stick
– repeat the sequence.

(b) When less support is needed – eg general unsteadiness, or when resident improves from (a)
– put stick and opposite leg forward together
– put the other leg forward past the stick
– repeat the sequence.

When a resident using (a) is walking faster and taking less weight on the stick, she is probably ready to change to (b) and may do so automatically.

If a resident needs the help of a person temporarily (eg when recovering from a bout of flu) it is best given from behind – with the care assistant supporting the resident's hips (one hand firmly on each side of the pelvis on the hip bones, just below waist level). Although help is often given under the arm on the opposite side to the stick, it is good to avoid this, as it can damage the shoulder of a resident who has had a stroke, which causes great pain.

Walking Frame

A resident who finds walking more difficult, who leans heavily on one care assistant or who needs two care assistants to walk, probably needs a walking frame.

All homes need a good stock of standard sized frames (approximately 33" height) as most residents needing a frame use this size. A few large adjustable frames (33" – 36") are needed for taller residents and an occasional tiny resident will need the junior adjustable size (approximately 27½" – 31½").

The following steps are necessary before giving a resident a walking frame:

1. **Decide on the height.** Try what "looks like" a frame of the right size first. With the frame on the ground, the resident holding the frame and leaning forward slightly on it (the back legs of the frame should be level with her feet) her arms should only be slightly bent. If she hunches forward and looks "bent" over the frame, it is too low; if her elbows are very bent and her shoulders pushed up, then the frame is too high.

If the standard size frame is unsuitable, try the appropriate adjustable frame, adjusting it until the resident looks and feels comfortable.

2. When you think you have a frame of the correct height, you will need to **teach the resident to walk with it.** Most people given a frame and no instruction will walk wrongly or even dangerously with it. In order to gain support and benefit from a walking frame, the following walking pattern is essential:

• put the frame well forward so that it can be leant on with arms nearly at full stretch

• take a normal-sized step with the "bad" leg (if there is one – if not, either)

• step *past* the "bad" leg with the "good" leg

• repeat the sequence.

NB: The walking frame should be on the ground when either foot is off the ground.

3. Before giving the frame to the resident **check that it has a strong, safe suction ferrule** on each leg.

4. Walking with a frame is a complex activity, so you will probably need **several training sessions** with the resident to make sure she has learnt to use it correctly.

5. If the resident needs the physical help of a person as well as a walking frame (hope-

fully only temporarily while gaining confidence in it or recovering from illness) it is best to give help from behind. As a walking frame is held and moved forward by the resident using *both* hands it unbalances the walking pattern and resident to help under *one* arm. Help should therefore be given from behind as described in the section on walking sticks. This is also safer for the care assistant. Should the resident suddenly collapse for any reason, the care assistant can lower her to the ground with full control, by bending her own knees and keeping a straight back.

This is impossible when holding a resident on one side – both resident and care assistant may well fall if this method is used. Another advantage of holding "from behind" is that help can gradually be reduced without the resident being aware of it.

How NOT to use a walking frame:
1. **Carrying the frame.** This is a hazardous activity and should be discouraged. This resident might try walking without an aid or using a walking stick.

2. **Pushing the frame.** This too is unsafe. The resident may need a frame-on-wheels.

3. **Lifting one side of the frame after the other** with a rotary motion. The resident who does this probably does not need a frame; a stick should suffice.

4. **Walking "into" the frame.** This happens when steps are taken which are too large. After two steps, the resident has her tummy right against the front bar of the frame, which is unbalanced and unsafe.

5. **Moving the frame and feet "at random"** with no pattern. This wastes the balance-aiding, weight-bearing value of the frame.

Residents using the frame in these last two ways should be taught the correct walking pattern.

The Frame-on-wheels
The frame-on-wheels is a walking frame fitted with wheel units on the front legs

which is pushed gently along. The ferrules at the back prevent any "running away" because as soon as weight is put on the frame it stops. Side-slip does not occur, as the wheels are restricted to forward movement. The frame-on-wheels is available in two adjustable sizes: for large/average adults and small adults/children.

The frame-on-wheels is very useful for elderly people who need a lot of help from one person or help from two people, but who cannot cope mentally with learning the walking pattern necessary to use a walking frame correctly. It is also surprisingly (it does not run away) useful for older people with Parkinson's Disease as the smooth movement can make their walking more fluent.

Decide on the correct height of a frame-on-wheels for a resident in the same way as for a walking frame. Any help required should be given from behind.

Special bags can be obtained which enable personal possessions to be carried on both kinds of frame. Handbag hooks can also be obtained.

Quadruped

Residents who have one "bad" leg (from severe arthritis in one hip or knee or a stroke), who need more support than a walking stick but less than a walking frame, may need a quadruped.

The following steps are necessary before giving a resident a quadruped:-

1. **Measure,** using the same principles as for a walking stick – the quadruped is itself adjustable.

2. **Check that the four small suction ferrules are safe** and replace them if necessary.

3. The quadruped should be **held in the opposite hand** to the resident's "bad" leg.

4. Teach the resident to walk using the following **walking pattern:**

• put the quadruped forward

• take a normal-sized step with the opposite foot

• take a normal-sized step with the other foot so that it lands level with or just past the quadruped

• repeat the sequence.

5. **If a resident improves** and starts to walk faster putting the quadruped and opposite leg forward together, she is probably ready to change to a walking stick.

6. If physical help is needed, give it "on the hips" from behind as for a walking stick.

When a quadruped is not in use, ie is free standing on the floor, it can be easily knocked over. This is a potential hazard which care staff need to remember.

Trolleys: Residents who usually use walking aids can be independent when transporting items (eg a cup of tea) by using a high trolley on wheels.

Assessment and teaching

It is essential for walking aids to be used correctly. Therefore all care staff must be able to teach how to use them, and continually remind residents of the appropriate correct, safe walking pattern. As it is difficult to teach a skill you have not mastered yourself, you should "try out" the walking aids covered above using the correct walking patterns.

As a resident's needs may change, it is important regularly to re-assess her walking, to ensure that she is still using the appropriate walking aid.

If a resident's walking deteriorates (which is usually very obvious) she may need a walking aid which offers more support.

If a resident's walking improves (which often goes unnoticed) she may need a walking aid which offers less support, or no walking aid at all.

Encouraging walking

Even when a resident has the correct walking aid and knows how to use it you may find she is reluctant to walk. Pain and stiffness caused by prolonged sitting may be the cause, in which case bending and stretching the legs a few times before walking may help.

However the usual reason for not walking is lack of motivation. Older people in a residential home need an enticing destination in order to feel that it is worth making the effort to walk.

The longer a person sits in a chair the more mental and physical effort it takes to get out of it. Therefore long periods of sitting must be "broken up" by providing many and varied destinations in addition to the basic reasons for moving, ie visits to the toilet, the dining room or returning to the bedroom.

A group of care assistants gave the following good list of activities to entice residents out of their chairs:

• providing tea and coffee in the dining room, rather than the sitting room

• group activities in another part of the home, eg keep-fit, disco, music and movement, bingo, craft sessions, card games, etc.

• gardening (indoor or outdoor)

• outings outside the home: to the pub, library, church, community centre or further afield.

If walking to another room is very difficult for a particular resident, start her off first and position chairs along the route for necessary rests.

If a resident *can* walk, always use *every* possible alternative to the dreaded independence-robber – the wheelchair. Do not give in to persuasion. Only use a wheelchair if the resident is really ill.

Risk and independence

Let us imagine an old gentleman who uses a walking stick as he is a little unsteady on his feet. It is Friday night and he wants to go to the pub nearby for a drink. He is perfectly capable of locating the pub and returning to the home from it, but he is discouraged from going by the staff at his residential home because "he might fall".

Is the slight risk of his falling such that he should be discouraged or even "not allowed" to pursue his usual (when he lived in his own home) Friday night activity? Or is this an acceptable risk which must be taken to enable this gentleman to remain independent and purposeful?

Just because he cannot continue to live alone at home does not mean that he cannot retain responsibility for some areas of his life when in a residential home. Indeed he must retain this responsibility if he is to stay truly alive.

Defining what constitutes "acceptable" risk for an individual resident is very difficult and can only be done after careful discussion of all the factors involved between the staff and the resident. There are very few, if any, situations in which a resident wishes to attempt an activity which in fact turns out to be an "unacceptable" risk. Encouraging elderly people to be independent, despite an acceptable level of risk, is to encourage them to remain active in body and mind.

Care assistants may also need to take the initiative in stimulating residents to take risks. An elderly lady who likes to walk holding a care assistant's arm, but who really does not require this help, may be taught to use a walking aid and then be encouraged to use it independently.

After the "supervision" stage has been successfully negotiated, this lady can walk around the home, albeit with a slight degree of risk. She could lose her balance and fall – but this is judged "unlikely", so the risk is "acceptable". If falling were thought to be "likely", then the risk would be unacceptable.

Getting up after illness

Elderly people must get up as soon as possible after illness because if they stay in bed the following threaten health and mobility:

• they become stiff and weak very quickly because they are not using their legs for walking

• their lung capacity becomes smaller

• they do not breathe deeply and fluid collects in the lungs

• they find this fluid difficult to cough up and they quickly succumb to pneumonia

• circulation deteriorates

• they are more likely to suffer a thrombosis, because of poor circulation. (This can cause a number of serious problems, any of which can lead to death.)

It is therefore essential for residents to be encouraged gradually to regain their previous mobility as soon as their illness has passed its acute stage (usually when the temperature has returned to normal).

When helping older people to get up for the first few times after illness into a chair by the bed, do everything *slowly* with them. For example, you might say:
1. "Sit over the edge of the bed *slowly*".
2. "Sit on the edge of the bed *for a few minutes*" (to get used to having legs down and head up).
3. "Stand up *slowly*" – use a walking frame for them to hold onto when in the standing position if necessary.
4. "Turn around and sit into the chair *slowly*".

Shoes or slippers?

Most residents wear unsuitable footwear. Slippers and soft shapeless shoes allow an elderly foot to spread and fall over so that shoes may eventually not be able to be worn and walking becomes unstable. They also "slop" at the heel which is dangerous and encourages elderly people to shuffle in order to keep the soft shoe/slipper on. Shuffling is dangerous as feet can catch on carpet edges or scatter rugs, causing falls.

High-heeled shoes, worn by a few residents, are clearly unsafe as they provide such an unstable base.

After explanation of the value of shoes for safe walking, all residents should be encouraged to wear shoes, if only for part of the day. Men should wear ordinary outdoor shoes. Women should be encouraged to wear a "sensible" pair of shoes. These can be difficult to find, but some mail-order firms provide excellent shoes for elderly women, often at very reasonable prices.

Surgical shoes are needed by a few residents with special (often arthritic) foot problems or when a surgical appliance (caliper or heel raise) has to be fitted onto the shoe. Incontinent residents may need machine washable shoes which some large department stores stock. They are not suitable for most other residents.

If a resident cannot get her shoes on she may need chiropody, new shoes or special shoes. Swollen feet may also be the cause; or if diabetic, the circulation in her feet may be deteriorating. These conditions should be reported to the GP. See also Chapter 10 on care of the feet.

Varicose ulcers

It is vital to notice a mark on the skin, or broken skin, early and treat it immediately as leg ulcers cause pain and immobility. As well as nursing treatment, walking must be encouraged as it boosts the circulation and maintains mobility.

A resident with an ulcer, however small, should never have her feet down on the floor when sitting. They should be up on a stool which supports the whole leg and raises the feet above hip-level. Only then can gravity help the circulation so that the extra fluid drains out of the legs, giving the ulcer the best possible chance of healing quickly.

Chairs

Chairs are probably the most important items of equipment in a residential home. Not only because so much time is spent in them, but also because much energy is used to get out of them and risk taken getting into them. Unsuitable chairs give care assistants unnecessary work and discourage independence.

Gradual replacement of obsolete dining room chairs without arms with stable chairs with arms is essential if the comfort and safety needs of frail elderly people are to be met. Even more important is the replacement of unsuitable low sitting room chairs (which only suit the needs of a few very frail residents) with supportive, high-backed chairs with a variety of seat heights and depths (most will need to be 18-20" high).

Once these are available, they are only useful if the correct chair is matched to the needs of each individual resident. A person who cannot get up from a low chair without help may be independent from a high chair. Providing a chair with a high seat for this resident will encourage her to maintain independence and dignity.

Getting out of chairs

If chairs are suitable, and a chair has been carefully chosen to meet a resident's individual need, yet she still says she cannot get out of it, what can care staff do?

Help her? No! *Teach* her how to do it by the method which works for most elderly people. The instructions to give her are:
1. "Wriggle to the edge of the chair" (by wriggling hips forward)
2. "Bring your feet back as far as possible" (knees should be bent to at least a right angle)
3. "Now put your hands on the chair arms"
4. "Lean forward" (when learning how to get out of a chair, a resident may need a firm but gentle hand on the top of her back to encourage her to bend forward)
5. "Now push with your hands on the chair arms, keep on leaning forward, and stand up!"

If after considerable teaching, the resident does need physical help, it should be minimal, and the helper should avoid dragging on the shoulder.

All care staff need to acquire the vital skill of teaching this method, to enable elderly people to get out of chairs independently. Getting out of a chair independently provides excellent muscle-strengthening and joint mobilising activity which helps to keep an older person fit and active.

Getting out of chairs with a walking aid

With a walking stick: Hold the walking stick in the curled fingers of one hand, while using the 'heel of the hand' to push up from the chair.

With a quadruped: Do not hold onto the quadruped while getting out of the chair (unsafe), but take hold of it when standing firmly.

With a frame: Do not hold onto the frame while getting out of the chair (unsafe), but take hold of it when standing.

Picking up items off the floor

Some residents find leaning forward to get out of a chair difficult and uncomfortable. This may be because they habitually avoid the bending forward position as it is awkward, makes them feel slightly dizzy and therefore anxious.

Thus when something needs picking up off the floor (a handkerchief or a newspaper) a "helpful" care assistant always does it – depriving the resident of the opportunity to practice and therefore retain the ability to bend forward at the hips.

Since "what you don't use, you lose" it is preferable for the elderly person to pick up the items off the floor with supervision or as little help as necessary.

For some residents a "helping-hand" aid can enable this activity to be carried out independently.

Getting into chairs

This is a hazardous activity because many elderly people have a compulsion to sit in the chair as soon as possible, once they are within reach of it. They therefore sit down in a great hurry before getting close enough to the chair, and may land on the floor. This can have disastrous consequences, including the possibility of a fractured neck-of-femur.

Uncontrolled movements like this are always unsafe; to avoid danger and to encourage controlled, safe movement the following sequence should be taught:
1. "Move towards the chair but do not try and sit on it yet".
2. "When you are close enough, turn all the way round until you have your back to the chair".
3. "Walk backwards until you feel the chair behind the back of your knees".
4. "Lean forward while feeling for the chair arms with first one hand and then the other".
5. "*Gradually* lower yourself to sit gently on the chair" (this last is important because it gives additional exercise to important muscles and prevents jarring of the spine).

It is essential to emphasise the first instruction and stop the elderly person *before* she lurches dangerously into the chair, by reminding her not to sit in the chair *until* she has turned all the way round and can

feel the chair.

Toilet and bathroom

The sequences for getting on and off the toilet are the same as those for getting on and off chairs, just described.

Many residents find it difficult to get on and off the toilet. Rather than care assistants helping them physically, which creates dependence, it is preferable to fix suitable rails for their use. A great variety of rails are available for different situations; it is therefore essential for an occupational therapist to advise on toilet fixtures. (Many homes have rails which are useless because they are the wrong type or fixed in the wrong place).

A removable high toilet seat can make a resident (e.g. with severe hip arthritis) who finds the toilet too low, independent. A hook in each toilet is useful for residents to hang their walking sticks on, as these are a nuisance or dangerous if just propped up.

Many residents will be able to manage the bath alone if they use a bath seat, bath board, non-slip mat and well-positioned grab rails. A range of smaller bath aids will enable many residents to wash in privacy. **NB** An occupational therapist should advise on the use of toilet and bath aids with particular residents.

Beds

Most homes have beds approximately 16" high (including mattress) which is rather on the low side. Low beds are difficult to get up from and more risky to sit down onto. The optimum height for an elderly resident to manage safely and easily is usually 18" – 20" high.

As a firm surface is easier to move on, sit safely down onto and rise from, beds should be firm. Softer beds can be made firmer with a board/boards under the mattress. Low beds can be raised on special, solid blocks.

Scatter rugs are dangerous for older people as they can easily be slipped or tripped on.

Moving while lying in bed
The basic instructions for moving sideways or up and down in the bed are:
1. "Lie on your back"
2. "Bend up your knees with your feet flat on the bed"
3. "Put your elbows firmly on the bed near you waist"
4. "Lift your bottom off the bed"
5. "Push on your elbows and feet and move your bottom up/down/to right/to left".

Rolling in bed
Usually achieved by:
1. "Turn your head to face in the direction you are rolling to"
2. "Bend up the leg of the side you are rolling away from with your foot flat on the bed"
3. "Reach with your arm for the side you are rolling to"
4. "Push on the foot of the bent-up leg and roll over".

Getting out of bed
Usually achieved by:
1. "Roll towards the edge of the bed"
2. "Swing your legs over the edge of the bed"
3. "Push up on your hands and sit up".
Having got to this point elderly people, particularly those with low blood-pressure, may need a little time to get used to the upright position before getting off the bed.

Getting off the bed
This is the same basic procedure as getting off a chair or the toilet:
1. "Wriggle to the edge of the bed"

2. "Bring your feet back as far as you can, so that your knees are bent to at least a right-angle"
3. "Now put your hands on the edge of the bed"
4. "Lean forward"
5. "Now push with your hands on the edge of the bed, keep leaning forward and stand up".

NB Residents who use walking frames should be taught not to pull on them when getting off the toilet, bed or chair, as it is dangerous. It is also dangerous for a care assistant to stabilize the bottom bar of the walking frame with a foot and the top by leaning on it, so that the resident can pull on the frame to get up. Why? If the care assistant is not there and the resident tries to get up by pulling on the frame, he or she may fall.

Getting on to the bed
This activity can be hazardous and worrying for elderly people. Using the following sequence makes the activity safer and more comfortable:
1. "Approach the side of the bed, but do not try and sit on it yet"
2. "Turn all the way round until you have your back to the bed"
3. "Walk backwards till you feel the bed behind the back of your knees"
4. "Make sure you are about half-way along the bed. If not move sideways till you are"
5. "Lean forward and feel for the bed edge with first one hand, then the other"
6. "Gradually lower yourself to sit on the bed gently".

Getting into bed
This is an awkward activity, which can result in a lot of unnecessary humping and lifting, if the elderly resident is not aware of how to position herself before lying on the bed.
These instructions should make it easier:
1. "Make sure you are seated about half-

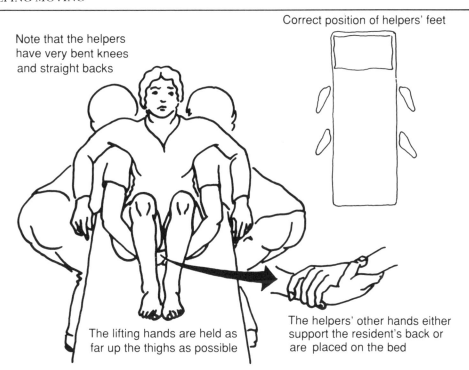

Correct position of helpers' feet

Note that the helpers have very bent knees and straight backs

The lifting hands are held as far up the thighs as possible

The helpers' other hands either support the resident's back or are placed on the bed

The Shoulder Lift - for lifting up the bed.

way along the bed"

2. "While sitting on the edge of the bed, move your bottom so that you are facing the foot of the bed"

3. "Swing your legs up on to the bed, meanwhile flinging your body back on to the bed". This must be done *quickly* or the resident may remain on the edge of the bed feebly trying to gather up sufficient courage to have another go; or she may get her body back on the bed and fail to get her legs up, which is uncomfortable; or worse she may just ask for and receive help – all of which may be avoided by following the steps above.

Wheelchairs: Transferring and lifting

Wheelchairs for individual residents

A permanently disabled resident who has been carefully assessed as needing a wheel-chair permanently, is entitled to one of her own from the DoH. The GP and a physio-therapist or an occupational therapist should be involved in obtaining the cor-rect chair individually chosen for the resi-dent. Once supplied, this chair should only be used by the particular resident for whom it was obtained.

The few residents who because of per-manent disability (eg double amputation) need a wheelchair of their own, but who can transfer independently from bed to chair, chair to toilet etc, should be encour-aged to do this, in order to maintain their independence. They should also wheel *themselves* from place to place whenever possible.

Wheelchairs for residents with declining mobility

The majority of residents who are in wheel-chairs need them because of deteriorating mobility. This chapter has looked at many ways of avoiding loss of mobility when this is possible.

However despite medical treatment and all attempts to keep them moving independently, some elderly people with diseases like arthritis and Parkinson's Disease do become less mobile and may eventually need a wheelchair.

It should then be used for as little of the day as possible and a maximum amount of walking should be encouraged. Even one short walk a day provides invaluable exercise, and will help the resident to remain active in body and mind as long as possible.

Wheelchairs for general use

A home for elderly people probably needs at least one communal wheelchair plus thick foam cushion, for residents who are recovering from illness. This wheelchair should *never* be used to save time wheeling residents who are capable of walking, as it eventually leads to permanent dependence.

Wheelchairs must be maintained as they are dangerous if tyres are flat, brakes do not work or foot plates get loose.

Wheelchair transferring – with help

Residents who are dependent and in wheelchairs for part or all of the day may still be able to do a lot of the work involved in transferring from bed to chair, chair to toilet etc. themselves.

Even if they require help in transferring, residents should be encouraged to use their arms to push with and to take as much weight through their legs as they can. This will help maintain their remaining strength, balance and concentration. Total lifts should rarely be necessary.

Principles of good lifting

The main problems which occur during partial or total lifts result from poor lifting techniques.

Good lifting does not need brute force, but a correct technique and careful planning. It avoids the problem of anxious,

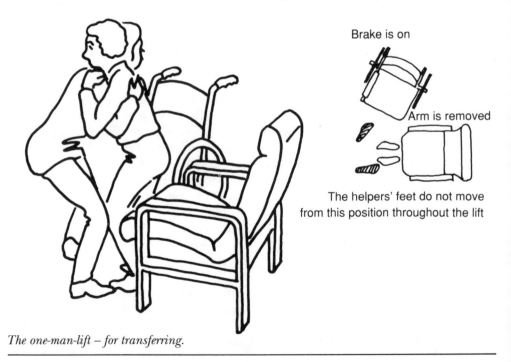

Brake is on

Arm is removed

The helpers' feet do not move from this position throughout the lift

The one-man-lift – for transferring.

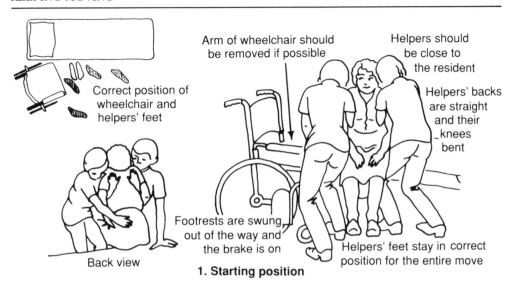

Correct position of wheelchair and helpers' feet

Arm of wheelchair should be removed if possible

Helpers should be close to the resident

Helpers' backs are straight and their knees bent

Back view

Footrests are swung out of the way and the brake is on

Helpers' feet stay in correct position for the entire move

1. Starting position

Hand changes position

2. Help the resident clear of the bed

Helpers' feet have not moved

3. Turn and lower her into the wheelchair

The two-man lift – for transferring.

tense, difficult-to-lift residents who unfortunately "know" from previous experience that being lifted is a painful, insecure business. Good lifting also protects care assistants from damaged backs.

A resident who is too disabled physically, mentally or both to take an active part in a partial lift should be encouraged to relax – as it is easier to lift a relaxed resident than a tense one. A tense resident who wants to hang onto the chair she is sitting in during the lift, can be encouraged to put her hands onto the shoulders of the lifter/s.

Rules for good lifting

1. Stop and plan the lift. Where is the resident and where are you trying to lift her to?

2. Arrange the room beforehand. Position the wheelchair or chair or both, so that only minimal turning is necessary. The turning part of lifting is the most difficult and dangerous. Remove the relevant arm of the wheelchair if it is removable.

3. Ensure that there is enough space to perform the lift safely. Don't have yourself squeezed into a corner. Move small items of furniture temporarily and larger items in a bedroom permanently to allow more space in which to lift a disabled resident.

4. Tell the resident what you are going to do and how she can help. Reinforce this by encouraging her throughout the lift.

5. Get into a good position before starting the lift. Stand as close as possible to the resident, with feet wide enough apart to allow good balance and with the lead foot pointing in the direction of travel.

6. Grip the resident under the arms and around the back thus avoiding strain on her shoulders and helping her to feel comfortable and secure.

7. Get down to lift by bending the knees while keeping the back straight.

8. If there is more than one person lifting, lift together on an agreed signal.

9. Bring the resident towards you and use your strong hip and thigh muscles to straighten your legs and lift.

Try to achieve a flowing technique using momentum and your body weight to balance the resident.

10. Keeping back straight but not stiff, and bending knees, lower the resident on to the chair within the same movement.

NB When trying a new lifting technique:
1. Warn the resident it will be different and explain how she can help.
2. Discuss it with your co-lifter and practise on another member of the care staff to check the principles and method carefully.

3. Persevere, although it will feel strange. It is worth lifting well for the sake of your back and residents' comfort.

4. Remember that the key rules above apply to lifting anything in any situation.

5. If possible, ask your local physiotherapist to visit the home to hold a demonstration/practice session on correct lifting.

CHAPTER 10

Care of the feet

by Judith Kemp

Normal feet and how they grow • walking • skin and nail care • special care for vulnerable feet • when to call the chiropodist • footwear

F oot care is of major importance to older people. Three out of four of them will have some foot problems. There are many simple tasks within the capability of any caring person, which I will describe. These can make the feet more comfortable, without needing the help of a professional chiropodist.

Normal feet

Each foot contains 26 bones joined by ligaments and moved by the actions of muscles in the leg and foot. Most children are born with normal feet, and at birth, the foot bones are mostly soft cartilage (like the end of your nose) which is gradually replaced by hard bone over the first eighteen years of life.

If the joints develop in an abnormal position, the way that the foot moves will be affected, and it will not function as efficiently as it should. This may not cause much discomfort in younger people, but often does in old age. Many foot problems are due to poor foot function, but the foot can also be affected by problems with the knees, hips and spine. Many so called "flat feet" are in fact caused by the relationship of the leg with the pelvis at the hip.

Walking

In a normal foot during walking, the outer edge of the back of the heel strikes the ground first. The shock is transmitted up the leg where the bent knee acts as a shock absorber. The outside edge of the foot then begins to take weight, followed by the ball of the foot, starting at the outside edge and then across to the base of the big toe. Whilst this is happening the heel is lifting off the ground and the foot finally leaves the ground as the big toe pushes off. The other foot does the same things but at a different time.

The muscles in the thigh lift the whole limb off the ground in walking whilst those below the knee control the movement of the foot. There are many more small muscles within the foot itself, which also affect toe function and stabilise the foot during walking.

When there is something wrong with the foot, knee or hip the normal cycle becomes disrupted and some parts of the foot may take too much weight, or take weight for too long. Other parts of the foot may not be doing their fair share of the work. This results in foot deformity, corns, callouses, foot strain and in some patients, ulcers caused by pressure.

Skin and nail care

The skin needs to be kept clean, supple and intact, because most germs causing infections like warm, dark, damp conditions. Because the feet are usually covered by hosiery and shoes, they are particularly vulnerable to bacterial, viral and fungal infections. In addition, older skin tends to be drier than young skin and may be undernourished if the circulation is not good. The following routine will help to prevent skin problems:

Wash the feet with warm water and good quality soap. Elderly people's feet may not need washing every day as do more active feet. The temperature should be tested with a thermometer and must not exceed 40 C (104 F). This is to avoid scalding fragile or insensitive skin. Unless instructed by a doctor or chiropodist nothing should be added to the washing water, nor should feet be soaked.

If the toes are very tight together, do not

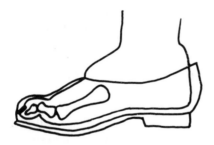

In a shoe without proper fastenings the foot pushes forward in walking.

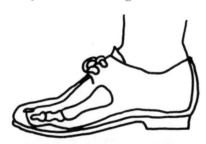

A properly fitted shoe allows for the foot to lengthen and spread out in walking.

pull them apart or pass the flannel between them, as this can split the skin. Use a cotton bud to gently wash between them.

Dry carefully, using a soft towel. Dry between the toes gently, using paper kitchen towels to absorb the water.

After drying, cut the toe nails if this needs to be done. If not massage the skin with a cream such as Simple Ointment BP, or a good quality hand cream. Pay particular attention to the heels which tend to be the driest part of the foot. Do not cream between the toes as this area tends to be moist in any case.

If the skin looks white, soggy or peeling, swab gently with Surgical Spirit, BPC. This may sting slightly but will quickly restore the skin to health. Repeat as often as needed to keep the skin texture normal.

Nail cutting

Cutting toe nails does cause some anxiety, especially if you are not used to doing this job, and because toe nails tend to become harder and thicker with age. Ideally, residents should be screened by a State Registered Chiropodist to ensure that anyone whose feet are potentially at risk, receives professional help (see below). If this is not possible, check the person's medical history. If they are diabetic, taking anticoagulants or steroids, check with their GP before proceeding.

One you are satisfied, gather together the equipment you will need:

1. A pair of **chiropodist's nail nippers** which can be bought from a good chemist shop. You will find them much easier to use than nail scissors, especially if you practise on your own finger and toe nails first.

2. A **diamond faced file** which can be boiled between use on residents, or disposable emery boards which can be kept for each individual. This is essential to prevent passing on fungal or other infections.

Fungal infections of the nails usually make them discoloured and crumbly. They can be treated with a paint or cream, but this takes about nine months to be effective.

Make the resident comfortable with their shoes and hosiery off. Their feet should be on a soft stool, covered with a clean, non fluffy cloth or disposable sheet, at a height convenient to you. Make sure the light is good, and place a low seat for you, facing the resident. Then wash your hands.

Start with the little toe nearest to your "nipper" hand. Hold the toe firmly (so that you do not tickle) with the thumb and finger of the other hand. Start by taking a small cut into the nail, making sure you are not going to clip the flesh before you shut the nippers. Shut the blades by pressing firmly on the handles. A "snatched" movement is less effective and may cause you to pull on the nail which can cause pain.

Continue to take small cuts until you reach the other side of the nail. Nails should not be cut too short. The nail should be as long as the fleshy part of the toe and you should not cut down the sides of the nail, nor round the corners with the nippers.

Once you have cut all ten nails, the corners can be rounded with the file or emery board. The free edge should be filed smooth. If the nails are thickened, the file can be used to reduce the thickness as well as the length. For residents whose nails do not grow very much, regular filing may be all that is needed.

Finish with a massage with cream as outlined above.

Special care

The feet can be affected by any disease which affect the body; in particular diseases of the nerves, muscles, circulation, skin, joints or the ability to fight infection. There are some groups whose feet are particularly at risk:

Diabetics. These people tend to have poor circulation especially in the toes, which leads to under-nourished skin, muscles and nerves. They may not feel their feet as well as normal, and can have bleeding blisters or grazes without feeling pain. They tend to develop pressure ulcers because they do not feel pain if they stand or sit in one position too long.

They are also less sensitive to heat and cold and may be scalded or get chilled without realising it. Any damage to the skin, however minor, needs good first aid treatment, careful daily observation and referral to a chiropodist or doctor at the first sign that healing is not occurring. Diabetics are less able to fight infections of all kinds.

People with **diseases of the nervous system** such as strokes, multiple sclerosis, spina bifida or who have had polio. The effects of these diseases vary but there is usually some loss of muscle power and nerve activity. The way in which the person walks (if at all) is altered, putting abnormal strains on the feet, and sensation may be lost.

People on **steroid drugs** or **drugs for cancer.** These drugs affect the body's ability to fight infection and relatively minor infections can become very serious in these people.

People with **poor circulation.** Many people find their circulation becomes poorer when they get older, but for some the problem is severe enough to need treatment from GP or hospital. They are at risk because the blood supply plays a vital part in fighting infection and healing. If it is diminished, these processes are severely restricted and infections may take hold much more quickly and with much greater damage than in the normal person.

Any resident who is taking **medication of any sort** or who has a foot problem should be seen by a doctor or chiropodist before care staff attempt foot care.

When to call the chiropodist

Ideally, each home should have a State Registered Chiropodist to advise and give treatment as necessary. The local District Health Authority should be approached for advice. They will not always treat on the premises if conditions are not adequate for good practice, but a screening service may be available. Residents should attend the local clinic wherever possible.

Once residents have been screened the chiropodist will advise on individual residents and should be called if anyone develops a new painful area, any increased redness or swelling in the feet, any colour change, any infection area which looks as if it might turn septic. This is especially important for residents with feet at risk as outlined above.

Footwear

Footwear plays an important part in foot health. The basic requirements for a good shoe are:

Length: the shoe should be about half an inch longer than the toes when standing with the fastenings done up.
Width: the foot should sit on the sole of the shoe and not hang over the edge, causing the uppers to bulge.
Depth: the front of the shoe should be deep enough so as not to rub on the toes or toe nails. This can be difficult to achieve if the toes are curly.
Fastenings: good shoes have an adjustable fastening across the instep to stop the foot sliding forward into the toe area and crushing the toes together. Laces, bars with buckles or "touch and close" (eg Velcro) all make good fastenings.
Heels: these should not be too high, and should be chunky rather than thin, to increase ankle stability.

Residents should be encouraged to wear shoes indoors for the greater part of the day, as slippers rarely fit the requirements of a good shoe as described. Slippers should be kept for early mornings or late at night, and it is essential that they are in good repair.

Further reading
The foot care book: An A-Z of fitter feet, designed for elderly people and their carers, by Judith Kemp. Published by Age Concern England, Astral House, 1268 London Road, London SW16 4ER.

CHAPTER 11

Pressure area care

by Elaine Barratt and Claire Hale

Who is at risk of developing pressure sores • what happens to body tissues under pressure • how to prevent damage • how sores should be treated

A "pressure sore" is a term used to describe an area of damage to the skin and tissue underneath it, which has been caused primarily by unrelieved pressure. Because they can easily occur in people who cannot move without help, they are a continuing problem for nursing and care. Evidence of sores has been found on mummified bodies from Egypt, suggesting that sores due to pressure are probably as old as mankind itself.

For patients and residents a pressure sore leads to unnecessary suffering, pain and loss of dignity, while nurses and carers are likely to develop feelings of guilt, frustration and confusion.

Today there is a vast amount of information available to carers, about the management of pressure areas. It is generally accepted that the goals of a systematic programme designed to prevent and treat pressure sores are:

• To identify the person at risk.

• To prevent or heal the pressure sores.

• To provide a nutritional programme to maintain or repair tissue.

• To teach the person how to prevent further sores.

Most of these are addressed in the following pages, where the causes of pressure sores, their prevention and their treatment are discussed in turn.

The causes of sores

Knowledge of the factors which contribute to the formation of pressure sores is essential for the effective prevention and treatment of sores. A pressure sore is caused by an interruption to the blood supply to that area. This interruption to the blood supply is usually caused by pressure, of which four types are usually recognised: compression, shearing, direct disruptive damage and friction. These are described below.

Compression: This occurs when tissues are squashed between an inside bone prominence and an outside resistant surface such as a bed (see diagram 1). The capillaries (tiny blood vessels) lying between the two surfaces become narrowed or blocked and the blood supply to the local tissues disrupted. The

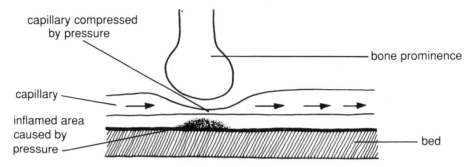

capillary compressed by pressure

bone prominence

capillary

inflamed area caused by pressure

bed

Diagram 1: The effects of compression.

tissues eventually die from lack of oxygen (which is carried to them in the blood). A patient left sitting too long in one position will suffer from this type of pressure, and a pressure sore will result.

Shearing: Shearing forces are caused by dragging the skin over hard material surfaces; the skin's surface becomes grazed and this damages the network of small blood vessels. Patients left in a semi-recumbent position are liable to this type of damage particularly at their sacrum (the base of the spine) and heels from sliding down the bed (see diagram 2).

Direct disruptive damage: This occurs when a severe blow to the tissues ruptures the circulation; this once again causes disruption of the blood supply to the local tissues, and tissue death due to lack of oxygen. A patient falling on to a hard surface would be likely to develop this sort of damage.

Friction: This causes burns and abrasions on the skin, and is likely to occur when two areas rub against each other. Sores developing under breasts are one example of this form of pressure.

Knowledge of the different forces that can contribute to pressure sores is important so that they can be avoided. However, carers also need to be aware of the fact that not everyone exposed to

pressure will go on to develop sores. A number of additional factors have been identified, which are known to make people more likely to develop sores. Such factors include both increased and decreased body weight, diseases affecting the blood and blood vessels, neurological factors, reduced mobility, pain and malnutrition. Other factors, which are in the control of the carer, include hygiene, poor lifting techniques, hard support surfaces, incorrect positioning and badly used "pressure-relieving" devices.

Some patients are generally more likely to get sores than others. These include elderly people, those with spinal injuries causing paralysis and loss of sensation, patients who are sedated or who are taking drugs that are likely to make them sleepy, the terminally ill and any patients with wasting, low resistance to infection, poor nutrition and impaired mobility.

Finally, chairbound people who may seem to be "better off" than bed-bound patients or residents are actually at greater risk of developing sores, because their body weight is not evenly distributed over such a wide area, and because preventive measures tend not to be applied so rigorously.

To help carers to identify the patients who are at risk of developing sores, a number of "pressure sore risk calculators" have been developed. The basis of these scales is to list the factors that predispose patients to sores, and score the patients on the absence or presence of these factors.

A well known and well used pressure sore risk rating scale is the Norton Score, developed for use with elderly patients in 1962. It comprises a numerical scoring system on five criteria: physical condition, mental state, activity, mobility and incontinence (diagram 3). A score of 14 or less indicates that a patient is at risk of developing sores; people scoring below 12 are considered especially at risk. Other risk calculators which are frequently used by nurses are: The Waterlow Scale, the Douglas Scale and the Pressure Sore Prediction Score.

Prevention

When you have identified patients at risk, preventive action must be taken. The main aim is relief of pressure, however it is caused. The traditional method of pressure relief is two-hourly turning of the patient or, more specifically, regular changing of the patient's position.

Care assistants in residential homes are unlikely to look after many patients needing such intensive nursing care. A knowledge of the principles is important, however, so that risks to less mobile residents can be avoided.

Barrier creams are thought to have a limited role in preventing superficial sores developing, and they should only be used to give protection from friction, dehydration, grazing and damage to the skin from urine or faeces. However, massaging the skin with these creams to promote circulation is a *misguided practice*. Rubbing or vigorously massaging the skin will cause tissues to break down and *increase* the likelihood of a pressure sore developing.

Washing with soap and water as a method of pressure sore prevention is also *an ineffective and potentially harmful practice.* Excessive washing lowers the acidity of the skin and removes the skin's protective substances, making pressure sore formation a greater possibility. Special soaps and cleaners are now available which do not reduce the acidity of the skin and these can be used on incontinent patients who may require frequent washing.

Other factors that aid prevention are **improved nutrition**, especially increased

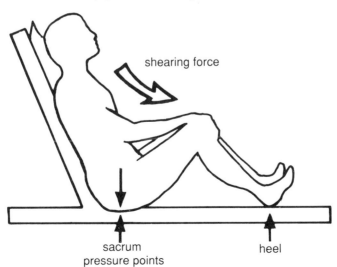

shearing force

sacrum
pressure points

heel

Diagram 2: Pressure points.

protein in the diet, **increased mobility** and appropriate medical treatment to **reduce oedema** (water retention in the tissues) and **treat anaemia** where appropriate.

For people sitting in chairs, **regular change of position, lifting and walking** will help prevent pressure sore development, and it is important that these people's needs are not forgotten.

Aids and equipment

When measures such as these are not possible or are impractical, there are a number of aids available that aim to minimise the forces that cause damage. However, it is important to note that any aid which reduces pressure due to compression may not reduce pressure due to shearing forces, and vice versa. For example, sheepskins placed under the sacrum and heels may minimise the damage caused by shearing in sliding down the bed, but will do nothing at all for the pressure caused by compression.

One of the primary causes of compression damage is the type of surface on which the person is placed. A major culprit here is the hospital-type mattress, because in many positions the bodyweight is supported by limited body contact with the flat, firm surface of the hospital bed. Ideally the support surface should have total contact with the body to enable the pressure to be more evenly spread.

Because of the need to spread body weight over a large surface area it is often better to look after someone lying on their back or front, with only limited time, not more than two hours, being spent lying on their sides at any one time. By taking this factor into account people can often be allowed four hours absolutely flat on their backs overnight, thus giving them a better chance to have uninterrupted sleep.

There are a variety of substances that can enhance a more even distribution of body weight. The most well-known of these are air and water. Air and water are used to suspend the body on a support surface, and the principle of suspension allows the body weight to be spread over a large surface area.

There are a number of pressure relieving aids that have been designed with this factor in mind: these include the low air loss beds and net suspension mattresses. The ripple mattress and vaperm mattress are based on the same idea, as are Ro-Ho cushions, Spenco Pads and slashed foam mattresses. Although many of these aids have not been evaluated, the principle upon which they are manufactured is sound and thus they should act to reduce pressure if they are used correctly.

The correct use of all pressure relieving devices is vitally important. For example, nurses often complain that ripple mattresses are ineffective, but researchers have found that many of these were wrongly set for the person's weight, that the tubing was often kinked and the machines poorly positioned. It is hardly surprising then that the ripple mattress does not appear to relieve pressure in such instances.

One often-used aid which does not, in fact, have any pressure relieving effect is the ring cushion. These placed under the sacrum are far more likely to cause pressure sores than to relieve them. This is because where the ring is in contact with the body, pressures are increased not decreased. Someone left sitting on a ring cushion for long periods of time will develop a ring of pressure damage where the body is in contact with the ring.

Pressure relieving devices are costly and it is important that they are used properly and effectively. Manufacturers usually provide detailed advice about the use and care of equipment and this should be followed for the best results. Finally, any equipment which allows forward slide should be avoided if possible, as while compression pressures are being reduced, shearing forces may be increased.

If, despite preventive efforts, someone develops a sore, then a positive approach to treatment is required. However, the treatment of pressure sores poses a number of problems, not least because everyone is an individual. The sore itself can range from a red area of skin to a crater involving deep tissue structures or bone, and complications such as infection and the presence of dead tissues.

Treatment of sores

Pressure sores are now usually classified into five stages. In stages 1 and 2, the skin is red but not broken. The redness of the skin indicates that tissue damage is occurring and will get worse if not treated. In stage 3 the skin is broken and there is usually a small ulcer. In stage 4, the ulcer has become larger and deeper, and in stage 5 the sore is usually infected with areas of dead skin, yellow discharge and an offensive smell.

Treatment of a pressure sore depends upon its stage of development. Pressure sores at stage 1 and stage 2 seldom require more than the prevention measures mentioned earlier. However, pressure sores of grade 3 and above are wounds and a qualified nurse should always supervise treatment. Nevertheless knowledge of the principles involved is useful to all carers.

As has been noted, knowledge about wound healing is increasing and earlier thoughts about the best environment for healing have altered. Previously a dry wound environment was considered important: this is why oxygen was used in the past to dry wounds.

However, it has now been established that drying a wound delays skin re-growth. In fact **wound healing occurs two or three times faster when wounds are covered with a dressing which closely covers the wound but allows the oxygen through,** compared with wounds covered with conventional dry dressings. These dressings are often in the form of an adhesive polyurethane membrane which is designed to retain the fluid produced by the wound and so create a moist wound environment.

Opsite is perhaps the best known of these: this membrane permits the exchange of oxygen and carbon dioxide, and the passage of water vapour, but will not allow bacteria, viruses or water to pass through. These membranes can be difficult to apply, and they should not be used on infected wounds.

When considering conventional wound dressings such as gauze, it is worth remembering that while they are effective at absorbing the fluid produced by the wound, they have little else to offer. They let the wound become too dry, they often stick to the wound surface, and when fluid soaks through to the surface of the dressing they provide a channel for wound infection. This also applies to some non-adherent dressings such as Jelonet or Sofratulle.

The use of stoma products (primarily designed for people with colostomies) to promote pressure sore healing has been reported to be effective. It is presumed that they work in much the same way as an occlusive dressing, and like Opsite retain wound fluid on the wound surface.

Numerous claims are made for creams, ointments and sprays as well as "desloughing" creams which claim to clean dead cells from the wound. Antiseptic preparations such as povidone iodine may have specific roles, but in general *the use of these substances to promote healing remains dubious.* Another factor important to wound healing is that the wound needs to be at body temperature for healing to take place. Carrying out a dressing and using cold lotions can reduce wound temperature so much that it can take several hours to return to body temperature. For this reason all lotions should be kept at room temperature if possible. Some dressings help to maintain the temperature of the wound; these include Synthaderm and Silastic Foam.

The choice of dressings available is increasing all the time: and when a nurse or carer is not sure what to use, it is advisable to seek help from a wound care specialist nurse. However, all wounds require a warm moist environment to heal and it is essential that carers help to provide such an environment.

Principles

1. If a wound is clean, leave it alone. If appropriate cover it with a special dressing as described.
2. If a wound has a small amount of exudate, wipe with dry cotton wool or gauze and cover with a sealing dressing.
3. When a wound appears to be infected, a swab should be taken or pus collected to send to the laboratory for analysis.
4. Mechanical or surgical treatment is the first choice when dead cells need to be removed from a wound. If this is not appropriate or possible, an enzyme desloughing agent can be used.
5. If there is a cavity, packing with ordinary ribbon gauze should be avoided because new cells can be damaged when the gauze is removed. A calcium alginate dressing can be used to pack a cavity. This dressing looks like gauze but gradually dissolves in the wound, does not damage new cells and promotes healing.

Even with all this, if someone is malnourished and debilitated it is unlikely that wounds will heal. Thus nutrition is very important and diet plays a major role in wound healing. A high protein, high carbohydrate diet is essential to provide the energy necessary for wound healing to take place.

In general, aim to provide the best conditions for wound healing - a clean, warm, moist environment. The use of "treatments" based on tradition rather than fact should at all costs be avoided.

Physical condition		Mental state		Activity		Mobility		Incontinence	
Good	4	Alert	4	Ambulant	4	Full	4	Not	4
Fair	3	Apathetic	3	Walks with help	3	Slightly limited	3	Occasional	3
Poor	2	Confused	2	Chair-bound	2	Very limited	2	Usually urine	2
Very bad	1	Stuporous	1	Bedfast	1	Immobile	1	Double	1

The Norton Score for pressure sore risk assessment.

CHAPTER 12

Mealtimes and nutrition

by Sue Thomas

Planning appetising meals • special nutritional and fluid requirements of elderly people • chewing and swallowing difficulties – help with feeding • special diets

---

Today's Menu
Boiled chicken
or
Flaked cod in white sauce
Creamed potatoes
Boiled cauliflower
Rice pudding

You can be forgiven for feeling that this menu sounds unappetising. It lacks colour, texture or flavour. Yet it is the type of meal traditionally thought to be the ideal "geriatric diet". This chapter aims to dispel such myths and offer some practical advice on how to help you residents to a healthy diet.

The nutritional needs of elderly people

The nutritional requirements of your residents will vary greatly between individuals. Nevertheless, we can make a few general observations.

Usually old people require fewer calories than younger adults, partly because the body's metabolism slows down with ageing, and partly because many old people become physically less active with advancing years. Requirements for all other nutrients, however, remain unchanged in old age. This is why elderly people benefit from a high quality diet: good food without too much "padding" from extra calories.

Fluids

Another requirement which does not alter in old age is the need for plenty of fluids. There is a danger than some old people try to cut down on drinks – for fear of incontinence, because they do not want to get up in the night or because they think that they should cut down on fluids when taking diuretics (water tablets).

Everyone needs about two litres of fluid (8-9 cups) daily – and this is especially important for elderly people living in warm centrally heated environments and during hot weather. Fluids such as tea, coffee, fruit juices, milk or water should be encouraged; but a word of warning about alcohol – it actually can cause dehydration, and so is not the ideal kind of fluid.

Mealtimes

Mealtimes are the highlight of the day for many of your residents and there is a lot that you can do to maintain a harmonious atmosphere in the dining room.

The residents will choose their companions at mealtimes. However, if there are one or two people with particularly offensive eating habits, a diplomatic segregation to another table might save embarrassment all round!

Try to make a note of those residents who eat slowly and serve them first to give them more time to eat. Never outface your residents with a huge plate of food – far better to give out a modest portion and then allow time to serve out seconds. Be sensitive to those with feeding difficulties and offer them a little help when you have the time.

Meal patterns

There are no strict rules about how many meals should be eaten daily, but it would be difficult for an elderly resident to get all the nutrition he or she requires from eating only once or twice daily. Those residents with a poor appetite might benefit from five small meals daily – the extra meals made up by nourishing snacks between main meals.

Special foods for elderly people

There are no special foods recommended for elderly people. However you may notice that many of your residents prefer familiar, traditional dishes to the more modern favourites such as quiches, pizzas or pasta dishes. If you are responsible for menu planning, certainly include a few "new" foods but try to give them English names. Cheese and onion flan may well be more appealing than the mysteries of Quiche Lorraine!

Another point to bear in mind is that, just as many elderly people may have impaired hearing or vision, others may have impaired taste or smell acuity, which reduces their enjoyment of food. Look out for residents who stir in three or four teaspoons of sugar to drinks, or those who need a lot of salt, pepper or ketchup on their food, just to give it some flavour.

Rather than the bland menu described at the beginning of the chapter, your residents need meals full of flavour and aroma. A pinch of chilli powder in the savoury mince or a little curry powder added to the chicken in cream sauce might reach the most jaded taste buds.

Risk factors leading to poor nutrition

Many old people will arrive in your home after an illness or a long period of failing to look after themselves adequately. In both circumstances their diet may well have been neglected and they could therefore be at risk of malnutrition. Signs and symptoms of poor nutrition include underweight, low resistance to infection and slow recovery from illness.

Once in residential care, with good food and companionship, most elderly people recover their appetite and make up for their past poor nutrition. However, for a variety of reasons, some residents will continue to eat badly and may remain malnourished. It is important to identify any residents in your care who might be poorly nourished. Some of the possible risk factors to poor nutrition are listed below.

Increased nutritional requirements

Extra calories, protein and vitamins may be needed by residents convalescing from illness, surgery, fractures or pressure sores. However it is at just these times that they have little appetite and eat less than usual.

If you have a resident who seems to be eating very little:

• Keep a record of all food and drink served to the resident, noting the amount of plate waste left. This will highlight their actual intake and whether it is a problem.

• Add extra nourishment to the resident's meals. For example high protein soup can be made by making up packet soup with all milk or using tinned/homemade soup with one dessertspoon of milk powder whisked in. One dessertspoon of milk powder can also be whisked into a portion of milk pudding or custard.

• Offer the resident small nourishing snacks between meals. For example: finger sandwiches with tasty fillings such as ham, corned beef, liver sausage, cheese and pickle, marmite; cream crackers or digestive biscuits and cheese; a small carton of fruit yogurt or fromage frais.

• Try them with a supplement such as Complan or Build-Up available from chemist shops. These supplementary drinks can be taken hot or cold and will add extra calories, protein, vitamins and minerals to the diet.

• Make a weekly or fortnightly check on their weight. The head of the home will need to inform the doctor if there is continued weight loss.

Confusion

It is common to find that new residents suffering from confusion are malnourished, simply because they have little awareness about the need to eat and may have spent weeks or months forgetting to eat or taking a badly balanced diet. This undernutrition usually rights itself after a few weeks in residential care.

However some confused people may continue to eat badly even in your care, either choosing a bizarre diet or eating very little. In such instances follow the advice given above for those with increased nutritional requirements. Draw your supervisor's attention to the problem because this sort of resident might benefit from a course of multivitamins from the doctor.

Lifelong "bad" eating habits

Once in care your residents might still be choosing a less than wholesome diet. Where improvements need to be made, introduce only small changes, one at a time, waiting for each new food to be accepted before trying the next.

Avoid the temptation to bring the residents in line with all the current views on "healthy" eating, because they are not necessarily as important to the over-75s as to younger adults. For example, it is well accepted now that a high fat diet is a risk factor for heart disease; but your residents have survived into old age, despite their high fat diet! Reducing their fat might deprive them of an important source of calories and the fat soluble vitamins A and D.

It is sensible to discourage your residents from having too many sugary foods between meals because they dull the appetite for the main meals. However the healthy eating recommendations to cut down on sugar and even salt in cooking are not appropriate because they may reduce residents' enjoyment of food, particularly if they have an impaired sense of taste.

Drugs

Old people are particularly at risk from nutritional problems caused by drugs. This is because the elderly tend to need more drugs, many of which are longterm. Drugs can affect nutrition in the following ways:

• Over-stimulating the appetite – which may cause obesity: for example certain drugs for psychiatric conditions or anti-anxiety drugs.

• Causing nausea and loss of appetite: for example high doses of digoxin, commonly used for heart conditions; chemotherapy drugs for cancer treatment.

• Causing malabsorption or nutrients: for example long courses of antibiotics such as tetracycline, regular use of laxatives; longterm use of anticonvulsants such as phenytoin.

Simple care and observation can help to prevent or minimise some of these harmful side-effects to medication:

• Always make sure that the residents take their drugs at the required times. For example, some medication must be taken with food, while other drugs should be taken between meals.

• If you notice a resident suddenly under- or over-eating, report it to your supervisor because it may be related to new medication.

• If medication regularly causes loose stools or diarrhoea, the doctor needs to be informed because it could eventually lead to malabsorption of nutrients.

Dental problems

Total lack of teeth or ill-fitting dentures can affect food choice, making the resident avoid foods such as chunks of meat or fresh fruit. Occasionally a resident may even demand pureed food because of dental problems. Ways to help include:

• Make sure that all your residents have regular dental checks. Make use of the domiciliary dental service, where local dentists will visit the home to treat residents with no additional charge for the travel.

• Encourage all residents to wear their dentures at mealtimes. Make sure that all dentures are regularly sterilised.

• Poor dentition is no excuse for requiring pureed food. Resist all such requests and encourage your residents to attempt as varied a diet as possible – helping them to soft rather than pureed foods where necessary.

Swallowing problems

Occasionally an elderly resident may experience problems with swallowing. This can be caused by a number of medical conditions including some physical obstruction in the oesophagus or the effects of a stroke. You may be able to help a resident with swallowing problems in the following ways:

• Inform your supervisor as soon as you notice a resident with swallowing difficulties. He or she will need a medical examination to discover the cause of the problem.

• If your resident has suffered from a stroke, there are ways that you can help them return to normal eating:

– make sure that the resident is sitting well supported to eat, with the arm affected by the stroke resting on the table.

– sucking a little crushed ice before each meal may help the resident to swallow.

– offer a soft diet, avoiding pureed food if possible. Puree is easier to eat, but it will not help the stroke sufferer to re-learn to eat normally.

– suitable foods include mince or flaked fish in sauce (without bones); root vegetables, cauliflower or tinned tomatoes (avoid peas and leafy vegetables); puddings present fewer problems – smooth consistencies such as semolina, yogurt or icecream are all ideal.

– drinks may be easier taken through a straw.

People who have speech difficulties often have special problems. See the section on feeding difficulties at the end of Chapter 6.

Institutionalisation

Meals are the highlight of the day for many residents, but eating the same menu week in, week out, in the same surroundings can become monotonous and even the resident with the heartiest appetite can tire of the cuisine. Here are some suggestions to increase residents' interest in their meals:

• Encourage them to make constructive suggestions for new recipes on the menu. Some homes have a "residents choice" day each week where some surprising dishes are chosen!

• Make regular changes to the dining area – different tablecloths, flowers or table decorations will make a great difference to the residents' enjoyment of their food.

• Make maximum use of events on the calendar. In addition to seasonal meals such as Christmas dinner, what about a strawberry and cream tea for Wimbledon or sausages and baked potatoes, preferably with some fireworks, for November 5th? This will help to bring the outside world into the home.

The following are common nutritional deficiencies found amongst the elderly in residential care, and ways to prevent them.

Vitamin C

Scurvy, caused by severe vitamin C deficiency, is rare nowadays. But a milder form of deficiency is common among the elderly, including those in residential care.

Vitamin C dificiency is caused chiefly by lack of citrus fruits and fruit juices in the diet and by the overcooking of vegetables, which destroys much of the vitamin. Symp-

toms of mild vitamin C deficiency are vague, but can include a reduced resistance to infection, poor wound healing, general apathy and even depression.

Any one of the suggestions below included daily in a resident's diet will ensure that they take sufficient vitamin C:

• A small glass natural orange or grapefruit juice

• One glass cold Ribena or fortified blackcurrant cordial

• One orange or two tangerines/satsumas (much easier to peel for arthritic hands).

If you are involved in either menu-planning or cooking in your home there are a few golden rules to remember which will boost the vitamin C content of meals:

• Always prepare potatoes and green vegetables just before they need to be cooked. If they are prepared and soaked in advance, a lot of the vitamin C is destroyed.

• Add the vegetables to a small amount of boiling water, cover and cook for as short a time as possible. If residents complain that the vegetables are "undercooked", you may have to compromise by cooking for a longer time initially and then slowly reduce their cooking times over a few weeks, gradually acclimatising the residents to more crunchy vegetables!

• Never add bicarbonate of soda to the greens because this destroys the vitamin C.

• Salads do not tend to be a popular choice amongst elderly residents, but many enjoy raw tomato. Served as an accompaniment to suppertime dishes such as macaroni cheese, raw tomatoes will boost their vitamin C intake. A wedge of fresh lemon served with fried fish will add both vitamin C and flavour to the meal.

Vitamin D

In the UK most of our vitamin D is obtained from the action of sunlight on the skin during the summer months, with just a little of the vitamin coming from food. Many old people who are housebound or have inadequate exposure to sunlight are at risk of vitamin D deficiency. This causes osteomalacia (adult rickets) – symptoms include muscle weakness, bone pain and an increased susceptibility to falls and fractures.

The most important way to protect your residents from vitamin D deficiency is to encourage them out into the sunshine, which is often easier said than done! Some of the suggestions listed below may prove useful:

• Serve tea in the garden on sunny summer afternoons – it might encourage even the most reluctant residents out.

• Direct sunlight is not essential for making vitamin D – a seat under the dapple of a tree will allow some ultra-violet rays to reach your residents.

• If you have residents who are unable to go into the garden, a seat on a verandah or in a shaft of sunlight by an *open* window would be helpful.

Dietary sources of vitamin D are useful, particularly in the winter months when body stores of vitamin D may be running low. Foods containing vitamin D include:

• Oily fish such as mackerel, herring, pilchards and sardines. These tend to be popular with older people and dishes such as sardines on toast might be a useful suppertime dish.

• Liver

• Eggs

• Evaporated milk – served with fruit or used in custards and puddings as an alternative to ordinary milk.

• Ovaltine

• Margarine – but a word of warning – not all catering packs of margarine are fortified with extra vitamin D. Check that yours is a fortified brand.

Fibre

Elderly people are particularly prone to constipation and it is usually caused by a combination of factors including insufficient fluids, side effects of medication, immobility and lack of dietary fibre.

Try to offer your residents plenty of fibre as food, rather than resorting to sprinkling natural bran on their breakfast cereal or porridge, because bran is fairly unpalatable and can affect the absorption of certain nutrients from the diet.

New residents must be introduced to a high fibre diet gradually, because too much fibre given to someone unused to it, can initially cause stomach pain and flatulence. They will also need to drink more fluid.

Easy ways to incorporate more fibre into the menu include:

• Regular use of wholemeal bread. Offer residents who dislike this a high fibre white bread.

• Offer a choice of higher fibre breakfast cereals such as Weetabix, porridge, puffed wheat, bran flakes.

• In cakes, biscuits and pastries 25% wholemeal: 75% white flour seems to be considered palatable by most elderly people. Fruit crumbles are delicious when made using all wholemeal flour mixed with a little brown sugar.

• Serve plenty of vegetables, jacket potatoes and fruit. A fruit salad, even one using some tinned and some fresh fruit, is a good way of increasing dietary fibre as well as giving extra vitamin C.

• If your residents are adventurous with their food, try them with wholegrain rice and wholemeal pasta which will boost their fibre intake.

Special diets

New residents requiring special diets can

cause consternation to cook and care staff alike. There are some basic rules which might help you sort out a suitable diet for each resident:

• Find out who prescribed the diet, for what medical condition and how long ago.

• If the diet seems old, check with the doctor that it is still required.

• If the resident has no diet sheet or a very old one (more than five years old), ask the doctor to refer the resident to your local hospital or community dietitian for a reassessment of the diet.

The following guidelines might help you deal confidently with two of the most commonly prescribed diets.

Reducing diets

If is difficult for an elderly person to lose weight because, as mentioned earlier in the chapter, calorie requirements drop with ageing. Even when an elderly person follows his/her diet strictly, weight loss will be slow.

Points to remember when helping a resident to lose weight:

• Only encourage them to diet if there is a good reason – for example weight loss required before an operation, or because obesity hinders mobility.

Meals are the highlight of the day for many residents.

• Plan short-term diets, eg 6-8 weeks, rather than placing a resident on a long-term diet, with no end in sight. This may give them far more motivation to stick to the diet.

• The diet should be gentle: cut out sugar in beverages, cakes, biscuits, sweets and chocolate; provide fresh fruit as an alternative to fattening puddings; allow starchy foods such as bread and potato (except chips) in normal amounts. If a stricter diet is felt to be necessary, ask the doctor to refer the resident to a dietitian.

Diabetic diets

The dietary treatment of diabetes has undergone radical changes in the past ten years. This has caused confusion for many elderly diabetics who are used to their old, strict diets. It has also been the source of many problems for the cooks and care staff.

Most elderly diabetics are controlled with a diabetic diet alone or diet plus diabetic tablets. A simple "low sugar" diet is all that is required for most of this group – but, if in doubt, check with the doctor.

Low sugar diet

Foods allowed freely:
  Meat, fish, cheese, eggs
  Vegetables and salads
  Tea, coffee, bovril, diabetic and sugar-free drinks, herbs, spices, pepper
  Saccharin and other artificial sweeteners.

Foods allowed in normal amounts:
  Bread (preferably wholemeal)
  Potatoes
  Rice and pasta (preferably wholegrain)
  Breakfast cereals (preferably high fibre variety)
  Fresh fruit, fruit tinned in water,

unsweetened fruit juices
  Plain biscuits
  Milk and milk puddings (using artificial sweeteners), icecream, yogurt
  Bedtime drinks, eg cocoa, Ovaltine, Horlicks
  Salt

Foods to avoid:
  Sugar and glucose
  Ordinary jam and marmalade, honey
  Sweets and chocolate
  Sweet biscuits and cakes
  Lucozade, lemonade, ordinary squash and other sweetened drinks
  Fruit tinned in syrup
  Condensed milk.

Diabetics who require insulin injections need a carefully controlled diet and should have an up-to-date diet sheet from a dietitian. In an emergency, if you have an insulin-dependent diabetic admitted to your care, make sure that they eat regularly, give them a "sugar-free" diet and, *very important*, give them a snack such as a milky drink and two biscuits both mid-morning and at bedtime. Contact a dietitian as soon as possible.

Gone are the days when the diabetic had to miss out on all food treats. There are even tasty biscuit and cake recipes, including birthday and Christmas cakes, available from the British Diabetic Association (address below).

Resources
British Diabetic Association, 10 Queen Anne Street. London W1M 0BD. 071 323 1531.

Further reading
Eating through the '90s. A handbook for those concerned with providing meals for elderly people. Produced by the Nutrition Advisory Group for the Elderly (British Dietetic Association). From Elizabeth Haughton, Dept. Nutrition and Dietetics, Gloucestershire Royal Hospital, Great Western Road, Gloucester GL1 3NN.

CHAPTER 13

Hearing difficulties and deafness

by Alastair Kent

How the ear works • causes of hearing loss • hearing aids and how to use them • communicating with deaf and hearing-impaired people • other aids and equipment

Losing your hearing is a very isolating experience because it cuts you off from much of everyday life. When hearing loss is accompanied by other problems associated with ageing the end result will, all too often, be an unhappy, lonely individual, withdrawn from contact with others and cut off from family and friends.

Too often people make assumptions about people with poor hearing that increase this feeling of alienation. Many people try to hide their deafness, perhaps because it is assumed by others to go with loss of mental agility. A recent advertisement by the Royal Institute for the Deaf tackled this head on with the caption "She's only losing her hearing, not her marbles" linked to a picture of an elderly lady struggling to hear.

Hearing loss is remarkably common. The Institute of Hearing Research estimates that as many as 10 million people in the UK have a loss of hearing that will cause problems for them in some circumstances.

The vast majority of these people are over retirement age. As many as 1 in 5 in this group have a significant hearing loss. If you work in a care home for elderly people, it is almost inevitable that some of your residents will have serious problems in hearing. This article aims to help you to help them.

How the ear works

The ear is divided into three parts – outer, middle and inner – each of which has a part to play in the process of hearing, and which will, if damaged or in some other way rendered non-functional, cause hearing loss or even deafness in the afflicted person.

1) The Outer Ear

This part of the ear includes the *Pinna*, which is the visible part. This acts like a funnel, channelling sound into the *External Auditory Canal*. This canal is really just a tube in the side of the head at the end of which is the *Ear Drum*. Sound waves entering the canal hit this membrane and make it vibrate. The higher pitched the sound, the faster the ear drum will vibrate.

2) The Middle Ear

This part of the ear is a small air filled cavity inside the head. It is connected to the outside world by a narrow passage called the *Eustachian Tube*. This opens up in the nose and throat. Its function is to ensure that the air pressure on each side of the ear drum is the same.

In the middle ear are three little bones. These are linked together and connect the inside of the ear drum with another membrane, known as the *Oval Window*. This leads to the inner ear. The names of the bones are *Malleus, Incus* and *Stapes*. When the ear drum vibrates these bones transmit the vibrations across to the inner ear.

3) The Inner Ear

The inner ear is full of liquid. It consists of a complex system of passages and is in two parts: the *Cochlea* and the *Semi-Circular Canals*. It is the cochlea which is concerned with hearing, while the canals control your balance. In the cochlea is a very sensitive organ called the *Organ of Corti*. This can be likened to a piano keyboard, but one with 17,000 keys!

Each "key" is a cell covered with tiny hairs, and each cell is connected to the *Auditory Nerve*. When the oval window is vibrated by the bones of the middle ear these vibrations are transmitted to the fluid which fills the cochlea. This then stimulates the hairs on the cells and, according to the frequency of the vibrations, a different combination of cells is caused to "fire" – or in other words, to send an electrical signal up the auditory nerve to the brain, where they are de-coded and we are able to perceive the sound in our consciousness.

Causes of hearing loss

The ear is a very complex and sensitive organ which can easily be impaired or damaged. There are many conditions

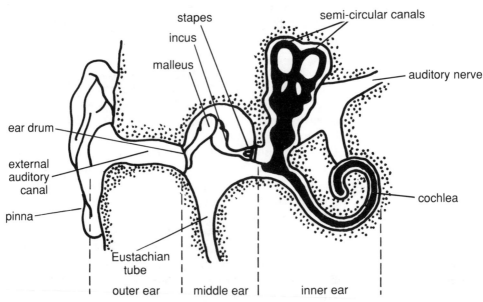

Anatomy of the ear.

which can affect hearing, but generally speaking, they can be divided into three broad groups: *Conductive Deafness, Nerve Deafness and Old Age Deafness.*

1. Conductive Deafness

This may be caused by anything which prevents the conduction of sound from the outside world to the point where the vibrations can stimulate the hair cells in the cochlea. Some of the commoner causes of hearing loss in elderly people include:

a) Blockage in the external canal: This must be almost total before hearing loss is noticed. Normally the ear's own clearance mechanism prevents a build up of wax. In some cases, however, it may be necessary to visit the doctor for the ears to be syringed. Poking with cotton buds usually makes the problem worse by pressing the wax down.

b) Otitis Externa: When the skin of the canal becomes irritated, it results in inflammation and sometimes infection. It may also affect hearing. Treatment is by careful cleaning and the application of ear drops.

c) Otosclerosis: This is the commonest type of conductive deafness. It is caused by an over-growth of bone in the middle ear, resulting in the link between the ear drum and the oval window becoming progressively more rigid and unable to transmit vibrations. It can be treated by surgery with a very good chance of improvement in the person's hearing.

d) Middle Ear Infections: These may be short term or long lasting, and may result in either temporary or permanent damage to hearing. They require medical treatment which varies according to the precise nature of the condition.

2. Nerve Deafness

Damage to the cochlea may occur as a result of illness, injury, exposure to some drugs or exposure to loud noises over prolonged periods. At present there is no known cure, and people with nerve deafness are dependent on others being aware of their problem and knowing what action to take in the circumstances.

3. Old Age Deafness

Hearing, like any other sense, tends to become less acute as we get older. There is little or nothing that can be done to prevent this, and it is a very common problem amongst elderly people. Where hearing loss is suspected, and other causes have been eliminated, the quality of life of the elderly person with diminished hearing will be significantly affected by the attitude and approach of those around. Practical suggestions for help are outlined below.

Hearing aids

Hearing aids are supplied to those who have been assessed as needing them, by the NHS free of charge. NHS aids come in two broad types – those worn behind the ear and those which are body worn. Whatever type is supplied, it is important to ensure that they have been issued as a result of professional assessment, that they fit properly and that they are in good working order. Hearing aids are also available privately.

Whatever the source of the aid, the following points should be observed to ensure that the user is getting the maximum benefit from it:

1. Is he/she wearing the aid(s)?
2. Is it working?
3. Is it switched on?
4. Are the batteries in good order? Batteries in a behind-the-ear hearing aid typically last for only two or three days, but may become useless in a shorter time than this.
5. Is the hearing aid clean? An ear mould that is clogged up with wax will be of limited use to the user. Ear moulds should be cleaned regularly.
6. Does the aid fit properly? A high pitched

whistling noise is a sign of feedback, showing that the aid is not properly fitted. This may be because the person has not put the mould snugly into his/her ear, or it may be an indication that the mould itself is poorly fitted and needs replacing. If it is the former, a little gentle adjustment is all that is needed. If it is the latter, new moulds will need to be fitted. If the mould appears to be fitting snugly in the person's ear, check that the tube leading from the earpiece to the aid is not split, as this too will often cause feedback.

Some people with impaired hearing seem unable to hear the high pitched whistle from feedback. It should not be ignored though, because it alters the hearing aid's ability to amplify other sounds that the hearing impaired person can hear without distortion.

It is also extremely irritating to those around who can hear it, and may result in feelings of anger or unpleasantness towards the person whose aid is whistling!

7. Can the persons with hearing aids adjust them properly to give maximum clarity? The controls on a behind-the-ear aid are very small and need a fair degree of fine finger control to adjust them. If a person is experiencing difficulty, they may find it easier to cope with a body worn aid. These have larger controls (they are similar in size to a personal stereo) which may be easier for stiff fingers to set.

Many people are issued with hearing aids but choose not to use them. Often this is because they feel embarrassed about owning up to their hearing loss. But hearing loss is widespread in the population over retirement age, and a sympathetic and matter of fact approach to the problem by you as the carer will help the person feel comfortable about admitting that they have a problem, and doing something about it.

It is also important to realise that a hearing aid will not "cure" deafness in most people. Hearing aids have a number of limitations:

1. They are unselective – many will amplify all sound picked up by their microphone without differentiating between those things you want to hear and those which are just background noise. Some more sophisticated ones will amplify some frequencies more than others, but even the best are very crude compared to the human ear.

2. Hearing aids work best at the distance of normal conversation – between three and six feet. Closer in they may distort the sound, further away they may not pick up a sufficiently powerful signal to amplify it clearly.

3. Hearing aids will not help in cases of nerve deafness. They can only amplify sound to compensate for problems associated with poor conductive mechanisms. They cannot make damaged nerves work again. People with nerve deafness need other kinds of help (see below).

What can you do?

There are a number of simple steps that you, the carer, can take to facilitate communication with the hearing-impaired person, whether or not they use an aid.

1. Avoid shouting. If a person is using a hearing aid then the sounds which they can hear will be amplified as well as those sounds with which they have difficulty. They will be made very loud, they may be distorted by the amplifier in the hearing aid and they may even cause pain to the hearing aid wearer.

Shouting also distorts your face. If a person is trying to lip-read you, this will make it more difficult. Try standing in front of a mirror and speaking normally. Now shout the same words and notice how different your face looks. (NB It is best to do this when you are on your own!) Clarity of speech, not volume, is the main require-

Hearing aids work best at the distance of normal conversation – between three and six feet.

ment, but again do not unnaturally emphasise words or articulate them in an exaggerated fashion as that will also change the shape of your face. Try this in the mirror too!

2. Give clues to what you are talking about in your face and by your body movements. Let your feelings show in your expression and try to move so as to help convey your meaning.

3. Think about the lighting. If a deaf person is to be able to lip-read you, good light levels are essential. Your face should be illuminated evenly, with no deep shadows. Do not stand in front of a window or a lamp, but turn so that the light falls onto your face. Do not get too close to the deaf

person – about four to six feet is best, so that they can see all your face easily. Further away the elderly person will probably not see you clearly enough.

4. Make sure that you have attracted the deaf person's attention and that they know you want to say something to them before launching in to a conversation.

5. Talk in a normal rhythm. Even if a person cannot hear or lip-read you very well, they may understand a lot from the context. If you speak in single words, rather than sentences, then the deaf person cannot get help from the flow of words.

6. Give clues. If you seem to have a problem in helping the hearing impaired person to understand you, then try saying to him/

her "I'm talking about . . .". If you get stuck with a particular word or sentence, do not repeat it over and over again. This will only cause embarrassment to both of you, and possibly result in anger or confusion. Try putting the same idea across in another way, using different words.

7. Control background noise. If the radio is on, or the vacuum cleaner is going, then it will be much more difficult for the person with impaired hearing to understand you.

The person with impaired hearing is most likely to understand you if you face them and speak clearly and with a normal rhythm, so he/she can use both sight and hearing to best advantage.

One final point: a person can only lip-read if they can see your lips. Droopy moustaches, covering the top lip, make this really difficult. Two minutes once a week with a pair of nail scissors could make a really noticeable difference to your communication skills!

Other aids and equipment

There are many devices other than hearing aids, available to help in a wide range of situations. These include:

1. Special alarm clocks which flash a bright light or operate a vibrating pad under the pillow or mattress.

2. Doorbells connected into special electrical circuits to cause the lights to flash when someone wants to come in. This may use a special signal lamp or be connected to the main lighting for the room.

3. Help to hear the television without annoying the neighbours. This comes in a variety of forms, including:

• Headphones

• Specialist TV listening devices

• Induction loops – these transmit the sound from the TV into a wire loop set up round the room. The person wearing a

hearing aid is able to adjust this to pick up the signal in the wire without interference from background noise.

• Teletext (also known as "Oracle" or "Ceefax"). Many TV programmes now are transmitted with sub-titles. To see the sub-titles it is necessary to have a special television or buy a de-coder to go with an existing set. These cost relatively little more than a standard TV set and help many people to follow what is going on much more easily.

4. Help with the telephone. Telephones cause a serious problem for many hearing-impaired people. Inability to use the telephone results in people becoming much more cut off from family, friends and the outside world than they need be; but again, there are a number of items that may be helpful.

• The bell may be connected to a flashing light so that a person with impaired hearing knows that the phone is ringing.

• The earpiece may be fitted with an amplifier and/or an inductive coupler (or a miniature induction loop) to improve the transmission of sound into the ear.

When these devices are fitted to a telephone, they can make a great deal of difference. There are some people who are too deaf to use the telephone and their problems are much more difficult to resolve. In such cases referral should be made to a specialist social worker with deaf people.

The aids and equipment mentioned above can make a major improvement in a person's ability to understand and take part in events going on around them.

However they can only help if everyone – you, the resident, management, family and friends – know that the equipment is installed and working and also know how to use it! There is no equipment in the world that can work when packed away in a box on top of a wardrobe.

Conclusion

We are all bound, in whatever capacity, to come across people with impaired hearing at some stage in our lives. Yet, despite this, hearing loss remains one of the most mis-understood impairments to which people are prone. I have given a few suggestions to help break down the barriers between people with impaired hearing and the everyday life of the community in which they live. Awareness and sensitivity are two of the most important attributes that you can have to help in this process, as these will help you to recognise the hearing loss in the first place and then do something about it.

Resources

Social Services Departments usually employ specialist social workers for deaf people. They can be contacted through the officer in charge of the residential home where you work, or directly.

Royal National Institute for the Deaf, 105 Gower Street, London WC1E 6AH (071 387 8033) offers advice, information and services to people with impaired hearing or those working with them.

British Association of the Hard of Hearing, 7-11 Armstrong Road, London W3 7JL (081 743 1110) runs local clubs in many parts of the country. It also provides information and a newsletter.

British Deaf Association, 38 Victoria Place, Carlisle (0228 48844). This organisation is mainly concerned with those born deaf and using sign language as a means of commun-ication. The BDA provides specialist services and deaf clubs for these people.

Local associations and societies in many parts of the country offer varying levels of service and support. Your local library should have this information.

CHAPTER 14

Sight problems and blindness

by Joan Mitchell and Rose Ashbee

How the eyes work • common disorders • normal changes with age • changes that need expert attention • caring for blind and deaf/blind people – communication, guiding, dressing, mealtimes, special help

Any disturbance of vision can be distressing and worrying. People may have a dread of permanent damage to their eyes, which might lead to blindness and consequent loss of independence.

This fear usually causes people to seek help early if they notice a deterioration in vision. However, elderly people may delay because they think that a reduction in their vision is simply due to old age.

Sometimes age changes are the cause of visual loss, and indeed with increasing age everyone suffers a change in his or her vision. For those who care for elderly people, an understanding of what is a normal age process and what requires further investigation, can be helpful.

The eyes

Each eyeball is a sphere, about one inch in diameter, and is protected by the bony orbit which is part of the skull. The eyeball has a tough white outer covering called the sclera. The curved area at the front of the eye is known as the cornea. This is trans-

parent like a window. It is unprotected and so can easily be damaged.

Behind the cornea is the iris, the coloured part of the eye, composed of muscle with an inner contractible circle known as a sphincter. This "hole" is known as the pupil and appears dark to the onlooker. The size of the pupil varies according to the intensity of the light (see below).

Behind the iris is the lens. This can change its shape by the action of muscles attached to it. In this way it can focus an image on the back of the eye. This region is known as the retina and can be likened to the film in a camera. Through a hole in the back of the orbit the optic nerve reaches the eye from the brain.

This is a simplified description of the eye, but it will serve in the understanding of changes which occur in the eye due to age.

External appearance

The eyes are suspended within the orbit in fat which acts as a cushion. Elderly folk lose some of this fat, so their eyes may appear to

114

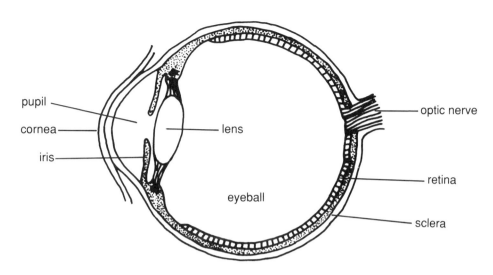

pupil

cornea

iris

lens

optic nerve

eyeball

retina

sclera

Anatomy of the eye.

be sunken.

Change in the size of the pupil. The pupils are round and equal in size, but with increasing age the pupil often becomes smaller because the iris becomes more rigid. When wide open the pupil lets in more light (like an open shutter in a camera). Thus the smaller pupil of the elderly person lets in less light and causes difficulty in vision if the light is poor. Elderly eyes adapt less quickly to changes in lighting.

Good lighting is very important in the home of an older person. It is a false economy to turn off lights in passages and to have dim lighting in dining rooms and reading rooms. Candlelit meals are best enjoyed by the young!

Arcus senilis. In a considerable number of elderly people, a narrow greyish white line develops near the margin of the pupil, leaving a clear rim outside it. This is due to fat deposits and has no effect on vision.

Pinguecula. Sometimes a triangular cream-coloured patch of fatty deposit appears under the conjunctiva on either side of the pupil. No treatment is necessary because it does not affect the eyesight. These patches can be removed for cosmetic reasons, but the resulting scar may be no improvement on the patch itself.

Xanthelasma. This is a long name given to the flat yellowish areas often seen in the skin of elderly eyelids, due to special deposits. They are usually symmetrical and have no effect on eyesight and do not require treatment. They can be cut away if they are disfiguring.

Disorders of the eyelids. The eyelids protect the eyes. They are covered with skin on the outside and a thin layer known as the conjunctiva beneath. As people grow older the eyelids become lax and the skin may be in folds. The eyelids frequently turn inwards or outwards due to weakness with increasing age.

Senile entropion is the term used for the lower eyelids turning inwards. This causes the lashes to turn inwards too and so irritate and damage the cornea and conjunctiva. Usually this can be corrected by a simple operation. Entropion does not affect the eyesight, but scarring of the cornea due to irritation and infection from the inturned lashes can impair vision if the condition is not treated.

Ectropion is the name given to the eyelid turning out due to the slackening of the skin and muscle of the lower lid. Tears cannot get away normally and soreness develops near the eye. The eyes also water a great deal. Again the condition can be corrected by a simple operation performed under a local anaesthetic.

Drooping eyelids may follow a stroke. Usually it is the upper eyelid which is affected. If the drooping hinders vision, special spectacle frames can be provided to raise the margin of the lid and clear the field of vision.

Changes in focusing

Ordinary visual difficulties such as long or short sight do not change much over the years until about age 45.

In youth the lens is transparent. It is covered by a membrane known as the lens capsule and the lens can change its shape by the pull of muscles attached to it, so bringing into focus objects at variable distances. In elderly people the lens becomes firmer and cannot change its shape so readily. It therefore becomes difficult to focus on a page of a book or other near objects including food.

This change becomes troublesome around age 45 although it has been going on long before this age. At first the printed page only needs to be held further away, but soon reading glasses become essential. The condition, known as presbyopia or long-sightedness, gradually becomes worse until by about 65 virtually everyone needs reading glasses. The process actually begins in early life. Distance vision usually improves.

Wearing glasses before or after the onset of long-sightedness has no effect on the course of the change, and there is no known method of preventing it. The changes vary from one individual to another and no exercises, diet or medicines have any bearing on the development of the condition.

Spectacles can be very helpful and there are many improved kinds on the market from which to make an individual choice. Variable focus lenses are particularly useful for musicians, painters, typists, etc.

Slow loss of vision

Slow loss of vision may not bother an elderly person, who may attribute the change to age. But it is very important that their eyes are checked regularly, because progressive loss of sight can sometimes be halted.

There are three main cause of blindness: cataract, glaucoma and senile degeneration of the macula. These three conditions nearly always develop very slowly and are not usually noticed until there is considerable loss of vision.

The first cause, cataract, can be remedied. The second, glaucoma, cannot be cured but it can be arrested. The third, senile degeneration of the macula, often progresses to blindness.

Cataract. This accounts for about a quarter of the applications for admission to the blind register.

As well as the covering of the lens becoming firmer with increasing age, the lens also becomes less transparent. Everyone over 65 will show some loss of lens transparency. Usually the lenses of both eyes are affected, although not necessarily to the same extent. Treatment is only required if the loss of transparency of the lens interferes with the vision enough to hamper a person's normal occupation or recreation.

Cataracts usually increase in thickness slowly, causing a gradual deterioration in vision, but there is no way of knowing how quickly the process will proceed. Some thicken very rapidly over a few months, others barely at all in a lifetime and may never give any trouble.

Cataract formation is a process of ageing and, as in the development of long-sightedness, no diet, exercises or other medical treatment can prevent it, any more than it is possible to stop a person's hair from going grey. Indeed, there is as much variation from individual to individual over cataract formation as grey hair.

Gradual obscuring of the lens leads to a subtle impairment in colour appreciation which is often not recognised by the victim until after surgical removal of the cataract.

The development of a cataract frequently increases short-sightedness. A change in glasses is all that is needed in the early stages. Sometimes drops can be used to dilate the pupil.

Cataracts do not necessarily need to "mature" before being removed. The decision to remove a cataract is made when poor sight interferes with an individual's lifestyle. Thick spectacle lenses are required after operation to replace the lens that has been taken away. There are also more complicated lenses that can be given after cataract operations, as well as lens implants. The choice depends on individual needs and on the person's ability to tolerate the aid.

Simple glaucoma. This is due to a rise in pressure of the fluid inside the eyeball. When glaucoma occurs gradually, the eye remains white and painless, but sight can be irretrievably lost.

It is probably due to ageing but the true cause is obscure. Heredity plays a part and therefore folk with a near relative suffering from glaucoma should be screened for the condition. It is usually detected by the optician, but sometimes elderly people notice a restriction in their field of vision which may cause them to blunder into objects. They may also complain of aching eyes.

Treatment by an ophthalmologist is nec-

essary and involves regular follow-up examinations.

Degeneration of the retina. Many degenerative changes affecting the lining of the eyeball (the retina) are a common cause of visual loss in the elderly, accounting for more than 25 per cent of cases of blindness. The degeneration frequently affects an important area of the retina known as the macula.

The only treatment for the resultant poor vision is strong reading glasses and the use of a magnifying glass or low vision aids.

Diabetics are more prone than others to vascular changes of the retina. Sometimes laser treatment can help. Diabetics are often more prone to cataract formation too.

Vitreous floaters. Age changes in the thick fluid behind the lens (the vitreous) often cause black spots to float about. These are called "floaters" and tend to move when the eye moves and settle when the eye is at rest. No treatment is needed for these and vision is not threatened, but it is important to be sure that the person has indeed a floater and not some other condition, such as retinal detachment.

Sudden loss of sight

The gradual loss of sight in one eye may not be noticed unless the good eye is covered up for some reason. If loss of sight occurs suddenly it is usually noticed soon afterwards. There are many causes for sudden loss of sight, including vascular causes, detached retina, or causes associated with other medical conditions. All require expert ophthalmological attention.

Toxic amblyopia. One uncommon cause of loss of sight, but one that is treatable, is toxic amblyopia. It is almost confined to heavy pipe smokers who complain of loss of vision in both eyes. Treatment with vitamin B12 and reduction in smoking bring about a marked improvement in vision. The improvement occurs in six to eight weeks after reducing smoking. Cigarette smokers do not seem to suffer from this condition.

Loss of vision associated with a painful eye. This usually happens suddenly, and the affected person is also ill. It is obvious that medical attention is urgently required.

There are four main causes of a painful red eye:

• Inflammation of the outer covering of the eye, eg conjunctivitis. In this case there is discomfort rather than pain and the sight is not threatened. Treatment is usually by appropriate antibiotic drops.

• Inflammation of the iris, known as iritis, is more painful and requires expert treatment. It is curable, but if neglected the sight can be affected.

• Similarly ulcers of the cornea are very painful and can lead to scarring and blurring of vision if untreated.

• Acute glaucoma is the most serious cause. The sufferer is usually prostrate and may even vomit. Prompt attention and admission to hospital is usually needed.

Herpes Zoster (shingles) affects one eye, but the other may be red and swollen "in sympathy". This condition usually follows the reactivation of the chicken pox virus which has lain dormant since an attack of chicken pox in childhood. Symptoms are more severe in the elderly and they are often left with severe pain at the site of the shingles for a long time afterwards. Expert medical treatment is needed as soon as possible.

Registration

Those who lose their sight to the extent that vision in the good eye is measured at less than "3/60" are eligible to be registered as blind. If below "6/60" with full visual fields they are eligible to be registered as partially sighted.

The registration is made by a consultant ophthalmologist and it opens the way to a large range of help from the services devoted to the care of the blind.

Braille or the more simple "Moon" can be learnt. Talking books and cassettes are available through a special Freepost service and there are many helpful devices which are being improved all the time. Large print books available at public libraries are valuable if visual loss is less serious.

Part two: caring for blind and deaf/blind people

There are some 190,000 registered blind or partially sighted people in the UK today, two-thirds of whom are aged over 75. But a recent RNIB survey has shown that the total number of people with some kind of visual handicap may be as large as 960,000 - most of whom, for one reason or another, are not registered. It is likely that some of these unregistered visually handicapped people may at some time find themselves in residential care.

There are also hundreds of people who are hard of hearing or deaf as well as being visually handicapped. The partial loss of sight and hearing together can cut people off from their surroundings and isolate them from companionship.

Being deaf *and* blind is not just twice as bad as losing either sight or hearing, the problems are multiplied. A visually handicapped person can still join in conversation and someone who cannot hear may compensate by lip reading or sign language. A person with both handicaps is unable to do so. It is rare for anyone to suffer a total loss of both senses. If an individual has some sight or hearing, opthalmic and audio examinations may indicate means of improvement.

Entering care

For many people coming to terms with losing their homes and (by implication) their independence, is a very traumatic experience, akin to that of bereavement. Pause for a moment and reflect how additionally disadvantaged an individual may feel coping with the extra burden of failing eyesight and hearing.

Try doing some every day activity like eating your lunch or trying to find something in the cupboard without using your eyes. Sit by the television with the sound turned down or try and listen to the radio that is slightly off tune so that it continually whistles and buzzes. Although no one can really understand what it must be like to be deaf and blind all the time, these exercises may help you to realise the enormous impact of these handicaps.

Adapting to change is difficult for most of us, and the older we get the harder it is to make any transition. For example, we have all moved house at some point in our lives and lived with the ensuing anxiety and fears that accompany such a move. These feelings intensify as we get older, and many elderly people coming into care may feel them insurmountable.

However there are many ways that we can help them to adjust to and enjoy their new environment. Encouraging independence, retaining dignity and maintaining self respect, are goals for which to aim for every individual.

Communication

When you approach a visually handicapped person, always introduce yourself, say who you are and what your job is. Do stop and chat if you have the time, and always say what you are doing. Try and remember to address each individual by name – after all, they cannot see that you are talking to them. Never leave a room without saying goodbye, it is frustrating and embarrassing for a person to realise that they are talking to an empty room. Do not shout, many visually handicapped have excellent hearing; speak clearly and at a normal pitch.

How easily someone who is deaf and blind can communicate depends on several factors. Firstly, how old they were when they lost their sight and hearing, secondly whether they lost both senses at once or one after another and thirdly whether they have learnt a language beforehand, either speech or sign.

Language and speech are not the same thing. Language is the ability to understand and communicate information. Speech is one method of doing this, gesture and touch are others. People whose first handicap was deafness may know British sign language and finger spelling. They should not find it too difficult to use the deaf blind manual (fig. 1) as it is an adaptation of the deaf manual spelled out on the hand.

An alternative is the Spartan alphabet, block capitals printed on the hand. If the individual has enough sight you may try using a thick, black felt tipped pen and writing (on paper) in large print. Whatever method you choose, you must use it consistently. It is best to start off by linking it to essential information about some activity, such as meals, dressing or bathing.

When you approach a deaf blind person, let them know you are there without startling them, by tapping them gently on the fore arm or wrist. To make sure they know who you are, let them feel a ring or a badge or a hair slide that you always wear. Or make a particular movement on their hand such as tickling their palm gently. Don't be put off if a deaf and blind person wants to use touch, remember it is the most important information sense they have left.

Do use every opportunity to communicate so that they feel part of the community and try and involve them in what is going on around them. At one RNIB home, the deaf blind enjoy a visit from a barber shop quartet as much as the hearing blind – try it! Most activities can be undertaken by the deaf blind although this means of course enlisting the help of volunteers and friends to interpret on a one to one basis. The manual alphabet can be learnt by most people in half an hour. My eight year old son confirmed this and took great delight in teaching his friends.

Guiding

Do ask first if a person wants assistance: no one likes to be grabbed and dragged. Let the person take your arm and walk slightly in front of them, watching out carefully for obstacles. If you need to walk in single file, through an open doorway for example, indicate this by tucking your guiding hand behind your back.

Always stop at the beginning of stairs and steps and say whether they are going up or down and about how many there are. If there is a handrail put the person's hand on it to help them. Do make sure you say when you have reached the last step.

Help the visually handicapped person to sit down by putting their hand on the back of the chair. Leave the rest to them; never lower them bodily into a chair they have not inspected.

Mealtimes

Do always ask what an individual likes and dislikes. There is nothing worse than putting an item of food into your mouth that you dislike. When serving a meal do remember to say that you have done so. Say what it is and the position it occupies on the plate and stick to the same system. For example, always place meat at 12 o'clock, potatoes at 6 o'clock and vegetables at 3 and 9 o'clock. Do ask if help is needed, perhaps by cutting up the food. Providing

a plate with an upturned rim will assist the visually handicapped person to feed themselves and reduce the risk and embarrassment of food sliding onto the table. When serving drinks say where you are placing them, and never overfill cups or glasses; this will reduce the risk of spillage.

Dressing

Just because a person cannot see how they may look does not mean to say that they do not want to look nice. It is helpful if clothes can be marked by differently shaped buttons (available from the RNIB) signifying co-ordinating colours. Never let a visually handicapped person go about with odd coloured shoes on, laddered stockings or grubby clothing. They will rely on you to tell them tactfully if anything is amiss.

General points

Make sure that the visually handicapped person knows the position of the call system, the radio, bedside locker and shaving points. Even people registered as blind may have some degree of sight. This does not mean that they are able to "see", but they may perhaps be able to distinguish between light and dark. Visual handicaps are so variable and the conditions that enable people to make the best use of their eyesight may vary considerably. Do remember to switch on the lights and make sure that the individual is aware of the position of the light switches.

Make sure that the visually handicapped person knows how to get to the bathroom, lavatory, dayroom and dining room. Try to mention easy to touch landmarks, such as pictures on the wall, or, a change in surface from carpet to tiling underfoot. Never leave hazards in their path such as hoovers, commodes, trailing flexes or tea trolleys. Always say if you have to leave something in the way or if something must not be

The deaf/blind manual alphabet. This chart is available from the Royal National Institute for the Blind. (Quick signs: Yes – two taps on palm; no – a rubbing-out movement across palm.)

touched. If you move anything always put it back exactly in the same place. Never put a visually handicapped person's belongings away before asking where they should go.

Do not worry about saying things like "Do you see what I mean?". Avoiding using such terms can often create more difficulties for everyone if a silence follows while you search for a different word.

Be natural. Your tone of voice and your manner is vitally important; it must convey what you intend it to. Visually handicapped people cannot see your face, whether you are smiling, worried or cross. Do not be afraid to touch. A friendly pat on the back or a squeeze of the hand can be reassuring and comforting.

But the greatest need for most deaf blind people is for companionship. Someone to talk to them at their own pace. To tell them what is going on in the world outside as well as in the house. Remember that visually handicapped people are normal people who just can't see. Treat them as you would treat anyone else, except at those times when they need a little extra help. Just as you would in their place.

Resources

National Deaf Blind Helpers League, 18 Rainbow Court, Paston Ridings, Peterborough PE4 6UP. Tel: 0733 73511. Information, advice and publications, including illustrated instructions for manual alphabets.

Royal National Institute for the Blind, 224 Great Portland Street, London W1N 6AA. Advice, information and publications, especially Braille books, periodicals and music, and Moon books and periodicals.

CHAPTER 15

Coping with confusion

by Una Holden-Cosgrove

What is confusion? What is dementia? • depression in elderly people • how to prevent or lessen confusion • how to communicate with confused residents • useful activities

Myths accepted by society are many, yet few of them can stand careful investigation and the real facts can be resisted or ignored. We smile benevolently at children and their belief in fairy tales, seldom realizing that we are influenced by them ourselves.

The terms confusion and dementia have become shrouded in myth, and it is hard to find clear definitions. Hardly anyone questions their meaning and everyone appears to be working in the dark.

What do these words mean to you?

Most people and dictionaries define "confusion" as mixed-up or perplexed. There are many meanings offered as definitions for "dementia" – the dictionary suggests that a person is behaving in a mad way. Other suggestions are:

Disorientation – not knowing who the self or others are and having problems with time and place.
A person can do strange things and conversation is odd.
There is a loss of ability to care for home and self creating a potential danger for others.

Dementia is a progressive, irreversible condition leading to total dependence.
There are two types – pre- and senile dementia.
Dementia is a speeding up of the ageing process.
The brains of those with dementia, or even all older brains, have shrunk and weigh less.
Vast cell death, or an emotional upset could cause dementia.

It is not just the man in the street who holds these beliefs, many professionals do too. Let us look at the problem in more detail.

What is confusion?

When were you last confused?
What sorts of things can confuse us all?

People get mixed up for many reasons, including:
1. The changing environment – waking in a strange bed, finding the way in a new town. Adjustment to this sort of change becomes much more difficult with age.
2. Daily living – being bothered by others

when trying to concentrate, learning new skills like driving, or not recognising an old friend.

3. Excesses – too much to drink or eat, drug overdoses.

4. Unusual upsets – bereavement, redundancy, unemployment, overwork.

5. Minor medical situations – anaesthetics, influenza, inhaling fumes, drug side-effects.

6. Illnesses – heart complaints, cancer, hypothermia, vitamin deficiencies.

7. Psychiatric disturbances – depression, mania, paranoia.

8. Neurological disorders – strokes, tumours, head injury.

9. Organic conditions which affect the brain.

The list is endless.

Acute confusion

This is recognised by the medical profession and implies that a person is disorientated, behaves strangely, feels distressed, neglects self care and may mix up day and night. It can be due to many things but usually means that the person is delirious. A delirium can occur at any age.

A seven year old suddenly staggers about, fails to recognise the family and says odd things. The doctor is called and expected to find the cause, prescribe medicine and cure the child. However, if exactly the same symptoms are observed in an older person the chances are that a "dementia" will be considered.

Because a person is over 60 years of age it does not mean that illness should be overlooked. Proper investigations must be carried out and if the state is a physical illness with a delirium, then suitable treatment should result in a return to normal living.

Have you ever experienced a delirium?
What was it like, what did you do and what did others claim you did?

Delirium is an acute confusion, but there are other acute confusions which are not due to physical illness. Depression is one example.

Depression

Here a person can become so cut off, miserable and self-effacing that he or she can look dilapidated, uncared for, weak, thin and fragile. Depression may give rise to delusional ideas: people may think they smell badly, have horrible infections or are untouchable in some way. Self-care will deteriorate, the home will become unkempt and sensible answers will be hard to obtain.

A little time and much encouragement will often provide good, reasonable answers and a useful history which would not be possible if the person was really deteriorating mentally. Depression is very common among the elderly and is frequently missed.

When you were recovering from severe influenza or other illness, how did you feel?
Did you want to get dressed up, clean your home, or go out?
Perhaps a stressful situation arose, did you not feel depressed and low?
What made you feel better?

To summarize:

Confusion can be caused by many things and be experienced by all ages.

When a person over 60-65 years shows signs of confusion it is just as important to investigate all possibilities as it is for younger people.

In many cases a good reason will be found which will respond to medical care, help in solving a problem or the provision of support in a crisis.

A case example
Mrs Mary Crisp was 81 years old. She had been totally independent, had few illnesses

and, until 10 years ago, ran a successful business with her husband. Unfortunately, he died 6 years ago but, though deeply distressed, she sustained the loss and rebuilt her life to fit in with her changed circumstances. She maintained her many friendships and although not well off managed to have some luxuries and an occasional holiday.

Suddenly she was admitted to hospital; her foot had caught in a rug and she had fallen downstairs. A week after a minor operation she became confused, failed to recognise her friends, rambled in speech and the staff had to feed and dress her. The fall had not caused any severe injuries apart from a broken ankle. It was assumed that she had "senile dementia" and would require long term care.

What do you think of such a "diagnosis"?

Assumptions can be made about people who become ill, are bereaved or suffer stress over unpaid bills, family problems and so forth. This situation can be called the "Dementia spiral" where a fit individual undergoes some trauma and becomes confused due to the emotional or physical stress, which in turn leads to neglect of self and poor nutrition. Frailty and isolation produce depression, withdrawal and apathy. The assumption that he or she is "demented" is easy to make.

Dementia

If all investigations to identify a confusional state fail, then it is possible that a real deterioration in intellectual and social functioning is under way. At this point it is important to consider the following:

What does the word "dementia" mean to you; what do you expect to see?
What is happening, what is the cause?
What is the difference between pre- and senile dementia?

Is dementia a disease in its own right – one that can be diagnosed?

Pre- and senile dementia
There is a long standing belief in the existence of these different states, but this belief is mainly due to ageism and an expectation of "senility" after the age of 65 years.

How many times have you said, or heard someone say, "Oh dear, I must be getting senile?"

This is said, usually, when something has been forgotten, badly done or mixed up. But anyone can forget; a child can 'forget' to do homework, a telephone message may not be passed on, or an appointment overlooked. Do we think children can suffer from dementia, do we call *them* senile?

An older person can forget in the same way. How often do we find ourselves at the top of the stairs but do not recall the reason until we go all the way down again? This is benign forgetfulness, and merely means that we have not been concentrating on what we had to remember. Our minds are on other things; senility has nothing to do with it.

A deterioration process can occur in young people. Causes include viruses, head injury, AIDS, toxins, poisons and a variety of diseases. These *could* be called pre-senile dementias but they can affect the over-60s too. The term pre-senile dementia was introduced by Alzheimer who found abnormal cells in the post mortem brain examination of a woman in her fifties.

Though dementia seems to be more common in the later years, recent investigations have established that age alone is of little relevance in relation to the actual disease process. The same thing is happening no matter what the age.

Although research has discovered that if Alzheimer's Disease (AD) develops in a person less than 60 years of age it is much more severe than if it develops after the age of 85 years, there is no point in using the prefixes pre- and senile, the disease process is the same and the terms are only insulting references to age. It is far more appropriate to diagnose the actual disease which is responsible for the dementia.

Other myths about dementia

Shrinkage and loss of brain weight indicate dementia. In the 20th century man is physically bigger and better fed, consequently his brain is probably bigger too. Furthermore, post mortem and scan investigations show a great variation in brain size and shape at all ages. There are variations in brains in much the same way as there are variations with other parts of the body.

After the age of 21 years there is a massive cell loss in all brains. There is some cell loss, probably since birth, but unless there is trauma or disease no great losses occur in normal brains.

Intelligence declines naturally with age. Most of the assessments used to reach the conclusion have been found to be incorrectly applied. Research is showing that intelligent elderly people continue to be intelligent, particularly if they use their ability. Sharpness may be somewhat blunted, but intellectual deterioration does not necessarily go hand in hand with age.

Definitions of dementia

Every book, every writer and certainly every profession working with the elderly has a different interpretation.

Persistent confusion, brain failure, organic brain failure or syndrome are among the many terms in use. The profusion of terms only makes it more complicated for the carers. Since the use of senile dementia has become unacceptable, "SDAT" has appeared – senile dementia Alzheimer's type – another term to contend with!

Some definitions still, incorrectly, define dementia as irreversible, progressive deterioration. In view of the ever-growing number of conditions which have responded to treatment, despite the presence of a dementia which also responds to the treatment, it is obvious that dementia is not necessarily irreversible and progressive.

Multi Infarct Dementia

Multi Infarct Dementia (MID) is the present term replacing "hardening of the arteries", arterio-sclerotic dementia, and refers to blood vessel damage. It implies multiple "strokes" and although not the commonest cause of dementia, accounting for only about 10 per cent of all dementia-related states, MID is frequently seen in hospitals and residential homes.

It has an apparently abrupt onset and the changes are step-wise. This means that there is a period of acute disability, recovery and then a stable period which can last for years, months or a few days. The next step would be another stroke attacking the same or another area of the brain, a repeat of the recovery and stabilising periods. The process may occur again and again, leaving more and more damaged areas on each occasion, until the person becomes severely disabled. There is usually a history of high blood pressure, and each attack can vary in intensity and degree of damage.

What do you think happens with a stroke?
Do all strokes result in irreversible damage?
Do you feel that strokes with older people result in deterioration and dependency?

Many old people recover very well from a stroke and may never have another one. Some are left with problems such as paralysis of an arm or leg, or both. Speech problems are also common, and obviously with severe strokes the outcome can be fatal. But for those who survive, it does not follow that intellectual loss occurs, or that improvement cannot occur over the ensuing years.

Unlike Alzheimer's Disease, MID may result in observable disabilities, but it can also result in hidden ones. The brain is a highly complex machine and damage to its parts can cause loss of performance: perhaps language is affected, or perception of the outside world, for example poor recognition of objects or sounds, or confusion in familiar surroundings.

These impairments of brain function differ according to the area of the brain in which the stroke occurs. Improvement or total recovery can occur, but another stroke could add to the damage in one area or cause loss of function in another area altogether. From a carer's point of view, however, the chances are that many functions are preserved, or only "bruised". It may be very difficult to identify the retained functions, but it is important to do so as these abilities are the basis for rehabilitation.

Alzheimer's Disease

Alzheimer's Disease (AD) is the commonest cause of a dementia even though, as yet, it is not possible to diagnose it clearly without a post mortem. However, the signs and history are good indicators.

It may start when the person is in his or her fifties, but it is more common in the 60-70 range (though it can appear earlier or later in life). In the very early stages a person can appear forgetful, unhappy when faced with a new or unusual situation and may often lose the way in both places and conversation.

As the disease progresses over months or even years, word-finding difficulties develop; concentration becomes poor; short term memory deteriorates and there may be difficulties with putting things together – the mechanic can no longer put the engine back, the knitter forgets how to do a purl stitch, and so forth. Personality remains intact for a long time, deteriorating only when, or if, the disease becomes really severe.

There are great variations from person to person in the effects of the disease. In the later stages these variations include lack of recognition of objects, smells, sounds and even faces. Dressing, washing and eating can prove hard, reading, writing and calculation can suffer, language, in general, can be affected. At this stage mood and personality can show changes. Perseveration – doing or saying the same thing again and again – can also occur.

Alzheimer's Disease is common amongst patients and residents, but is being carefully investigated. The full story is incomplete, but the facts are being established at a surprising rate. It is now known that large numbers of cells in particular parts of the brain of afflicted people become abnormal; that cell losses occur also in particular areas; certain vital transmitting substances are not produced properly; and that certain toxins or poisons might have a role to play. In a small percentage of cases the disease may be inherited.

Investigations are worldwide and new information is flowing through. As yet there is no definite treatment to cure the disease but researchers are optimistic. There is also the possibility that there are sub-types of AD; new conditions have been identified and indicate that there are exciting findings to come. Research has also shown that the caring professions using positive approaches are limiting or even halting deterioration.

The other disease processes with which dementia occurs are not often found in residential homes so will not be outlined here, but there are a considerable number of them. It is relevant to point out that strokes and multi-infarct dementia can complicate the picture by occurring with AD, Parkinson's Disease and other conditions. A confusional state resulting even from constipation can add further problems.

Prevention

It is impossible to guarantee to prevent mental deterioration or the disease processes which cause it. Healthy living is in vogue and the brain also needs to be "oiled" to keep it in good working order. Interests and activities are vital to everyone; so is a good diet with fish on the menu.

Society's expectations of ageing need to be modified and the expression "It's to be expected at my/your age" should be dropped from the vocabulary. Education of the public on the real facts about ageing should be stressed, and professional training for care staff should include an eye-opening visit to a club for normal, healthy, independent older people.

Without further research there is no remedy to reverse *all* forms of disease attacking brain function. However, there are methods which can be used to minimise the effects and to avoid misdiagnosis and misinterpretation. These include:
1. Full and proper investigation.
2. Appropriate treatment for an illness.
3. Consideration of psychological influences and respect for elderly people as individual, intelligent beings.
4. Appropriate help from the community for particular problems – bereavement, loneliness, finances etc.
5. Preservation of dignity, choice, independence and self-respect.
6. The use of retained abilities.
7. Avoidance, as far as possible, of misinterpretations and assumptions.
8. Simple and individual goal setting using achievable stages.

Under stress

Imagine that you are 61 years old. You have been admitted onto a geriatric ward due to a minor illness. Many patients are over 80 and many are confused and noisy. You are treated in the same way as they are. How do you react?

At the age of 82 years you are in care. The dormitory has beds down each side and there are no curtains or screens. You are dressed and undressed in public and as you cannot walk unaided, washing and toiletting are public too. You were independent until admission. How do you react to this loss of privacy?

As a physically, but not mentally, disabled person you are seated beside someone you cannot see properly. This neighbour, other than swearing, does not speak clearly, seems to be spitting and is frequently incontinent. Things are spilt on you, a hand grabs at you and the smells are nasty. One day you lash out, protest and demand attention. What are the reactions and how do you feel?

These are just some of the situations which occur in care settings. The resulting distress can precipitate a confusion: who would want to come to terms with such degradation? Many factors should be considered when caring for an apparently deteriorating older person. Two questions could be posed:

Is this person really deteriorating or reacting to stress?
Are we precipitating a confusional state?

Apparent deterioration will lift if and when circumstances change for the better. On the other hand, true deterioration can become excessive – show more signs than are truly present – particularly when the person has insight. Older people are influenced by the same mistaken beliefs as anyone else.

An active, stimulating, supportive environment is as vital as correct medication, relevant social help and recognition of the individual's special needs. Depression, physical illness and emotionally based problems will quickly respond to such treatment and the exaggerated effects of an organic disease process will also lessen considerably. However, more specific approaches may still be required for those with more severe conditions.

Good practice

Positive approaches start with attitudes and often basic common sense. Looking at a situation as though it was happening to you *can* help, but not always as your dislikes and needs may be totally different from the client's, in much the same way as your tastes in music vary widely. There are, of course, things that most people have in common: regard for personal independence, privacy and identity for instance.

A popular training experience is an attempt to understand what it is like to be blind, deaf, unable to move freely or to recognise objects by touch alone. Trainees act the role of a patient or resident and are treated as such for anything up to a whole day.

This does provide some insight into the situation and shows how frightening and lonely it can be, as well as how easy it is for misunderstandings to arise. Suddenly the warm, friendly touch and guidance become precious and highly valued while personal contact becomes supremely important.

Good communication is vital, but because frail, perhaps disabled, elderly people cannot move away from threatening situations or into desirable ones, problems can intensify. If, without being aware of it, you are threatening or boring, the person is unable to escape and is forced to withdraw by using inappropriate excuses. Seating is often unhelpful, as the chairs can be placed in such a way that people cannot see another's face, and cannot judge if conversation is possible or even desirable.

Even if the chairs are properly placed what is there to say to one another, and what is there to do together? People need to have something in common, some interest, experience, the opportunity to offer a drink, a biscuit, a newspaper or some item of mutual interest before conversation can flourish and friendships are possible.

Goal setting

Each individual is different, has particular strengths, needs or weaknesses. Each person should be assessed carefully, discussed in detail and priorities for care programmes set in easy stages. The individual's views on these priorities are as essential as those of the staff. Long term goals should be reached a step at a time with each stage, or "mini aim", in writing and understood by all concerned including the resident.

It is not helpful to use negative statements. eg "Tim Green has dirty habits", or "Tim Green must stop being dirty". A positive statement could be "Tim Green will wash his hands and face every morning before breakfast", and build on this.

To see only the problems and faults is to limit the individual's personality. It is always wise to start by listing the good things about a person; apart from anything else strengths and abilities can be used to improve faulty skills. Reading ability will increase social contact by helping a friend to keep up with the news and an ability to cook could increase self confidence whilst giving pleasure to other friends.

Goal setting is important and not difficult to do. Lists of strengths, needs, priorities and written, staged aims can show progress and lead to setting another stage when the time is right. Each success will encourage the person, the staff and even the relatives.

The environment

Our environment plays a major role in influencing our lives and we are in control of it most of the time. Homes are chosen or changed to suit our needs, organised to make things easy and decorated to express our personality and provide comfort. Visitors are welcome if they are people we wish to know and belong to familiar groups. Work is part of the environment as are the

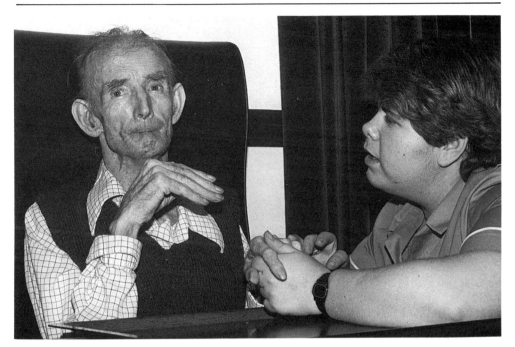

A warm friendly touch is precious, and personal contact becomes supremely important.

town, school and community. Our distress on being parted from familiar, loved and necessary people and places is intense.

Think of when you were alone in a strange place where you knew no one. Was this a pleasant experience?

Elderly people are often forced to leave their homes and become lost beings on a ward or in a home; without identity, a role or the support of those who know and love them. Suddenly their achievements, previous status and experience are of no importance and they have even lost the familiarity of their own home, own possessions, routines and choice in what they do.

No longer is there a private place to go, control over events or circumstances, or the admission of visitors. The person becomes the permanent visitor in a strange place filled with unfamiliar things and routines, strange faces, noises, objects and rules. How long could we tolerate this kind of loss?

How many people visit your home in a week?
How many people appear each day in a residential home?
How important is your own bedroom?
How private is the bedroom in a residential home?
How do we find our way around in a strange environment, do we make mistakes?
Do we find signs and directions helpful?
How easy is it to find toilets in your unit?

Remember how long we take to familiarise ourselves with a new place. Certain things can increase problems: lighting may cast shadows making reading difficult, and floors look dangerous. Corridors can confuse by appearing unending and threatening to those with a Zimmer frame. Other corridors go round and round leading nowhere. Rows of beds or bedrooms can be obstacles to finding the right personal space. Walking through your home or unit examining the environment can prove enlightening.

The psychological environment is as important as the physical one.

Is there something for the residents to do other than eat, sit or sleep?

Are there any group activities or things to do alone?

How much conversation or interest in others is there?

Do staff make time for social contact?

How independent are the residents? Do they do their own simple washing or cooking?

How often do staff wash, dress and feed residents rather than give them time to do it themselves?

In what way are residents encouraged to use the abilities they have?

Groups

Every human being has the right to belong to a group, ignore it or leave it as he or she wishes. Life begins in the family group and further group attachments grow and play a major role throughout life – apart from the hermits amongst us. In care, help is needed in setting up and developing group involvement. Staff time is limited, but it can be saved through groups which eventually maintain themselves. There are various useful guides to setting up groups (see Resource list).

Group activities can vary from simple things like painting, exercise to music, quizzes etc; or reminiscence, for which there are numerous aids such as postcards, photographs, slides, video-tapes etc; reality orientation; and visits from the local carol singers, reminiscence theatre and others as well as outings to the pub or interesting places chosen by staff and residents themselves.

Activities

These do not need to be day-long and do not require expert leaders. We all enjoy a leisurely breakfast with a newspaper or radio which are activities in themselves; so are good TV programmes, a radio play, *our* sort of music, or even writing a letter or doing a jigsaw. A mid-morning or afternoon nap can be welcome, but we do need company at some point.

Every staff member has some interest or skill – gardening, making up, fashion, football, even looking through a magazine are all activities that can be shared and enjoyed by all concerned.

It is worth spending some time learning about reminiscence and reality orientation (see Resource list). Neither are highly skilled techniques and staff often find that they have been using them quite naturally already. These approaches do help confused people to keep in touch and even to improve some abilities. The methods are not hard to use and staff find it satisfying to learn more about their clients and to see improvements in response and behaviour as a result of their own efforts.

In conclusion

It is important to understand more about the disease processes that cause confusion and dementia; this helps in understanding individual needs. Appreciating that each person is different and that the cause of apparent intellectual and behavioural changes varies in nature and degree is also helpful.

Furthermore it is important to know that some conditions can be reversed, some result in specific impairments and others require special help in order to slow down the process as much as possible. Understanding this can lead to individual planning, specially designed programmes for each person and tremendous sense of achievement for all staff.

Something can be done for each client, even if the person has chosen to give up and wishes to be left alone to die. Comfort, understanding and awareness can work miracles in restoring self-respect and dignity – things we all cherish. It is no longer correct to accept a dementing process as progressive and irreversible. Research is finding answers and each year the extent of knowledge grows.

The caring role is exciting as research findings show that the optimistic and positive attitudes in hospital and residential home are creating stimulating, carefully planned care approaches which are playing a major role in achieving and maintaining better levels of functioning and living for those whose future was once one of total dependency.

Resources

Barraclough C. and Fleming I. (1986) *Goal Planning With Elderly People.* Manchester University Press.

Bender M., Norris A. and Bauckman P. (1987) *Groupwork With The Elderly.* Winslow Press.

Garland J. 1991. *Making residential care feel like home,* Winslow Press.

Holden U.P. and Woods R.T. (1982 2nd edition 1988). *Reality Orientation: psychological approaches to the "confused" elderly.* Churchill Livingstone.

Holden U.P. (1988) *Looking at Confusion,* Winslow Press.

Holden, U.P. 1991. *Day into night.* Winslow Press.

Aids and activity materials

Age Concern England, Astral House, 1268 London Road, London SW16 4ER.

Help The Aged, 16-18 St James' Walk, Clerkenwell, London Lane, London E8.

Orientation Aids (books and reality orientation materials). Dalebank, Glencaple, Dumfries.

Winslow Press (books, including practical handbooks on confusion, reminiscence, wandering, aggression etc, aids, games – catalogue available). Telford Road, Bicester, Oxford OX6 0TS. Tel: 0869 244733.

Nottingham Rehab Ltd, 17 Ludlow Hill Road, Melton Road, West Bridgeford, Nottingham NG2 6HD. Tel: 0602 234251. A variety of activity materials and aids – catalogue available.

CHAPTER 16

Care of the dying person

by Sheila Mackie Bailey

Talking about death • the chance to choose a way of dying • stages in the dying process • physical, psychological and spiritual care • how death affects the carers

The main task when caring for a dying person is to ensure that they experience an "appropriate" death; the kind of death that the person would have chosen for himself, given the opportunity. The ways in which we can help people to express their preference will be discussed later. However when a person is dying others are affected, especially their family and friends, and those who care for them. How they can be helped to cope will also be discussed.

Close contact

Up until very recent times not only did both birth and death take place in the home, but after someone had died the body remained in the house until the funeral. A consequence of this was that people grew up with first-hand experience of dying and death. Not only that, but the death rate amongst all age groups was high. Nowadays the infant mortality rate is much lower and generally speaking people are living much longer.

However a more significant change is that most babies are born in hospital and that is where most people die. Their bodies are then taken to the undertakers where they remain until the funeral. As a result most of us have grown up with only very limited personal experience of dying and death, making contact more difficult to cope with.

Distressing

Not only that, but being faced by death reminds us of our own mortality. Although we know we won't live for ever, regular encounters with death can be distressing. This is particularly true when caring for elderly people, when dying and death occur regularly. In order to protect ourselves from the anxiety and stress we use a variety of coping tactics, which will be discussed in detail.

But even in everyday life the words dying and death are rarely used. We substitute euphemisms, milder words and phrases, such as "he's on the way out; he's slipping away; he won't last much longer; he's had it; he's snuffed it; he's a goner; he's passed away; she's lost her husband" and many others.

Cultural needs

Another important feature is that we live in a very diverse society made up of people from a variety of countries and cultures, with different life styles and values, and certainly different attitudes to dying and death. When caring for the dying person, his family and friends, consideration must be given to this, and every effort must be made to ensure that in trying to achieve an appropriate death consideration is given to cultural and spiritual needs.

The dying process

Death used to be accepted as the natural conclusion of life, the ultimate experience. Advances in technology have changed that, prolonging life beyond previous expectations of the course of diseases. A better standard of living has also meant that people live longer, both of which make death less acceptable, even resented.

Elderly people approach death in a variety of ways. Some certainly do resent it, while for others it is a welcome release. The important thing is that carers should not assume that they know what the dying person thinks and wants. Ageing itself may impair a person's mental faculties, and certainly prolonged illness and the fatigue it brings will make somebody mentally less alert. It is therefore essential that carers try to find out at the earliest opportunity what he would want for himself at the time of his death.

In the late sixties Dr Elisabeth Kubler-Ross described five stages of dying which provide useful guidance for carers. The stages are: denial, anger, bargaining, depression and acceptance. However what she also made clear was that not only the dying person but also their family and carers may experience these stages. Each stage is a way of coping, and the role of the carer is to help the person through the stages, to share the experience with them, but not to try and rush them through.

Denial: In this stage the person denies what is happening. He needs support, but the carer should neither encourage nor contradict what he is saying about his illness. This stage gives the person time to get used to the idea that he is terminally ill. At this stage the person or his family may try to "shop around", to get another opinion. Carers should realise that this is a normal coping mechanism and should offer them realistic hope, but should not lie to them.

Anger: This next stage is probably the most difficult for the carer to deal with – the "Why me?" stage. The anger may be understandable but the abuse is frequently directed at those closest to the person, and that often includes the carer. During this time both family and carers feel guilty because they feel helpless and frustrated and this makes them angry as well.

It is important that the carer should realise that any abuse and anger is not directed at them personally but rather at the impending death. All care at this time should be directed towards supporting the dying person, meeting all their physical needs and maintaining a pleasant attitude – without being too jolly as this is likely only to provoke further anger.

Bargaining: During this stage, which is often quite short, the person seeks ways of postponing the time of their death, "If only I can live . . . to see my grandchild born . . . to have one more Christmas . . . to have a chance to go to visit my son . . . I'll die happy" or other similar remarks are not uncommon, but most common is to try to bargain with God.

"If God lets me live until then I'll be a better person . . . pray more regularly . . . go to church . . ." or something similar. Again the responsibility of the carer is to encourage the person in their realistic hopes and to make their family and friends aware of them. But also to be prepared to cope with the disappointments if the bargains, especially those with God, are not apparently kept.

One possible response to this dilemma is to remind the person that although God always listens He doesn't always say yes. But then the carer must be prepared to cope with whatever direction the dying person then tries to take the conversation.

Depression: This may be quite a long stage as the person realises that the bargaining has failed, that their impending death is getting ever closer, that they will soon be losing their life, their family and those to whom they are closest. Often the person is very quiet during this stage and just being beside them holding their hand is all they need the carer to do.

Crying is a healthy sign as this usually shows that the person is coming to accept their state and the closeness of death. They should never be told off for crying but rather assured that it is okay to cry, and comforted while they weep. This is a time when the carer should be particularly aware of the person's spiritual beliefs and make sure they are visited by a clergyman or religious representative if that is important to them.

Acceptance: This is a time of contentment for the dying person and of sharing with family and friends, a time so to speak of tying up loose ends, putting their house in order, and saying their farewells. The person's interests tend to be very narrow, their interest in external matters not very great, but this should not result in their being neglected.

At this time, apart from care to ensure that they are comfortable, all they require from their carers is some physical contact, touching such as stroking the hand and forearm which is very comforting. Family and friends when they visit should also be encouraged to do this and respect the dying person's wish for silence.

It is important to remember that these stages are coping mechanisms, and are unconscious. Not only that but a person who is dying does not necessarily move through them in a systematic way, but may move or even jump between them. Anger may return at intervals, and some stages may last a lot longer than others. Also, not everyone has arrived at acceptance by the time they die.

Physical care

Physical care is described in detail in other chapters of this book. However it is important to remember that carrying out physical care provides an ideal opportunity to talk to the dying person, to offer comfort and support and to find out about his real feelings, hopes and fears.

The main problems when caring for a dying person are management of pain, control of sickness, care of the skin, control of constipation and of respiratory secretions. All of these may cause the person unnecessary distress.

Psychological care

Death may be the loneliest experience all human beings face. How we care for somebody who is dying can make this experience worse, or better. Many people who are dying feel abandoned; they are physically cut off from those around them, either because they are in a room on their own or because they have curtains or screens pulled round them. The only time they receive any attention is for cleansing, toileting and feeding. This applies whether the person is in their own home or in an institution.

Some elderly people already feel that their bodies have let them down, that they are worthless and have nothing to contribute to their family or to society, and this belief is reinforced by the isolation which they experience when they are dying.

Some people if asked would say they would prefer to be alone, but they are probably in a minority. The carer should try to find out what each individual would like. One danger is that the routine of the institution determines the care a dying person receives, rather than that care being of their choosing, and planned to meet their needs.

But how do carers find out what the dying person would like? A direct question would probably be inappropriate, but if the carer listens to what someone says about other people's deaths, they may learn a great deal.

Discussion with family and friends can also be very helpful. For example, should the family and/or friends be present at the moment of death? People who are well will often comment about what happened to another person:

"It's a shame his children weren't here."

"He shouldn't have been alone like that."

"I can be doing without all that nonsense."

"If they do that to me I'll come back and haunt them."

There are many ways in which people make their wishes clear. We must listen and then discuss with them what we have heard. A simple response to any of the above statements, such as "What would you like if it was you?" is frequently all that is needed. Then any preferences expressed should be discussed with other members of the staff and the person's family, and noted on the person's casenotes, or in a file kept for that purpose.

It is perhaps a privilege of old age that one is allowed to express a choice; at other times death is often the result of a traumatic episode and so choice does not come into it. Therefore elderly people should be given every opportunity to express their wishes either directly or indirectly, and those wishes must be noted and respected. This applies not only to their dying but to

their funeral and the disposal of the body, whether they prefer burial or cremation.

Again, neither of these are subjects which can easily be discussed, but frequently can be deduced from comments about other people. Alternatively the family may be aware of what is wanted because of what has happened to other close relatives. Close friends should also be consulted as often this is something that is discussed with friends but not with family.

Sometimes people will make a note in their Will of special wishes they may have for the disposal of their body, the style of their funeral or other such matters, but unfortunately unless somebody is made aware of these special wishes they are often not known until too late. For example, although an elderly person's organs are not generally suitable for transplantation, the cornea may be useful. If it is to be used, however, it must be removed soon after death. Donor cards may be a useful way of encouraging the elderly person to discuss their wishes about the events of their death.

Spiritual care

We live in a diverse society, and it is essential that carers should be aware of the spiritual beliefs of everyone they care for. In particular they need to know what influence that may have on their attitude to dying, and to the ritual which should be observed at the time of death, including care of the dead body.

The simplest thing is to have written notes readily available, to which all members of staff can refer. Many religions already have these printed out and are willing to discuss what is required with carers.

However it is also important to remember that some people are atheists and their beliefs must also be respected. Because somebody is an atheist does not mean that they value life less than other people, and certainly they still need the support of loving family and friends. Whatever your personal beliefs it is important that you do not impose them on the dying person, but rather respect and meet their spiritual needs. A mistake at this time could cause the dying person, their family and friends a great deal of distress.

Ministers of religion and religious leaders have an important role to play in the care of the dying person and their help should be enlisted as soon as possible. One of the worst things that can happen is a minister of religion being called to the bedside as a stranger at the moment of death. This is usually most unhelpful, and could even be frightening. The best approach is to treat the minister of religion or the religious leader as a valuable member of the caring team and to involve them in the care of the dying person at every appropriate opportunity, ensuring that the person is able to practise their religion as they wish.

Care providers

As I have mentioned before, carers, family and friends may all go through the same stages as the dying person, which adds to the stress for the carers. In order to protect themselves from these stresses carers may adopt a variety of tactics. These include:

Avoidance: The carer may avoid going anywhere near the dying person. If contact cannot be avoided, then the carer does the very least that is necessary but ignores the person.

Passing the buck: The carer doesn't answer any "awkward" questions, but responds by saying things like: "You'll have to ask the doctor/nurse/warden when you see them." Family members are treated in the same way.

Miracle cures: The carer hopes that some form of miracle cure will become available to save the person's life. This is especially the case if the dying process is prolonged or painful.

Careful conversation: The carer avoids asking questions which would encourage the dying person to discuss how they feel about their forthcoming death. Rather than asking "How are you feeling?" the carer may say "You're looking better today" or "You're feeling better, aren't you?" Then they quickly move on to another subject before the person can answer.

Isolation: As described previously the dying person is separated from other inhabitants, and of course this means that family and friends are also isolated and the carer doesn't have to come into contact with them either.

Selective hearing: The carer only hears the most comfortable things the dying person says. If for example he says "I'm frightened, I'm in pain, my leg hurts" then the carer will only respond to the last statement, and do something about it, but ignore the rest.

Denial: When talking to the dying person the carer will deny that death is the probable outcome, saying such things as "Don't be silly, you're good for another twenty years" or, "Don't talk nonsense, whatever gave you that idea?" and talking optimistically but unrealistically of the future.

Person's awareness: In some circumstances the carer may assume that the dying person is unaware of what is going on around him. The carer therefore talks freely, with others or to the person about what is wrong with him and about what will happen to him, even to the extent of making jokes about what might happen.

It is important to recognise that these tactics are adopted unconsciously; they are the way our minds protect us from a situation that might otherwise be difficult for us to deal with. This is especially the case when we have known the elderly person for a long time and feel they are more of a friend than a patient.

It is vital, however, that these behav-

Carers need to support each other in coping with the stress of their work with dying people.

iours are recognised and changed, as they prevent the carer from giving the best, most appropriate care and helping the dying person to have an "appropriate" death. To facilitate this, many institutions, recognising that carers often need as much help as the dying person and their family, have organised regular staff meetings which allow staff to discuss their feelings and experiences. In this informal way staff offer each other mutual support and an opportunity to share. Being able to discuss one's feelings about death and dying reduces the amount of stress and unhappiness felt by carers. In addition some time can be allocated to discuss ways of dealing with awkward questions and difficult moments.

In addition carers should be encouraged to pursue interests in their off-duty time that are not related to work, and to make sure that they do not discuss their work when they are off-duty.

Significant others

Perhaps the first thing to remember is that not every elderly person is loved or cared about by their family, and this feeling may be mutual. In some cases a close friend (or friends) is more important to the dying person than their family. This friend or whoever it is they are closest to, should be allowed to be as involved in the caring as they and the dying person would wish them to be. This may mean assisting with quite intimate aspects of care, or simply being allowed to sit and keep the dying person company. Family and friends should be included as part of the caring team. To shut them out at this time is cruel and may cause both them and the dying person a great deal of distress and misery.

Both the dying person and the people they care most about should be supported in their grief, especially at the time of death. If they have not previously witnessed a death then it is helpful if somebody, a carer, nurse or religious minister describes for them what it might be like. Being present at the death helps the survivors to come to terms with what has happened, and to begin the next stage of their grieving.

If they are not present then every effort should be made to ensure that they view the body as soon as possible, in the company of somebody they know well, preferably a member of the caring team. At times it is most suitable that carers and significant others share their grief together, even crying or praying together – whatever is appropriate.

In conclusion

Death is the inevitable end of all life. "It is not death, but dying, which is terrible," wrote Henry Fielding.

The responsibility of carers is to ensure that the dying person's experience is not terrible, but an "appropriate" death, one in which they have been involved in the planning and one where their wishes and their beliefs are known and respected.

CHAPTER 17

Accident and emergency

by Teresa Mearing-Smith

The aims of First Aid • what to do in an emergency or following an accident • common conditions and how to cope • when to call for help

Sooner or later, as you work with elderly people, you will find yourself having to cope with an emergency. There may be an accident; someone may suddenly become very ill and distressed; or they may collapse and become unconscious. Whatever the situation, there are important and simple principles of First Aid which you can apply, while waiting for qualified help to arrive.

First Aid

The aims of First Aid are:

• To preserve life

• To prevent the condition worsening

• To help recovery

No one will expect you to make a precise diagnosis, but you are in the ideal situation of knowing the residents, what medical conditions they may have, what drugs they are taking, and whether or not, for instance, they have a tendency to fall, or suffer from fits, chest pain or breathlessness.

The following steps will help you to act in the right order of priorities:

Assess the situation

You must appear calm and confident. This is important not only to help you to cope, but also to prevent fear and anxiety spreading to other residents or staff who may witness the emergency. If appropriate you should take charge, and make use of any other residents who are well enough to fetch another member of staff. You must ensure the safety not only of the casualty, but also of yourself and other residents. There is for instance no point in a second resident slipping on the wet patch on the floor on their way to get help.

Decide what has happened

There are no marks for getting the answer right, but it will be helpful for both yourself and others who may take over to know exactly what has happened. Ask other residents or relatives what they saw or heard, or even smelt. Of course, if the resident can tell you herself, that makes life much easier.

Now have a look at the resident. What

can you see that might give you a clue. Has the resident fallen and hit her head, or cut herself? Is she conscious? What is her colour like? Then use your hands gently to remove any harmful object, undo clothes to get a better look, or feel her skin or limbs. Is she hot? Cold? Sweaty? Or is one limb swollen, indicating a fracture?

Obviously you must get the right balance between finding out what is wrong, and preventing further deterioration or doing unnecessary harm. If you remain calm and confident it is unlikely that you will do the wrong thing.

Treatment

The first and most important steps are to ensure the person has:

• An open airway

• Adequate breathing

• Sufficient circulation

· The **Recovery Position** is important here. This is similar to the position in which you would put a very frail or dying person; on her side with the upper leg bent and resting forwards to take the weight of the lower half of the body while the upper half rests forwards on the upper arm (see figure 1). The importance of this position for someone who is unconscious is that the head is on its side and there is less obstruction to breathing. The tongue is less likely to fall backwards, and vomit or mucus is less likely to collect at the back of the throat. You may need to place a resident in this position; certainly if their breathing becomes noisy this is the best position for them to be in.

The next important step is to **dress any wounds** using a simple gauze dressing and micropore tape, or gauze held on with a bandage. If bleeding has not stopped you will need to apply pressure on the wound until it does. More serious large wounds or fractures can be covered with a clean (non-

fluffy) cloth, but dressing should be left to a trained nurse.

Put the casualty in the correct position. I have mentioned the recovery position, but a conscious patient may well wish to sit up, propped slightly forwards. She will probably tell you which position is most comfortable. If the situation appears serious and you have taken the preliminary steps I have listed already, it is probably better not to move the person more than is necessary.

Perhaps most helpful of all in this situation is the care assistant who **remains calm and has a calming influence** on the victim and others around. **Be sympathetic**, reduce pain and discomfort as far as you can, handle the person gently to prevent more harm or pain, and protect them from cold and damp.

It is your responsibility as the first person on the scene to **make sure the resident is not left in an unsafe condition**. Therefore you should call the doctor, or officer in charge or other staff as appropriate and inform the relatives if necessary. This is where your account is important, for other people whether trained or not will want to know what has happened, and what treatment, if any, you have given. If you have managed the situation yourself, you should enter the details in the Kardex or Day/Night Book as appropriate.

When to call for help

It is a good idea to discuss with the officer in charge and other staff, what the home's policy is on calling for help in an emergency. You should know whether you are expected to call the doctor or an ambulance yourself, or whether other trained staff or the officer in charge will do this. You should know which residents often have little "turns" from which they recover quite quickly with basic help, and which residents have more serious conditions. If you are unsure of what to do, it is far better to call for help than to struggle on by yourself.

Do you know?

Telephone:
Where all the telephone extensions are
GP's number(s)
Nearest Accident Centre number
Officer in charge or other staff at their home (if appropriate)
Where to find residents' relatives' numbers

How to switch off:
Gas
Electricity
Water

Fire:
What the Fire Drill is
Where the Fire Extinguishers/Fire Blankets are

Medical:
Where the First Aid box is
What drugs each resident is taking
How to open the drugs cupboard

It is worth finding out all this *before* the emergency happens!

Now I will describe some emergency conditions and how to cope with them.

Breathing

Choking: Try to feel in the mouth for the obstruction (eg food or false teeth) and remove it. To do this, gently open the mouth and use two fingers to sweep around inside, but be careful not to push the object further in. If a resident turns blue while eating, puts a hand to their throat and cannot speak, use the Heimlich manouvre (Figure 2).

Asthma: You will know which residents suffer from this condition and how badly it

affects them. A sudden deterioration may be helped by an inhaler if the resident has one; occasionally they may need oxygen. Try propping them up in a chair or in bed, talk calmly, offer a drink to sip and call for further help if there is no improvement.

Winding: This occurs with a heavy blow or fall onto the upper abdomen. Sit the resident down, loosen tight clothing and gently massage the stomach. This treatment normally works well.

Hiccups: These can be very distressing if prolonged. Holding the breath, taking long drinks or breathing in and out of a paper (not plastic) bag often stops the attack, but seek further advice if the hiccups persist for more than three hours and the resident is distressed.

Circulation

Shock: This can happen if blood or other fluids are lost from the body, (from severe cuts, burns or diarrhoea and vomiting). The resident will be weak and faint, pale, cold, and sweaty, and may be breathing faster.

If you think shock is the problem, you must seek further help, but you can reassure the resident, lie her down on her back with her head on one side and elevate the legs, cover with a blanket and loosen clothing; but do not give anything to eat or drink until advised to.

Fainting: This is a brief loss of consciousness caused by insufficient blood reaching the brain. It may occur as a result of sudden pain, a fright or sometimes hunger. Lie the resident down. Tell her to take deep breaths and loosen any tight clothing. Make sure there is plenty of fresh air; sometimes a sip of cold water will help.

Angina and heart attacks: Angina is a temporary problem, usually brought on by exercise or stress; it causes pain in the chest and sometimes the left arm. There may

The Recovery Position: when you have positioned the casualty's body, readjust her head to make sure her airway is kept open.

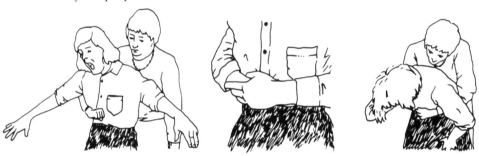

The Heimlich Manoeuvre. 1. Stand behind the choking victim and clench one fist, thumb towards her stomach. 2. Hold this fist tight with your other hand – it should be placed under the ribs, between the navel and breastbone. 3. Pull sharply inwards and upwards, three or four times (pushing the upper abdomen against the lungs to force air violently upwards).

also be sweating and difficulty in breathing.

Get the resident to rest by sitting or lying propped up, and loosen clothing. Here your knowledge of the residents is important: if you know that she suffers from angina and has little tablets or a spray to put under the tongue (Glycerin Trinitrate) or other treatment for an attack, give it or find someone who can.

A heart attack is a blockage in one of the blood vessels carrying blood to the heart muscle and may look like severe angina (therefore use the same treatment) or it may cause death, either sudden or pre-ceded by severe chest pain.

Summon help and make sure that other residents are not distressed by what is going on. Put the person in the Recovery Position, whether or not there are signs of life. Sometimes, although apparently dead, a person may start breathing again and this position will aid their recovery.

Bleeding: One day you may discover one of the residents in a pool of blood. This may have resulted from an injury, perhaps to the scalp or shin.

Don't panic! A little blood goes a long way and the resident may have spread it around herself, either in confusion or in an attempt to clear it up. Aim to control the bleeding and prevent the wound from becoming infected. So first quickly wash your hands and find the First Aid box or supply of cotton wool and gauze. If small, clean the wound itself either by gently placing under running water or with cotton wool swabs, then cover the wound up with a piece of gauze and clean the surrounding skin. In this way you can tell exactly how big the wound is and what other damage if any has been done.

If you think you are competent to put on a suitable dressing then do so. If you are unsure then ask a trained nurse to put on the bandage. If the cut is more serious then call for help straight away. If the bleeding persists, press firmly on the wound for five to ten minutes, or until the bleeding stops, and elevate that part of the body if you can.

Nose bleeds: These may cause the loss of a lot of blood which can be swallowed or inhaled, and could cause vomiting and/or difficulty in breathing, so the resident may be very frightened at the sight of all the blood she has lost.

Remain calm and sit her down with her head forward over a bowl or basin. Pinch the soft part of her nose just below the bone and get her to breath through her mouth avoiding swallowing, coughing, spitting or sniffing; carry on pressing for ten minutes then release. If the bleeding persists carry on for another ten minutes. If after thirty minutes the bleeding still has not stopped, then summon help. If the bleed has been a severe one it is probably a good idea for the resident to sit propped up in bed for a few hours, and avoid any exertion.

Varicose veins: These may bleed quite dramatically, and frighten the resident, so remain calm, apply pressure on the site of bleeding, and elevate the leg. Lay the resident on her back, remove any clothing over the leg and press directly on the vein with either your fingers or the palm of your hand over a dressing. Make sure there are no tight stockings or suspenders constricting the leg higher up. If the bleeding is not controlled quickly then get help.

Bruising: This is caused by bleeding just under the skin which causes a bluish purple mark, and sometimes swelling. The elderly bruise very easily so you should know how to help. If the injury has just happened, raise the injured part, if possible, and place in a comfortable position, apply a cold compress (ice-pack – or a bag of frozen peas is ideal). Once the acute stage is over, it is important that the resident is encouraged to move, so as not to become stiff.

Nervous system

Concussion: This is caused by a fall or a blow to the head. Injuries of this sort often cause unconsciousness, if only for a few minutes. If the resident comes to very quickly, place her in a chair or lying down and comfort her. She may well feel sick or actually vomit, so be prepared.

If she is unconscious place her in the Recovery Position if possible, and seek help. Head injuries in elderly people do not always follow the usual pattern, so always tell a trained member of staff if you think the resident has suffered such an injury.

Stroke: This is caused by the blood supply to part of the brain becoming suddenly cut off, either because of a clot or a haemorrhage into the brain. This is another condition that is common in elderly people, and is often associated with high blood pressure.

In its mildest form, a stroke causes weakness on one side of the body or face or difficulty in talking, which may last for half an hour or less, and is followed by complete recovery. More serious is the weakness that is very severe and shows only minimal improvement after days or weeks.

The most serious form of stroke is associated with loss of consciousness and total inability to move one or the other side of the body: death commonly follows.

Your role here is to help and comfort the resident who is probably very frightened and confused. You may not be able to understand her, but she may well understand you. Get her to a safe comfortable position if possible.

If she is unconscious, place her in the Recovery Position or at least in a position where she is not a danger to herself or others. Those who have had a stroke usually cannot move themselves and are a dead weight, therefore if you want to preserve your back, do not attempt to move them alone: get help!

Epilepsy: The disease results from abnormal electrical discharges in the brain and causes involuntary movement of the body, usually lasting no more than five minutes, and followed by confusion or a dazed feeling. You should know, if any residents in the home suffer from epilepsy, what may cause the attacks, and how they are best treated. While the attack continues you should help the resident into a safe position on the floor (unless they are in bed at the time). Loosen any tight clothing, do not try to restrain and do not put anything in the mouth.

Allow the spasms to stop, and the resident to regain consciousness, and then help them into bed or a chair until fully recovered. There is no need to call for an ambulance or the doctor immediately unless the fit lasts for more than fifteen minutes, several fits occur in short succession, or the resident has not had a fit before. The fact that a fit has occurred should be noted in the records and the doctor informed in due course.

Diabetes: This is caused by the body's inability to use sugar properly, and is common in the elderly. Most diabetics will have treatment either with diet or tablets rather than insulin injection. It is unlikely that a diabetic with dietary control alone will suddenly deteriorate, but conditions such as chest infection or stomach upset could upset the blood sugar levels. Those on tablets, however, may become suddenly ill if they have not eaten (and therefore become very *low* in sugar) or if an infection or other illness causes the blood sugar level to become *high*.

Low sugar (hypoglycaemia) causes paleness, sweating, rapid breathing, trembling and confusion. The treatment is to give the person a sugary drink or boiled sweet. Symptoms should improve dramatically; if not, seek help quickly. High blood sugar (hyperglycaemia) should be suspected in any diabetic who has become unwell. Drinking excessively and passing water very frequently are the first signs, followed by deep breathing and drowsiness. This is serious and needs immediate attention.

Injuries to bones, muscles and joints

As you will know from experience, elderly people are often unsteady on their feet, perhaps from arthritis, a previous stroke, painful feet or poor vision, and are therefore liable to fall and injure themselves. Older ladies in particular often have brittle bones (osteoporosis) and can break a bone very easily.

If you suspect that one of the residents has fallen, it is important that you report this to the officer in charge, as the resident herself may not remember what has happened. Sometimes an elderly person becomes confused or takes to her bed, with no complaints of pain or a fall, but a broken bone, especially in the hip, must be suspected.

A fractured hip bone (head of the femur) is a serious injury. It typically causes the leg to appear shorter and to be turned outwards, sometimes with swelling and pain around the hip, but this may be difficult to see. In fact you may be amazed to find that an elderly person has walked on a broken hip with very little complaint. Normally a doctor would need to confirm the diagnosis, but the home may have a policy of calling the ambulance immediately if the diagnosis is obvious. An operation is normally needed, and it is remarkable how quickly elderly people can recover from this, and are back on their feet within a few days.

Another common fracture is of the wrist (Colles fracture) caused by falling on to an outstretched arm. This is normally easy to see, as there is pain and swelling at the wrist, and sometimes an obvious "bend" in the bones. Again this requires hospital treatment; usually the results are very good, but there may be permanent stiffness, swelling and pain.

Other bones may break, such as the collar bone (which normally heals by itself with the arm in a sling) and the ribs which can be very painful, but again heal by themselves. The shoulder can dislocate in a fall and require hospital treatment. Although elderly people often fall and cut their heads, fractured skulls are uncommon.

Sprains and strains: A strain occurs when a muscle is overstretched and torn by a sudden movement, while a sprain occurs at a joint when it is suddenly wrenched. There is swelling, pain and stiffness. Treatment for these injuries is rest, ice (a bag of frozen peas is particularly good), compression with a thick layer of cotton wool and bandage followed by elevation.

These may not all be possible; for instance you may find it difficult to elevate a leg when there is bad arthritis of the hip. It is also important that an elderly person does not get put into bed for days on end, as they then risk developing pneumonia, pressure sores, constipation or incontinence, and will have difficulty in getting mobile once again.

Cramp: This occurs when a muscle suddenly goes into spasm, and can be very painful. It often happens to elderly people during sleep. Gentle stretching of the muscle and massage will help. You need to straighten out the leg or the toes carefully and gently massage the area that hurts.

Burns: It is often difficult to assess the seriousness of a burn: if in doubt, call for help. Any significant burn requires medical attention, and any burn affecting the leg, arm, chest, back or head requires hospital treatment. Elderly people are less able to stand the shock of a burn, and will need hospital treatment more often than fitter, younger people.

You can help further damage occurring in a minor burn by cooling, either by placing the area **gently** under running water or soaking the skin in cold water. Hot, wet clothing should be removed as quickly as possible as in a scald (which happens with wet heat such as steam, hot water or fat). Cooled dry burnt clothing should be left in place.

Once the burn has been cooled it may only need a simple dressing to protect it. If a blister forms, do not burst it, as infection is then possible, delaying healing. New skin will grow under the blister, and over the next week or so the skin of the blister will gradually dry and peel off. If a blister is large and does break, then you will probably need to ask a trained nurse to dress it.

Hypothermia: This develops when the body temperature falls below about 35 degrees Centigrade (95 degrees Fahrenheit). One would hope that elderly people living in residential care would not suffer from this condition, but a resident could well fall out of bed and be unable to attract attention for some hours. In this case it will be obvious that she is cold, and the possibility of hypothermia, like that of a stroke or a heart attack, must always be considered.

Re-warming should be done gradually, with any wet clothing removed first and the resident placed in bed in a warm room. You must ask for further help.

CHAPTER 18

Rules and regulations

by Deirdre Wynne-Harley

• The law that affects you • registration and inspection of homes • keeping accurate records • residents' rights • complaints • health and safety at work • employment legislation

This chapter explains the law as it relates to people in residential care and nursing homes.

The most important thing to remember is that whatever dependency, disability or illness your residents suffer from, they are individual people first and foremost with all the normal rights of citizenship. Carers have a duty to protect these rights and ensure that residents' autonomy and civil liberty is not infringed by the care and treatment given.

The legislation which regulates life and work in homes falls into three broad categories:
– registration
– residents' rights
– employment and health and safety

Each of these topics is discussed below.

NOTE: The legislation quoted applies specifically to England and Wales. Requirements in Scotland and Northern Ireland are similar and the acts are listed at the end of the chapter.

The legislation – what it says

The Registered Homes Act 1984 governs residential care and nursing homes. This Act, together with the regulations and guidance, sets out the requirements for registration and operation of homes. Some homes are "dually registered": that means they have both beds for residential care and for people who need nursing care.

The law requires that all care homes with more than three residents and all nursing homes regardless of numbers must be inspected and registered by the appropriate authority. Until 1991 this has normally been the local social services department for residential care and the health authority for nursing homes. Under the 1990 Community Care Act new multi-disciplinary inspection units will take on this responsibility for residential homes. They will still be locally based and work closely with the health authority.

The registration covers client groups and the numbers of residents who may be cared for in the establishment. Sometimes registration will be refused or cancelled; in these cases the proprietor may appeal to the Registered Homes Tribunal, which will either confirm the decision of the registration authority, uphold the appeal against this decision, or vary the conditions of the registration. The registration authority must comply with any directions made by the Tribunal.

How it works

1. Starting up

Anyone wishing to open or take over an existing home MUST apply for registration.

2. The Certificate

When a registration certificate is granted, the home must abide by its conditions as to number and type of resident/patient. When registration authorities consider applications, they will specify certain criteria regarding the suitability of the applicants and the premises. They will also issue guidelines about the services and facilities to be provided and the level of staffing. Criteria and guidelines will be based on the 1984 Registered Homes Act and Regulations, *Home life: a code of practice for residential care*, the NAHA *Handbook on Registration and Inspection of Homes (1985)* and guidance from the Department of Health. The certificate must be displayed in a prominent place.

3. Inspection

Inspection is an essential element of the registration process and includes continuing checks on standards. The Registration or Inspection Officer will visit the home at least twice a year and one of the visits is likely to be unannounced. These visits ideally provide opportunities for residents and staff to meet and talk to the officer from the inspection unit. The manager of the home will receive a written report after the inspection. The registering authority will also require that the home continues to comply with the demands of the fire department, environmental health department and the building regulations. These requirements will be reviewed from time to time and the registration officer will check that they are up to date.

4. Records

When the home is registered and operating normally, certain records must be kept, and be available at all times for inspection by authorised officers of the registration authority.

These records must include:-

• A statement of the aims and objectives of the home, of the care and attention to be provided in the home and of any arrangements for the supervision of residents, which has been supplied to the registration authority and has been agreed with that authority. In practice this means that staffing levels, therapeutic and rehabilitation facilities and services agreed must be provided.

• A daily register of all residents (excluding persons registered or persons employed at the home and their relatives) which must include the following particulars:

(a) the name, address, date of birth and marital status and whether the person is the subject of any court order or other process

(b) the name, address and telephone number of the resident's next of kin or of any person authorised to act on his behalf

(c) the name, address and telephone number of the resident's registered medical practitioner and of any officer of a local social services authority whose duty it is to supervise the welfare of that person

(d) the date on which the resident entered the home

(e) the date on which the resident left the home

(f) if the resident was transferred to a hospital or any other home, the date of and the reasons for the transfer, and the name of the hospital or home to which the resident was transferred

(g) if the resident died in the home, the date, time and cause of death

(h) if the resident is an adult who is subject to the guardianship of a local social services authority, the name, address and telephone number of that authority and of any officer of the authority whose duty it is to supervise the welfare of that resident

(i) the name and address of any authority, or organisation or other body which arranged the resident's admission to the home

- A case record in respect of each resident shall include details of any special needs of that resident, any medical treatment required by the resident, including details of any medicines administered and any other information in relation to the resident as may be appropriate, including details of any periodic review of the resident's welfare, health, progress
- A record of all medicines kept in the home for a resident and of their disposal when no longer required
- A record book in which shall be recorded the dates of any visits by persons authorised to inspect the home, that is any registration or inspection officer, fire officer or environmental health officer
- Records of the food provided for residents in sufficient detail to enable any person inspecting the record to judge whether the diet is satisfactory, and of any diets prepared for particular residents
- A record of every fire practice drill or fire alarm test conducted in the home and of any action taken to remedy defects in fire alarm equipment
- A statement of the procedure to be followed in the event of fire
- A statement of the procedure to be followed in the event of accidents or in the event of a resident going missing
- A record of each person employed at the home to provide personal care for residents, which shall include that person's full name, date of birth, qualifications, experience and details of that person's position and dates of employment at the home, and the number of hours for which that person is employed each week
- A record of any relatives of the registered persons or of persons employed at the home who are residents
- A statement of the facilities provided in the home for residents and of the arrangements made for visits by their parents, guardians, friends and other visitors
- A record of the fees applicable from time to time including any extras for additional services not covered by that scale and of the amounts paid by or in respect of each resident
- A record of all money or other valuables deposited by a resident for safe keeping or received on the resident's behalf, specifying the date on which such money or valuables were deposited or received and the date on which any sum or other valuables was returned to a resident or used, at the request of the resident, on the resident''s behalf and the purpose for which it was used.

This may all seem to be very complicated, but is usually made easier by the use of standard recording systems.

Care staff will often be involved in providing some of the necessary information. Through recording in a day book their observations of the residents' health, activities, appetite and so on, a valuable contribution may be made. It is very important to ensure that any accidents to residents or staff or incidents such as a missing resident, or sounding of the fire alarm (whether this is a false alarm or not) are recorded. It should be standard practice in all homes for staff to exchange information when shifts change, so that staff coming on duty understand any notes in the incident book or in the residents' records.

Residents' rights

It is important to remember that the legal rights of residents in residential care and nursing homes are exactly the same as those of any other citizen, and staff must always bear this in mind in their day-to-day duties. It is all too easy when caring for people to diminish an individual's basic rights without being fully aware of doing so. This happens most commonly through the use of forms of restraint, through medication and health care, by withholding information, and most of all by the erosion of choice in daily life and activities.

Sometimes it will be necessary for decisions to be made on behalf of an individual who has become incapable of doing so themselves. The legal position is often unclear as physical and mental conditions may change dramatically or almost imperceptibly over a long period. There are often also variations, ups and downs which can create uncertainty about a resident's true mental state.

The common law test of "capacity" is to the effect that the person concerned must at the relevant time understand in broad terms what he is doing and the likely effects of his action. Thus, in principle, legal capacity depends upon understanding rather than wisdom: the quality of the decision is irrelevant as long as the person understands what he is deciding.

The Mental Health Act 1983 itself contains three different approaches. The first in Parts II and III governs compulsory admission to hospital and guardianship, the second in Part IV governs consent to particular forms of treatment for mental disorder, and the third in Part VII governs the management of property and affairs.

Whatever the situation, care staff should never make decisions or even assumptions about a resident or patient's mental capacity without guidance from the home's medical advisers.

Managing finances

Many older people have informal arrangements for the management of their finances and property. Often these will be handled by a close relative or friend. Sometimes a solicitor or bank manager will act on their behalf.

On no account should care or nursing staff become involved in residents' affairs.

Where an individual has no one to assist with their affairs, the registration authority should be asked to recommend someone to act as his or her agent. There is an increasing number of advocacy groups which offer specially trained volunteers to help elderly people in this way. Social services, Age Concern and Citizens Advice Bureaux will usually know of local advocacy schemes.

Some residents will be under the jurisdiction of the Court of Protection and all their affairs, property and money will be managed through the Court of Protection. Increasingly, as people get older, they are making Enduring Powers of Attorney (EPA). This means that they give someone else the power to represent and act for them in matters of property and finance at some time in the future if the need arises. Then if they become unable to make decisions for themselves the EPA is registered with the Court and the named representatives takes over. No one connected with the home should be appointed an attorney.

Restraint

Physical restraint should never be used in residential care in any form – including restraining chairs. If it appears that restraint is necessary, the home is clearly not an appropriate place for that resident to be, either in terms of staffing or in the facilities and environment provided. Restraint in this situation is an assault on the person and consequently could give rise to legal action against the manager or member of staff involved.

In nursing homes restraining chairs should only be used in exceptional situations. They should never be a substitute for adequate staff cover. The use of cotsides is more likely to cause accidents than provide protection as residents may fall while trying to get out.

Consent to treatment

Admission to a home does not change an

individual's right to choose his or her own general practitioner. Neither does it change the rules on consent to treatment. The law provides that no medical treatment can be given to any person without his valid consent. Any breach of this rule will result in the person concerned being liable to legal proceedings. For consent to be valid, the patient must be given information about the proposed treatment or medication, be competent to give consent and give consent voluntarily. If the resident has difficulty in understanding or communicating in English, every effort must be made to find an interpreter to explain the purpose and effect of the treatment. When a resident or patient is not able to understand because of their mental state, treatments prescribed by the GP or consultant must be in the best interests of the individual but keeping in mind any strongly held views they have expressed in the past.

Medication

No drugs except simple "household remedies" should be given without a doctor's prescription. Whether residents retain and administer their own medicines or these are kept by the manager, proper arrangements must be made for safe keeping. All medicines must be in individual containers, clearly labelled with the name and dosage. When held by the home, they must be administered ONLY by a responsible person authorised by the manager. Staff responsibility does not include insisting, forcing or tricking residents into taking medication. If residents refuse, this should be noted and the GP informed. Medication must not be used for control or punishment. As with restraint, inappropriate or forceful administration of any medicines is in effect a physical assault.

Access to information

Changes in the law over the past few years have given people greatly increased rights to know what is said about them in personal records. This applies to residents also. Therefore, subject to adequate safeguards and counselling where necessary, individuals should be able to see the records about themselves kept by the home. Any decision to withhold information should only be taken at a senior level in the organisation and the reason for doing so explained to the satisfaction of the registration authority. All residents' records should be kept securely with strictly limited access.

Residents' finances are often a matter of concern and a recent amendment to the legislation [Residential Homes (Amendment) Regulations 1988] requires that homes keep detailed records for each resident of any money or valuables (including social security benefits) received on his or her behalf and indicating how this was spent or disposed of. Residents or their representatives must have access to these records.

Complaints

Residents and their families have a right to know how and where to contact the registration authority if they wish to make a complaint or discuss some matter which has not been resolved between them and the management. Information about who to contact must be displayed clearly, preferably near to the registration certificate.

Health and safety and employment legislation

The Health and Safety at Work (etc) Act 1974 obliges all employers to ensure as far as reasonably practicable the health and safety at work of all employees.

Accident prevention

Safety is also covered in the 1984 Registered Homes Regulations. This states that "the person registered shall, having regard to the size of the home and the number, age, sex and condition of the residents, take adequate precaution against the risk of accident, including the training of staff in first aid". Inspectors from registering authorities will enquire into accident prevention arrangements, when making visits. The home will also receive occasional visits from the health and safety or environmental health officers who are responsible for enforcing the Health and Safety at Work legislation. Properly authorised inspecting officers have legal rights of access to homes.

In matters of safety, staff must be alert, observant and careful. Accident prevention in residential homes, as in our own homes, is often a matter of common sense. Legislation and special precautions will be ineffective if equipment is not used correctly or defects reported. All accidents in the house or grounds, however minor, affecting residents, staff or visitors should be recorded in detail without delay. Any witnesses should also make and sign written statements. This is very important and should be done immediately.

Policy statement

Where five or more people are employed, the employer must have a written policy statement regarding safety at work, including arrangements for carrying out that policy. All staff must be made aware of this policy and any subsequent changes.

For staff in residential and nursing homes, special risks may be associated with lifting and helping residents to move. These risks are to residents as well as staff and illustrate the importance of having a clear safety policy and appropriate accompanying arrangements for training. Every home must have at least one first aid box clearly marked. All staff should know where this is kept.

Emergency procedures

Emergency procedures must also be clearly stated and understood by all staff. These should cover
– procedure in the event of a fire
– procedure in the event of accidents
– procedure if a resident is missing

Food hygiene

Food hygiene is another aspect of safety which may involve care staff, especially in small homes where job specifications are more flexible.

The Food and Drugs Act 1985 and the Food Hygiene (General) Regulations 1970 apply in residential and nursing homes and it is the responsibility of the manager to see these are observed. Staff must be aware of regulations which affect them directly, like the requirement for wearing clean washable over-clothing when handling, preparing and serving food. Any members of staff who have kitchen or dining room duties should follow the basic rules of hygiene displayed in the kitchen. The Food Safety Act 1990 now requires that *all staff* who handle food attend approved training courses in basic hygiene.

Health

There are also health requirements and staff must inform their employer if they are suffering from or are a carrier of:
– typhoid
– paratyphoid
– other salmonella infections
– amoebic dysentery
– bacillary dysentery
– any infections likely to cause food poisoning, eg septic cuts, boils, burns, sore throats or nasal infections.

Any of these infections will have to be reported to the local medical officer for environmental health who will advise the person in charge about necessary precautions.

Your employment

Employment law is very complex. Both employer and employee have rights and duties and these should be clear to both parties when the appointment is made. The Employment Protection (Consolidation) Act 1978 provides that all new employees (who work over 16 hours a week) should be given a written statement of terms and conditions of employment within 13 weeks of starting. This statement must give the names of employer and employee and the date when the employment starts. It must also detail:-

– job title
– rate of pay and whether this is weekly or monthly
– hours of work
– holiday entitlement, including public holidays
– arrangements for such pay
– notice period
– pension schemes

Information about disciplinary rules, grievance procedures, and persons to whom application should be made if the employee is dissatisfied with any disciplinary action against him should be available in the contract or a separate specific reference document.

If any terms or conditions change, the employee must be informed in writing within one month of what such changes are.

Trade unions

In law every employee has a right to membership of an independent trade union; they also have an equal right not to belong to a union. This is regardless of whether or not the employer recognises the union. An employer may not prevent or deter employees from being members of independent trade unions or compel them to join one.

The employer is free, however, to choose whether or not to recognise a union. "Recognition" means the employer recognises the right of the union to represent its members in collective bargaining. The relevant legislation is The Employment Act 1980.

Rehabilitation of offenders

Under the Rehabilitation of Offenders Act 1974 a person who received a non-custodial sentence of not more than 30 months, and is not convicted during a specified period, becomes a rehabilitated person. His conviction then becomes "spent", in other words it is regarded in law for most purposes as never having occurred.

There are, however, certain types of employment (listed in the 1975 Order) where this does not apply, provided that when asked about previous convictions, the person is told that by virtue of the Order spent convictions must be declared. The exceptions include occupations concerned with carrying on an establishment required to be registered under the Registered Homes Act 1984.

Data protection

Many homes now use computers for keeping personal records of staff and residents. Under the Data Protection Act anyone storing personal information about other people must register with the Data Protection Registrar. The onus is on the computer users to declare themselves. As with the residents, staff have a right of access to information about themselves held by the employer.

Conclusion

This chaper has highlighted the areas of legislation which are most likely to affect care staff directly or are concerned with the registration of the home.

There may be occasions when a member of staff becomes aware of acts or incidents which breach some aspect of the law. These may be minor and perhaps arise from a genuine oversight or of a much more serious nature. Whatever position an individual holds, they have a duty to residents and colleagues to take some action. The first course would normally be to discuss the matter with the head of home and in the case of a safety hazard to alert colleagues until the danger is removed.

If the matter appears to concern the work of a senior colleague and affects the residents' well being, the advice of the registration officer should be sought. The registration authority has a duty to investigate any possible offences against the Registered Homes Act. Similarly serious concern about matters of health and safety should be reported to the Environmental Health Officer if no remedying action is taken by the Head of Home.

Fortunately staff are rarely in a situation where they have to report incidents or practices in a home. However, if this does happen, they should not be deterred from taking the correct course of action through fear of the consequences.

Work with people who are mentally frail or have dementing illness can be very stressful and it is often easier to provide a regime which assumes a generally low level of ability in all residents. But each resident is a different person and, however ill, will respond differently. By treating each one individually, whatever their disabilities, their rights as citizens will be protected and maintained to the greatest degree possible. This will also be seen to enhance the work of the carers and the quality of life of the home as a whole.

Main legislation quoted

Registered Homes Act 1984 and Regulations 1984, amendments 1988 (England and Wales).
Nursing Homes Registration (Scotland) Regulations 1988 (came into force November 23 1988 and covers both residential and nursing homes).

Health and Personal Social Services order (Northern Ireland).
Health and Safety at Work (etc) Act 1974 (whole of UK).
Employment Acts 1980, 1982, 1988.
Employment Protection (Consolidation) Act 1978 (whole of UK).
Food Safety Act 1990 (whole of UK).
Guidance:
Home life: a code of practice for residential care, published by the Centre for Policy on Ageing, 25-31 Ironmonger Row, London EC1V 3QP. Tel: 071 253 1787.
NAHA Handbook - Registration and Inspection of Nursing Homes, 1985, published by the National Association of Health Authorities.

Points to remember

1. Residential care and nursing homes must be registered and work within the terms of their registration.
2. Proper resident records must be kept on the premises and any accident or incident should be recorded immediately by care staff in the day book.
3. Residents' property must be safeguarded and a record kept of all valuables deposited for safe keeping.
4. Staff of homes should never take responsibility for residents' finances or accept a power of attorney.
5. Physical restraint of residents is an assault and may give rise to legal action.
6. Residents and their families must be given information about how to make a complaint.
7. Think safety – staff should always be alert and observant.
8. Be aware of all the emergency procedures.
9. Staff have a duty to report accidents or incidents which they believe are wrong or illegal.
10. However frail the resident, their civil rights must be protected. Personal and nursing care should not reduce their rights or dignity.

CHAPTER 19

Opportunities for training

by Richard Banks

How to select the right form of education and training for you • How to use the National Vocational Qualification System to ensure that your skills, knowledge and understanding are recognised for employment and career progression

This chapter is intended for all people involved in personal care, including those who care for elderly people with varied physical and mental disabilities, in residential care and nursing homes. Education and training are matters for constant attention as we gain a better understanding of how best to work with other people, and the changing ways care is provided. What sort of training and education are suitable for you will depend on your individual needs.

The way in which education and training are provided also has to be organised to match the time you have available and the type of education or training that suits you. It is also important that the skills, knowledge and understanding you gain, by whatever means, should be properly recognised and recorded. This is important whether you intend to improve your work practice, have your present skills identified or carry on to further qualifications.

You're in charge

Therefore there are two main aims to this chapter. To show you:

1. How to select the right form of education and training for yourself.

2. How to use the National Vocational Qualification (NVQ) /Scottish Vocational Qualification (SVQ) system to ensure that your skills, knowledge and understanding are recognised for employment and career progression.

In thinking about how to find and select the correct education and training in personal care, the things people consider generally fall into the following categories:

How can I get help in working out what I want?

How can I identify the skills, knowledge and understanding that I have now - so I know my starting point? (As a general rule people find that they can do, and know, more than they imagined).

What is the end result that I want from this education, training and assessment?

What are the practical issues to be solved, such as finding time?

How can I be sure the education and training will be organised in ways that help me to learn and not repeat negative experiences of the past?

Will I experience discrimination? Or will anti-racism and anti-discrimination be part of the content and part of the experience?

All of these are legitimate concerns, but until recently people have often felt unable to ask about them because of the difficulty in gaining any education or training opportunities at all, or the fixed nature of some courses. A way of looking at this problem is to separate three issues about education and training that are often confused:

1. The opportunity to obtain education and training.

2. The assessment of individuals.

3. The requirements of employers.

Confidence

The NVQ/SVQ system has separated assessment from education and training. This means people requiring education and training can approach the matter with a greater sense of confidence and assertiveness. It is now the education and training providers' task to ensure that what they offer is what is wanted in terms of success in assessment, the needs of the workplace and the needs of individuals.

There will still be potential for conflict between individuals and employers, possibly about what a person needs to be able to do in order to do a particular job. The standards upon which the National Vocational Qualification system is based, and the awards given, are approved by employment interests (the Care Sector Consortium) but are not attached to any particular job. So they do provide a basis but cannot in themselves solve any conflict between what an employer will spend on education and training and what the staff as individuals or as a group want. The care sector trades unions (who are represented on the Care Sector Consortium) have information about NVQs/SVQs and will be able to offer some assistance to members.

The outcome of your learning must be clear. With the introduction of NVQ/SVQs for care staff there is now a developing system which enables those employed or contemplating employment in personal care to gain recognition for their skills, knowledge and understanding, even if they have received little or no formal training. This is a major change: there have been some excellent courses, but no proper national recognition of the work involved in social care.

The actual existence of these awards is however only part of the change; the way people are assessed for these qualifications is another. NVQ/SVQs are not courses; people will be able to gain an NVQ/SVQ without taking any formal training. This is possible because the qualifications are based on the idea of COMPETENCE IN THE WORK PLACE.

"Competence" in personal care is described in National Standards, which have been developed in consultation with people working in the care field and approved by employment interests. These standards are used in the assessment by gathering evidence of a candidate's work practice by direct observation or, when this is not possible, by the nearest possible method.

The evidence gathered is then compared to the standards. Candidates are found competent when they consistently fulfil the criteria described in the standards. If a candidate is not able to fulfil the criteria consistently they are judged "not yet competent" and will be helped to develop their practice so that they will be able to show evidence of their competence.

Helpful experience

The assessment system of NVQs/SVQs is intended to be a positive and helpful experience because it focuses attention on what people can do, not what they cannot do yet. Many people find it helpful when finding out about NVQ/SVQ to put aside anything they know about other assessment systems and start from scratch, because this is for most of us an entirely new system.

NVQ/SVQ assessment allows people who have gained their skills, knowledge and understanding by previous education or training, experience in work or in caring for relatives, or as volunteers, to have nationally recognised qualifications. The qualifications themselves are organised so that individuals can build up UNITS as they are able, which add up to a full qualification. Qualifications are awarded at different levels to make progress routes clear and to enable a person to transfer between jobs and work settings more easily.

Discrimination

It is sometimes difficult for care staff to gain education and training. Employers often undervalue the complexity of the tasks in social care and make inadequate provision for teaching new staff or for in-service training. Shift work combined with family responsibilities makes it hard for staff to undertake evening classes. In addition staff have often experienced unfair discrimination in their past education/schooling, leaving them understandably unwilling to risk further negative experience. There may be discrimination in their present work place which has prevented them from gaining promotion or training. It is vital therefore that the introduction of NVQs/SVQs is not only free from unfair discrimination but that the NVQ assessment system is itself actively anti-racist and anti discriminatory. This means that not only the standards against which the assessment is done are anti-racist and anti discriminatory but that the assessment process and access to the assessment is anti-racist and anti-discriminatory.

The end result of the introduction of NVQs will be that by having better qualified and competent staff the quality of care

available to service users will be improved.

It is often assumed that the only way to gain education and training is to go on a course. While this may suit many people it is important to recognise that this is only one way. The over-riding issue is what will work best for you. The separation of training and education and an individual's assessment offered by the NVQ/SVQ system means that how you gain your skills, knowledge and understanding is not part of the way your competence in the work is assessed. This places you in a position where it is up to you to decide how to get the education and training you require. If you are in employment or a volunteer this will obviously be done in conjunction with who ever is in charge of training in your organisation and the resources available will affect what is possible. One of the best ways to identify your training, education and assessment needs is to make a plan of what you want, what you need to get what you want, and how you will put it into action.

Your choice

This can then be the basis for you to negotiate your programme of learning. Then within the constraints of the opportunities available you can choose your way or ways to learn. At the same time you should identify your needs for assessment, which can, and I believe should, be a continuous process. In other words, you don't need to wait until you have everything settled. Indeed, one way to use the NVQ/SVQ system is to plan to begin assessment on the units you are confident in and progress to units you are not sure of. Then with your assessor's help you can identify areas of work where you need to improve your practice, and discuss what is the best way to do this.

Planning how you will use education, training and assessment is a difficult thing to do on your own. The ideal person to help you would be someone who will encourage you to think things through and express what you want, but will not try to tell you what is best before you have worked it out for yourself. They should also know about the assessment system, so that they can continue to help as you are assessed. They may also be able to help you work out where there is evidence of your competence. Some organisations arrange for a member of staff to fulfil this helping role; they are often called "mentors".

The following five headings may be useful in organising your plan. The questions in each heading are intended to get you thinking: you can ignore them, use them or add to them as you need.

SKILLS NOW

Will the education and training recognise and value the experience, knowledge and understanding that I have already?
I have been doing this work a long time; how can I get recognition for all that experience?

OUTCOME

What changes do I want to make to the way I work?
Do I want to get a different job?
How can I be sure the education and training, once completed, will mean something to employers?

PRACTICAL

Who will pay for it?
Will I get time off to do the education and training?
Do I have to do it all at once or can I do it in parts?
Will I be able to get there?
Is the education and training going to be run at a time suitable to me?

EDUCATIONAL EXPERIENCE

How can I find education and training that is about the real work?

How can I find education and training that I can do?
Will I have to do things I don't like, or know I am not good at?
What will the other people on the education and training be like?
Will I be able to understand?
Will I be able to manage the work?
How will the education and training help me to do the work better?
How will I have a say in the education and training's content?

ANTI-RACISM / ANTI DISCRIMINATION

Will I be discriminated against? You may have this fear because in the past you have been discriminated against. Common examples of discrimination are: because a language other than English is your first language, because you have to leave at a particular time to pick up children, or the building has not been designed for people with disabilities.
Will the education and training help me improve my anti-racist and anti-discriminatory practice?
How can I help to bring about change in the place I work to cater properly for the cultural needs of the people we work with?

ACTION

Work out what is the best way that you learn. Is it:
On your own? With a group of people? Away from work or at work?
Over an extended time, or in short pieces? What works best may depend on what it is you are learning at the time.
When are you able to do this education and training? If you live a busy life, space will have to be made and this space will have to be at a time when you are in the right frame of mind. Education and training is about providing an opportunity for you to learn. For it to be successful it has to be something you can engage with and feel is yours.

Ways to learn

Education and training is offered in a large number of ways, none of which is perfect for all people or all of an individual's needs, so choose what suits you at the time and for the purpose you require. Here are some of the ways you might find useful to learn:
• Learning at work: this may be a pre-planned activity or by planned supervision.
• Short courses: away from your work place or run in the work place for a group of staff.
• Courses in a college: these may be day release, blocks of time, night classes or full-time.
• Open learning: this can be done on your own or with a group of others, using learning materials provided with either tutor support, correspondence or support from other learners. The learning materials used for open learning are also varied - books, work and task sheets, VHF video and interactive video.

Last, and most difficult, you will have to decide how to get what you have decided you want. This may involve some compromise because of what is available. If you are in employment you may find that your employer is only able to offer education and training that is directly linked to the work you do now. This may be fine but it does no harm to ask and to indicate that you may want more in the future. If you are not working in the care field at present, the problems to solve are to locate college or open learning packages that suit you, and to get a grant or another form of financial help.

All about NVQ/SVQs

You can only be assessed for NVQs/SVQs in approved assessment centres. These are places that have proved to the awarding body (the organisations that actually give the NVQ) that they can operate assessment in the proper way. Because NVQs/SVQs are assessed against standards that are work based, approved assessment centres are usually employers or organisations that work with employers who provide assessment. If you cannot gain access to an approved assessment centre you can not be assessed for an NVQ/SVQ, but of course you can prepare yourself to be assessed. The system for operating assessment centres has been in place since September 1990 and it may take some time before there are sufficient assessment centres. If your employer is not part of an assessment centre yet it may be worth enquiring what their plan is. There are costs involved for employers in training staff to be assessors, for example, and for releasing staff to operate the assessment system but it is anticipated that the advantages of the system will outweigh these costs.

All-embracing

NVQ/SVQs in care are part of a much larger system in that will cover all areas of employment. This new system of vocational qualifications is intended to:
• provide qualifications that are valid in the work place
• be easily understood
• enable people to progress
• indicate the level of qualifications so that people can transfer between different types of employment

The focal point of the assessment system is the standards, which are statements of what has to be achieved to do the job well. These standards are agreed by the Care Sector Consortium (representing employment interests) It is important that as you begin to plan your own assessment, you read and become familiar with the standards, which are available in all approved assessment centres. They often appear rather daunting, looking more like telephone books than anything to do with caring for people. Don't let this put you off!

The parts you are likely to use will be reasonably easy to find. Do have a browse through the standards; you may well find units which are about your particular skills which you had not thought of. As the system is developed, more "user friendly" ways of printing the standards are being produced. These will often contain just the units for an award; this is easier to use but do not forget to look at all of the units and awards that are available, since they may suit your needs now or in the future.

Standards are expressed as PERFORMANCE CRITERIA - things that are actually done. These performance criteria are grouped into ELEMENTS, which are in turn grouped into UNITS which describe recognisable pieces of work. Units are grouped together into AWARDS which are set at a level within the NVQ/SVQ framework.

Values in care

The best way in which the "value base" of care can be expressed in the standards, is under review. At present the values are in the CORE PERFORMANCE CRITERIA: candidates have to show evidence that they are fulfilling these core criteria at the same time as they are fulfilling the performance criteria.

This may sound complicated but what it would mean, for example, is that when you are working you are showing respect for your clients (and they are experiencing that respect) as you actually work with them, rather than merely talking about respecting them. The value base of care is clear to most but we are all aware that these values are sometimes absent in the way some individuals and work places operate. The standards have been agreed at a level of best practice, producing minimum requirements of candidates - things they must do to be found competent. The issues to be dealt with in operating assessments

for NVQ/SVQ and the effect on care practice may be seen by looking at one core performance criterion:

The candidate recognises and takes account of the client's culture, political beliefs, race, religion, sexual identity, age, gender, physical and mental condition.
From the Residential, Domiciliary and Day Care Standards.

The evidence that candidates show of fulfilling the criterion will be different, depending on where and how they work, but to be found competent candidates will have to show that they consistently fulfil the criterion.

It is recognised that in some work places there is racism and discrimination towards the staff and the clients. It will clearly be difficult if not impossible for a candidate to provide sufficient evidence in such work places. This may appear unfair since the racism and/or discrimination may not be the fault of the candidate (indeed they may well be discriminated against themselves). The alternative, of ignoring the candidate's lack of evidence, would be to allow some bad or incomplete practice which would devalue the awards and not contribute to the development of improved practice. Therefore in such circumstances the assessment for NVQ/SVQ will have assisted in identifying an important task for the work place - removing the discrimination or racism. This is a task primarily related to the requirements of justice, good care practise and the law. NVQs/SVQs can not in themselves achieve such improvements, but because the standards are based on good practice, assessors do work within organisations that are taking action to improve practice, anti-racism and anti-discrimination.

The assessment process

The basics of the assessment process are:
• Evidence is gathered of the candidate's

The "value base" of care means that you are showing respect for your clients as you work with them.

competence in conditions as close as possible to the conditions under which they would normally work.

• The assessor must ensure that the candidate is consistently fulfilling all the performance criteria of the unit(s) on which they are being assessed, before they can be found competent.

• If a candidate does not show sufficient evidence for one or more performance criteria in a unit, then they are not yet competent in that unit.

Filling the gaps

Assessment is not therefore a one-off examination. There will be many people who on the initial gathering of evidence will have evidence gaps. Such gaps are of three types:

1. There is some difficulty in gathering the evidence which will have to be overcome. (Assessors are prepared for their task and to find other ways of gathering evidence.)

2. The timetable to gather sufficient evidence has been under-estimated and the candidate and the assessor will have to plan again.

3. The candidate is not performing up to the standard required and therefore needs to improve their practice. (It is important to recognise that one reason for this may well be that the policy and practice of the work place itself is at fault.)

The only way for the assessment process to start is for the candidate to request assessment. Once the assessor has been assigned to the candidate they need to plan the assessment. They must ensure that they are both clear about the basis they will work on. Before the candidate and the assessor can begin the actual assessment process a number of questions have to be talked through and agreed by both the candidate and the assessor:

• What are the units of competence the candidate wants to be assessed?

• How is the candidate going to provide the assessor with evidence of their competence?

• What evidence gathering methods will be appropriate, for example how will the rights and privacy of clients be ensured?

• What is the type and range of evidence that will need to be shown for the assessor to be satisfied that the candidate consistently fulfils the criteria?

• How will the evidence be recorded, and who will have access to those records?

• Can the records be used for anything other than the assessment?

• How will the assessor ensure that the evidence gathering methods used will not unfairly discriminate against the candidate?

• How will the candidate be given feedback on their performance?

• When will the evidence gathering start and the assessment made on the evidence be finished?

• What is the appeals procedure?

• What are the education and training opportunities - especially if there are areas where the candidate is found not yet competent?

Competence

Once agreed, the evidence gathering can begin. This is primarily the candidate bringing to the attention of the assessor actual evidence and/or parts of their work that they believe will show evidence of their competence. This evidence may well be about work that the candidate has done before and records in some way their achievement. This is one of the times when the candidate will be glad that they have spent time planning for the assessment. As more people use the NVQ/SVQ system there will develop a better understanding of how best to use it. Therefore do seek out others who are going through assessment; you can offer each other support.

As the candidate is found competent in the units they have asked to be assessed on they will receive a certificate for each unit. When they have been found competent for all the units in an award they will get a certificate which will give the name of the award and its level. Awards at the same NVQ/SVQ level in the care sector, even if from different awarding bodies, are recognised as being equivalent. You are advised to keep these certificates (and any others you have) safe. The National Record of Vocational Achievement(NROVA) is a grey plastic box file designed to keep certificates and records together.

Your future

The NVQ/SVQ system is designed to encourage people to build up their qualifications, either to progress in their present work or to transfer into other areas of work. When you have achieved your first award, consider how you would like to progress. Such progression may be into other areas of competence at the same level or into higher levels including full professional qualification. For example level 3 NVQ/SVQ Awards in Care are recognised as part of an entry to the Diploma in Social Work.

The work that has gone into the development of National Vocational Qualifications, Scottish Vocational Qualifications and associated education and training has been undertaken by a large number of individuals and groups. One of the major strengths of these developments is that they are based on collective work which draws upon the perspectives of all involved and associated with care work. In this chapter I have attempted to represent this collective work in a concise manner, but the work remains that of the original authors and working groups.

Views and opinions expressed are mine and not necessarily those of the Central Council for Education and Training in Social Work.

CHAPTER 20

Useful addresses

Resources you can draw on for practical help, information and publications

All these organisations welcome a stamped, self-addressed envelope sent with your enquiry.

Action for Blind People, 14-16 Verney Road, London SE16 3DZ. Tel: 071 732 8771.

Action for Dysphasic Adults, Canterbury House, 1 Royal Street, London SE1 7LN. Tel: 071 261 9572. Advice and information for people with speech difficulties, their families and carers.

Age Concern England, Astral House, 1268 London Road, London SW16 4ER. Tel: 081 679 8000. Information and publications. Practical volunteer services through local groups.

Age Exchange Reminiscence Centre, 11 Blackheath Village, London SE3 9LA. Tel: 081 318 9105. A unique reminiscence centre and hands-on museum. Activities include reminiscence groups, youth theatre, professional touring reminiscence theatre company, book publication, exhibitions and a comprehensive programme of reminiscence training courses such as "Introduction to reminiscence", "Making shows, books and exhibitions", "Reminiscence with mentally infirm elderly people" and "Cross-generational reminiscence".

Alzheimer's Disease Society, 158-160 Balham High Road, London SW12 9BN. Tel: 081 675 6557/8/9/0. National Association and local branches providing carers with information and support; newsletter and other publications.

Arthritis Care, 5 Grosvenor Crescent, London SW1X 7ER. Tel: 071 235 0902. Self-help support group (local branches) for arthritis sufferers.

Association for Continence Advice, at the Disabled Living Foundation, 380-384 Harrow Road, London W9 2HU. Tel: 071 289 6111. Network of professional nurse continence advisers.

British Association of the Hard of Hearing, 7-11 Armstrong Road, London W3 7JL. Tel: 081 743 1110. Runs local clubs in many parts of the country; also provides information and a newsletter.

British Colostomy Association, 38-39 Eccleston Square, London SW1V 1PB. Tel: 071 828 5175. Officers and volunteers give personal advice and help to those with colostomies.

British Deaf Association, 38 Victoria Place, Carlisle. Tel: 0228 48844. Information, services and clubs for people born deaf and using sign language.

British Diabetic Association, 10 Queen Anne Street, London W1M 0BD. 071 323 1531. Information, publications and services for diabetic people and their carers.

British Epilepsy Association, Anstey House, 40 Hanover Square, Leeds LS3 1BE. Tel: 0532 439393. Advice, information, self-help groups.

British Red Cross Society, 9 Grosvenor Crescent, London SW1X 7EJ. Tel: 071 235 5454. Volunteer beauty care and other services.

Centre for Policy on Ageing, 25-31 Ironmonger Row, London EC1V 3QP. Tel: 071 253 1787. Publications and information on old age, policy and service provision, including practical handbooks on aspects of residential care. Publishes Home Life: a code of practice for residential care, the guidance document for the Registered Homes Act 1984.

Christian Council on Ageing, The Old Court, Greens Norton, Nr Towcester, Northants NN12 8BS. Tel: 0327 50481. Information and publications on spiritual needs in old age; local branches.

Counsel and Care for the Elderly, Twyman House, 16 Bonny Street, London NW1 9PG. Tel: 071 485 1550. Assists elderly people into residential and nursing homes. Advice and casework counselling service.

Cruse-Bereavement Care, Cruse House, 126 Sheen

Road, Richmond, Surrey TW9 1UR. Tel: 081 940 4818. Service of counselling, advice and opportunities for social contact for all bereaved people.

Disabled Living Foundation, 380-384 Harrow Road, London W9 2HU. Tel: 071 289 6111. Publications and information, especially on incontinence, clothing, aids and equipment, music, visual handicap and footwear.

Gardens for the Disabled Trust and Garden Club, Mrs Julia Sebline, Hayes Farmhouse, Hayes Lane, Peasmarsh, E. Sussex. Tel: 0424 882345. Practical and financial assistance for disabled people wanting to take an active part in gardening.

Help the Aged, 16-18 St James's Walk, Clerkenwell, London EC1R 0BE. Tel: 071 253 0253. Publications and information. Specialist services include skilled reminiscence work with confused elderly people.

Horticultural Therapy, Goulds Ground, Vallis Way, Frome, Somerset BA11 3DW. Tel: 0373 64782. Technical, advisory and support service to gardening projects.

MIND/National Association for Mental Health. 22 Harley Street, London W1N 2ED. Aims to promote mental health and help mentally disordered people. Local associations throughout the country.

Multiple Sclerosis Society of Great Britain and Northern Ireland, 25 Effie Road, Fulham, London SW6 1EE. Tel: 071 736 6267.

National Deaf Blind League, 18 Rainbow Court, Paston Ridings, Peterborough PE4 6UP. Tel: 0733 73511. Information, advice and publications, including illustrated instructions for manual alphabets.

National Schizophrenia Fellowship, 28 Castle Street, Kingston-upon-Thames, Surrey KT1 1SS. Tel:081 547 3937. Advisory service through the national office. 120 local groups.

Nottingham Rehab Ltd, 17 Ludlow Hill Road, Melton Road, West Bridgford, Nottingham NG2 6HD. Tel: 0602 452345. A variety of activity materials and aids – catalogue available.

Nutrition Advisory Group for the Elderly (British Dietetic Association). Information and a handbook, Eating through the '90s, for those providing meals for elderly people. Available from Elizabeth Haughton, Dept. Nutrition and Dietetics, Gloucestershire Royal Hospital, Great Western Road, Gloucester GL1 3NN.

Orientation Aids, Dalebank, Glencaple, Dumfries. Books and reality orientation materials.

Royal National Institute for the Blind, 224 Great Portland Street, London W1N 6AA. Tel: 071 388 1266. Advice, information and publications, especially Braille books, periodicals and music, and Moon books and periodicals.

Royal National Institute for the Deaf, 105 Gower Street, London WC1E 6AH. Tel: 071 387 8033. Advice, information and services to people with impaired hearing those working with them.

Schizophrenia Association of Great Britain. Bryn Hyfryd, The Crescent, Bangor, Gwynedd LL57 2AG. Tel: 0248 354048. A telephone and postal advice service is offered to psychiatric patients, their relatives and mental health professionals.

Social Service Departments – at your local authority. The address will be in the telephone directory, or available from your local library. Residential home registration officers are a source of information and advice; specialist social workers can help with handicaps such as deafness or blindness.

Talking Books for the Handicapped (National Listening Library), 12 Lant Street, London SE1 1QR. Tel: 071 407 9417. A postal lending library service of literature recorded on long-playing cassettes.

TFH, 76 Barracks Road, Sandy Lane Industrial Estate, Stourport-on-Severn, Worcestershire DY13 9QB. Tel: 0299 827820. Games, puzzles, pastimes etc for older people.

University of the Third Age, 1 Stockwell Green, SW9 9JF. Tel: 071 737 2541. Promotes and organises self-help educational activities for older people.

Winslow Press, Telford Road, Bicester, Oxfordshire OX6 0TS. Tel: 0869 244733. Books, especially on aspects of caring for the elderly mentally infirm, activity aids and games, reminiscence materials.

Glossary of terms

Aids (acquired immunodeficiency syndrome). A disease in which the human immunodeficiency virus (HIV) is acquired by sexual activity (usually) and less commonly by other routes such as blood transfusion, sharing contaminated needles and breast milk.

Alzheimer's disease. A form of dementia which is notable because it can affect middle-aged people in their forties and fifties. No cause is known. The frontal and occipital lobes of the brain are affected causing loss of memory and intellectual abilities, apathy, difficulty with walking and talking, and disorientation.

Amnesia. Loss of memory.

Anaemia. Shortage of the oxygen – carrying part (haemoglobin) of the blood's red cells. This may be because the body is losing too much haemoglobin (for example bleeding from the rectum), or because it is not making enough (for example due to a shortage of iron in the diet).

Anaesthetic. A substance that can cause temporary loss of the sensation of pain or consciousness. As a 'local' anaesthetic it numbs a specific part of the body only. As a 'general' anaesthetic it causes the patient to lose consciousness.

Angina. Chest pain due to oxygen shortage in the heart muscles. Caused by narrowing or blockage of the coronary arteries which supply the muscles with oxygen.

Antibiotics. Medicines which either kill bacteria or stop them multiplying and spreading. They have no effect on viruses.

Anti-convulsants. Medicines which are used to treat epilepsy.

Asthma. A condition in which the tubes of the lung have a fluctuating and reversible tendency to narrow causing breathlessness, coughing, wheezing or chest tightness. The triggers to this narrowing may be allergic such as housedust mite, animal fur, pollens or something quite different like infections, fumes, smoke, cold air or exercise. Some people are sensitive to certain medicines, food colourings and alchohol.

Atheroma. The fatty deposit, largely of cholesterol, which lines arteries causing them to become 'hardened', thick, and weak (known as arteriosclerosis).

Arteriosclerosis. See atheroma.

Arthritis. Pain and stiffness in a joint or joints. Common causes include osteoarthritis, rheumatoid arthritis and gout.

Autopsy. See post mortem.

Benign. When describing a tumour means favourable, non-cancerous, usually contained within a capsule and not spreading to other parts of the body.

Bradycardia. A marked slowing of the rate of the heart.

Braille. A system of writing and printing by means of raised points representing letters which allows blind people to read by touch. From Louis Braille (1809-1852), a French teacher of blind people.

Bronchitis. Inflammation of the air tubes of the lungs. This may be 'acute' due to a bacterial or viral infection. Or it may be 'chronic' due to excessive production of mucus caused by many factors including pollution or smoking. Known as the 'English disease'.

Bruising. The discolouration of skin which results from leakage of blood from a blood vessel, usually due to trauma.

Cancer. A large group of diseases which are linked together because in each case there is uncontrolled tissue growth of the affected part of the body. This tissue growth is always abnormal, may spread into organs nearby or far away (e.g. by blood or lymph spread to lymph glands, lung or brain), and may cause death. The outlook (prognosis) for each sufferer is very different depending on the site and type of their cancer.

Capillary. The tiny blood vessel which lies between arteries bringing blood to the tissues and veins taking it away.

Cataract. A clouding of the lens of the eye which prevents light passing through it easily, making vision dim and sometimes lost altogether.

Catheter. A tube which is passed into the body to drain fluids from or inject fluids into an organ. The most common is the urinary catheter for draining the bladder.

Cerebrovascular accident (CVA). See stroke.

Chemotherapy. The treatment of disease by medicines or chemicals. Often used in the context of treating cancer.

Chorea. Strange, uncoordinated movements of the body, particularly limbs. Huntington's chorea is an inherited variety accompanied by mental deterioration.

Circumcision. An operation to remove all or part of the foreskin of the penis.

Conjunctivitis. Inflammation of the white of the eye caused by a bacterial or viral infection, or by an allergy.

Coronary artery disease. Narrowing or blockage of the arteries supplying the heart with oxygen. Usually due to atheroma, a fatty coating of the inner lining of the arteries. Also known as coronary heart disease (CHD).

Coronary heart disease (CHD). See coronary artery disease.

Cramp. Muscular spasm of a muscle usually due to lack of oxygen reaching it.

Defaecation. The act of opening the bowels.

Diabetes mellitus. Failure of the normal production of insulin by the pancreas or failure to use it properly by the body leads to excessively and persistently high levels of sugar in the blood. This can have serious consequences for some organs of the body including blood vessels, kidneys, and eyes.

Digoxin. One of the earliest discovered medicines which was found to have a beneficial effect on the failing heart.

Diuretic. Medicine which stimulates the kidneys to produce more urine. Commonly used for the treatment of heart failure.

Diverticulitis. A condition in which there is inflammation of small pockets (diverticulae) of large bowel which stick through the muscle surrounding the bowel at weak points. Generally caused by long-standing constipation.

Dysarthria. Difficulty with articulating words, often due to a stroke.

Dysphasia. Difficulty speaking, particularly arranging words in an understandable way.

Encephalitis. Inflammation of the brain, usually due to a virus.

Enuresis (nocturnal). Bed-wetting.

Epilepsy. A condition in which disorganised electrical activity in the brain causes fits. These may involve the whole body, known as 'grand mal' fits, or they may be less serious involving perhaps a short loss of full consciousness known as 'petit mal' fits, or they may be confined to one part of the body (e.g. leg or arm) known as focal fits.

Fainting. Temporary loss of consciousness which causes the person to fall to the ground usually because of reduced supply of blood to the brain. It may be due to pain, terror, standing for too long in one place or illness. Recovery occurs immediately the head is lowered to restore the blood supply.

Floater. A moving object which is found within the field of vision. It is usually not important and has many causes.

Fracture. The medical word for a broken bone.

Gangrene. Death and destruction of a part of the body (e.g. a toe) following the loss of the blood supply to it. If there is no accompanying infection the gangrene remains 'dry'. If infection is present it becomes 'wet'.

Glaucoma. An illness in which abnormally high fluid pressure inside the eye can damage it permanently.

Heart attack. Damage to an area of heart muscle (see infarct) due to obstruction of the artery supplying this area with blood. The main symptom is usually sudden severe chest pain. It may be accompanied by shock and an abnormal pulse rate (either very fast, irregular or slow). If the damaged area is large, the person may die. If it is less extensive the person will survive and the heart gradually recover.

Heart failure. The failure by the heart to perform its function of pumping blood round the body efficiently. The most common symptoms are breathlessness on minimal exertion, tiredness and swollen ankles.

Hemiplegia. Paralysis of one side of the body as a result of injury or disease of the brain or spinal cord. Most commonly due to stroke.

Hernia. Protrusion of an organ from its normal position in the body into another. The most common is the inguinal hernia in which bowel pushes through defects in the muscle of the groin. Also known as a 'rupture'.

Herpes zoster. The virus which causes the painful skin condition shingles.

Hypertension. Raised blood pressure. Doctors are increasingly wary about giving hard-and-fast figures for hypertension but most would agree that diastolic pressures persistently over 100-105 mm Hg and systolic pressure persistently higher than the range 160-200 mm Hg are worthy of treatment.

Hypotension. Low blood pressure.

Hypothermia. Body temperature abnormally below the usual value of 37 degrees centigrade. At about 35 degrees centigrade confusion and listlessness may begin, below 33 degrees centigrade the breathing and pulse rate and blood pressure may start to fall. If prolonged death may occur.

Incontinence. The inability to retain faeces or urine until a suitable time and place is found for their release.

Infarct. An area of the body which is damaged or dies as a result of not receiving enough oxygen from its arteries. This supply failure is usually due to a blockage of or haemorrhage from the artery. Frequently used as 'coronary' or 'myocardial' infarct to describe the damage done to heart muscle after a heart attack.

Insomnia. Difficulty getting to sleep or remaining asleep for long.

Lumbago. Pain in the low back.

Malabsorption. The failure of the normal absorption by the gut of some or all of the contents of food. This can cause symptoms of malnutrition such as failure to grow (children), loss of weight, diarrhoea, or anaemia.

Melaena. The production of black, tarry stools containing blood from the upper part of the gut.

Metastasis. Secondary tumours which have spread by blood or lymph from primary cancerous tumours. The commonest sites for metastases include glands, lung and bone.

Micturition. The act of emptying the bladder of urine.

Motor neurone disease. An usually fatal disease in which there is progressive destruction, for reasons unknown, of some of the nerves responsible for stimulating muscles. This causes increasing weakness of groups of muscles, most notably those involved with breathing and swallowing.

Multiple sclerosis. An often fluctuating, sometimes progressive, disease of the brain and spinal cord in which plaque replaces areas of normal nervous tissue. Depending on the site and extent of plaque this causes a range of symptoms including difficulties with co-ordination, incontinence and problems with vision and speech.

Neoplasm. See tumour.

Neurological. Relating to the body's brain and nerves.

Neuro-transmitters. Chemical substances which help to pass a signal down a nerve.

Oedema. Excessive collection of tissue fluid, often round the ankles or at the base of the spine.

Paralysis. Loss of movement (but not sensation) in a muscle or group of muscles normally under the person's control. May be due to damage to the muscle itself or to its nerve supply.

Paraplegia. Paralysis of the lower part of the body usually due to a spinal injury.

Parkinsonism. Symptoms similar to those of Parkinson's disease i.e. shaking or trembling, rhythmical muscular tremors, rigidity, mask-like facial expression.

Pick's disease. A form of dementia which particularly affects people aged 40-60. The frontal and temporal lobes of the brain are involved causing loss of memory and orientation, apathy, disordered emotions and speech difficulties.

Post mortem. After death. Also used as a noun to describe the process by which a pathologist investigates the cause of a person's death by examining all organs (autopsy).

Pressure sore. An area of skin and underlying tissues which die as a result of pressure persistently preventing the flow of blood through its blood vessels (e.g. from lying with heels in the same position for long periods). This causes an ulcer or sore to develop. Also known as a bed sore.

Prognosis. Describes the outlook for a person with a disease in terms of death and disability.

Pneumonia. Inflammation of the lungs due to bacterial, viral or fungal infections.

Prolapse. The abnormal descent of any organ from its normal anatomical position. The most common organs to prolapse are the womb and bladder.

Pruritus. Itching.

Pyrexia. Fever.

Recovery position. The safest position in which to place a person who has had a serious accident or suffered a catastrophe like a heart attack or stroke. The purpose is to make sure the airway is kept open and fluids like vomit or blood can flow out of the mouth rather than down into the lungs. If a back injury is suspected only move the person if it is unquestionably life-saving and then as gently as possible because movement may make the back injury permanently worse.

Rehabilitation. The process by which a team of health workers restores a person who has had a serious illness to as near a health state as he or she had before the illness.

Sacrum. Part of the lower end of the spine.

Shock. Physical collapse resulting from impaired blood circulation to vital organs. Common causes include severe bleeding or a heart attack which prevents the heart pumping the blood effectively.

Speech therapist. Professional specially trained to help people with speech difficulties.

Sphincter. The ring of muscle which surrounds the opening of a hollow organ like the bladder and which controls the escape of the contents of the organ until a suitable time.

Spina Bifida. A congenital disease in which there is a defect in the bones of the spine. This can be mild (spina bifida occulta) and cause no symptoms. However in more serious forms the spinal cord can be damaged causing paralysis of the legs and incontinence of urine and faeces, often accompanied by mental retardation and hydrocephalus.

Sprain. An injury to a ligament when the joint it is supporting is forced through a range of movement greater than normal, without dislocation or fracture.

Stroke. A rapid brain disorder usually caused by a blockage in or haemorrhage from one of the main arteries of the brain. Speech and movement are most commonly affected but other functions may be damaged depending on which artery is affected. The speed of recovery depends on the extent of the blockage or haemorrhage. Also known as a cerebrovascular accident (CVA).

Tachycardia. A marked increase in the rate of the heart.

Thrombosis. The formation of a blood clot (thrombus) on the lining of an artery or vein which may partially or completely block the blood flow through it.

Thrush. An infection due to the yeast-like fungus candida albicans. Common sites of infection include the vagina and mouth.

Toxin. Poison.

Tumour. A lump or swelling in the body. It may be benign or malignant (cancer).

Ulcer. A persistent break in the surface of the skin or the lining of a body cavity (like the stomach).

Ureters. The tubes which drain urine from the kidneys into the bladder.

Urethra. The tube which carries urine from the bladder to the outside.

Vascular. Relating to blood vessels, usually arteries or veins.

Vertigo. A feeling of dizziness accompanied by a feeling that either oneself or one's surroundings are spinning.

Index